AF668036

RECONSTRUCTING

THE BENGAL PARTITION

RECONSTRUCTING THE BENGAL PARTITION

The Psyche under a Different Violence

Jayanti Basu

Samya

Reconstructing the Bengal Partition:
The Psyche under a Different Violence
was first published in 2013 by SAMYA,
an imprint of Bhatkal and Sen,
16 Southern Avenue, Kolkata 700 026.

© 2013 Jayanti Basu

ISBN 978-81-906760-9-0

Rs 650.00

All rights reserved. No part of this book may be reproduced
or utilized in any form or by any means
without prior written permission from the publisher.

Design by SAMYA and Krishna Gopal Das,
typesetting by Krishna Gopal Das,
74T Sultan Alam Road, Kolkata 700 033,
and printed at Bengal Phototype Co.
46/1 Raja Rammohan Roy Sarani, Kolkata 700 009.

Published by Mandira Sen for SAMYA,
An imprint of Bhatkal and Sen,
16 Southern Avenue, Kolkata 700 026.

To my parents

Foreword

THE PROJECT

At long last! This is the second book to emerge after the first one entitled *Aftermath: An Oral History of Violence* by Meenakshi Verma in 2004 from the project that Ashis Nandy, then Director of the Centre for the Study of Developing Societies in Delhi, initiated in 1997 with limited funding from a number of sources and then with larger support from the Ford Foundation. It was in collaboration with a number of organizations and scholars, including some from Pakistan and Bangladesh. The project was to study the violence and uprooting that took place during the partitioning of British India, mainly through interviews with the victims, perpetrators and other witnesses who went through the experiences of the events of 1946-48. Nandy believed that much of the present-day dissensions and altercations between India and Pakistan have resulted from the bloodshed and mass dislocations of Partition. Further, that although reams have been written about Partition from political, economic, sociological, and other viewpoints, there has not been any systematic psychological study of how the trauma of the violence and uprooting of Partition has affected those involved.

In a broader perspective, this is not so unusual. The psychological effects of the Holocaust were not initially explored until some twenty years later. The emotional effects of such trauma are usually papered over with a wall of silence, while their legacy lives on in current-day life. Nandy, himself, as a child witnessed the violent riots of Calcutta, which left a lasting impression.

The project included interviewers, often social scientists, social workers, psychologists, even journalists and others from India, Pakistan and Bangladesh who interviewed over 2,000 persons, not only victims but also perpetrators. Verma's book concentrates on the western border. While occasional papers have been published from those who participated in the project, no comprehensive book especially on the Bengal border has emerged until now. While some novels and films depict the violence of Partition, to my knowledge the only psychological book published on this subject prior to the project was by Urvashi Butalia from interviews of women in the early 1990s of those who crossed the Punjab border.[1]

The numbers affected by Partition are overwhelming. The estimates of those who died range from a minimal number of 200,000 by the British to the official Indian government figure of 1,000,000. More recently, Ashis Nandy from his research puts the figure as over 2,000,000, and Jayanti Basu cites a figure as much as 3,500,000.[2] Added to this are the refugees, or those uprooted, with estimates by Ashis Nandy of 16,000,000 and Jayanti Basu for as much as 18,000,000. This is by far the largest refugee flow in world history. Moreover, most of these people—Hindus, Muslims and Sikhs—who were uprooted had lived in their areas for multiple generations.

Then there were the attacks on women to dishonour their families and communal groups, a figure of 100,000 or more rapes and some 30,000 women abducted from their families and taken by the other side, whether Hindu, Muslim, or Sikh.[3] Compounding this trauma two years after Partition, the governments of India and Pakistan decided this was unfair booty and demanded they be returned to their original families. Many already had children and all were considered dishonoured. At one of the meetings of the project, a young Pakistani journalist reported that he had gained access to an aunt who seemed highly secretive about her background. He gradually learned that she had been abducted by a Hindu family, married into it and had a child. On her journey to Pakistan, the child died, and she was then married to his uncle. All of this was kept completely secret over the years.

Partition has often been written about as genocide. Certainly the numbers killed would seem to justify calling it genocide. However, I question this. I see it as being uniquely different from genocide. In the usual recorded major genocides of the twentieth century—for example, the Turkish army killing Armenians, the Holocaust where the Nazis tried to exterminate Jews and Gypsies, Rwanda where the government encouraged the Hutus to exterminate the Tutsis, and in Cambodia where the government tried to eliminate the educated classes—the government played a central and decisive role, there was an ideology that fuelled the killings, and there was no ambiguity over the effort to eliminate one or another group.

In Partition, however, the British government did not try to exterminate anyone. Nor did they have any overarching ideology that would fuel the violence and uprooting. Rather, their decisive role before and after Partition was not to provide any protection against the communal riots and assaults. If anything, it was a sin of omission, not commission. In contrast to the British, the rulers of the princely states of India immediately called out the troops to quell any riots or attacks, thus preventing violence. They, in contrast to the British, exercised proper, protective governmental control. No wonder Jayanti Basu cites a number of sources as seeing partition violence and uprooting as an enigma or a riddle. An enigma compounded by the ambiguity that each group had up to that time rather close relationships with the other, and were often helped by some from the other group to safety.

I should briefly mention my own involvement in the partition project. In early 1999, I was invited by Ashis Nandy to join a small group of interviewers in May in Kathmandu as an outside commentator to discuss interviews with partition victims and perpetrators. The meeting was held in Nepal as at that time Pakistanis and Bangladeshis could not get visas to India, and Nandy wanted persons from all three countries to get involved. I subsequently went to two other meetings in New Delhi in 2001 and 2003. I then reflected on my own psychoanalytic treatment with a number of Indian patients both in India and in New York to see if any were affected by Partition. I found that the family dynamics of a Hindu man I had seen some years ago in long-term psychoanalysis in New York could have been much better understood, as well as how their trauma affected him, if I knew about Partition then. In addition, before one of the meetings in New Delhi, I had the unusual occasion to interview a Hindu family twice in Long Island, New York, where the husbands as boys were in a train massacre leaving Pakistan. One of the wives who is a psychologist could recount how this trauma affected the entire family in different ways over three generations.[4]

THE BOOK

It is significant that this first book on the eastern border to emerge from the project is written by a psychoanalyst, one who, herself, comes from a family who had to flee East Bengal. This cannot simply be a neutral subject for Jayanti Basu. It is rather one she must have struggled to understand for years, to penetrate the silence of what was not said but emotionally communicated within her family and by their relatives and friends amongst those who fled from East Bengal. As a psychoanalyst she is eminently suited to explore the effects of the emotional trauma both in her family and those others who were refugees, as well as the effects on herself.

Also as a psychoanalyst, she is extremely well suited to undertake interviews of those who were dislocated from the towns and lands of East Bengal to Kolkata. I should emphasize that the hallmark of a psychoanalyst is that of a highly trained, sensitive and astute listener. Similar to other psychoanalysts, she is adept at drawing a person out, creating a safe space for a person to express thoughts and especially feelings that are not usually communicated. She is sensitive to what is not said as well as what is said, and can understand innuendos and all kinds of defensive manoeuvres. She is particularly sensitive to emotions and defenses against them, and to the play of the unconscious.

She also listens to herself and her own emotions as well as to the person being interviewed as a further way of knowing the other. Moreover, she is extremely sensitive and reflective on the nature of memory, how it is affected by the age of the person and the particular experiences he or she has undergone since Partition, as well as by their personality. It is a truth about the nature of the person, less so than on actual events that happened. Thus, she takes into account the particular self of each person and the age at which he or she left East Bengal, as it affects their memory of Partition, the trauma undergone, and how they dealt with it.

Thus, Jayanti Basu assesses the rich complexity of the human psyche in response to the trauma of Partition, and has as it were, a postmodern sensibility that the memory of past events is to a great extent psychologically determined. This study is therefore a highly qualitative and contextual one. The validity of her relatively small sample is bolstered by the depth of her interviewing and her psychological understanding of each person. She is then able to delineate how these personal variations in response to the trauma of Partition can merge into a collective self, and in so doing, she describes major aspects of Bengali culture.

At the core of the book, Jayanti Basu makes a highly important distinction between what she terms the 'soft violence' of Partition in Bengal, where there were relatively few violent attacks and killings, with the 'hard violence' of the Punjab where there were multiple deaths. In soft violence there is the prolonged threat of violence and a terrifying fear for one's life, with little if any sense of personal control, resulting in people fleeing for their lives and living with fear and insecurity within themselves for years. Undoubtedly, there was also soft violence in the Punjab as evidenced by my Hindu patient whose family fled well before the major violence. And a patient of a few years ago was also affected by the reactions of her father and grandfather to the trauma of Partition in Sind, although none in the family was affected by actual violence. Their trying to maintain strict control over themselves and their children had surfaced as a major problem in her own life when she tried to do the same. When I related this to a friend, a social scientist, who fled as a child from Austria just before the Holocaust began, she mentioned having to maintain a similar tight control over herself and her children years later as a reaction to the trauma of dislocation, which she eventually dealt with in her own psychoanalysis.

There is another contrast between the soft and hard violence of Bengal and the Punjab, respectively. One gets the impression that those being interviewed in this book were able to speak sporadically about their trauma and experiences over the years although much emotionally has been silenced. Not so with most of the interviewees in the project from the western part of India and what is now Pakistan. Interview after interview started with the person saying more than fifty years after Partition, 'This is the first time I have ever spoken about this.' A dramatic example of this came with the appearance at a meeting of the project in New Delhi by Dr. Ravi Kapur, the late renowned psychiatrist. He had refused to come to previous meetings but said he would come to this one. The night before, he called that he would not come, but then unexpectedly showed up. He would only speak of his own experiences as a child: seeing the killing of Hindus in Lahore by a Muslim mob as his family were leaving, then of the train he was on refusing to stop to let on board Hindus fleeing from Muslim attackers, of coming to New Delhi and witnessing a well-to-do Muslim man coming out of a bank in an upscale neighbourhood, who was then confronted by Hindu soldiers and soon after bayoneted. He said he has never spoken about any of this to anyone since he was a child, not even to his wife, a well-known psychologist, nor to his two children. Thus, Jayanti Basu's distinction of the reactions to the trauma of soft and hard violence is a very important one. Her spelling out the nature of soft violence with its repercussions is a major contribution.

This book not only presents extremely sensitively done interviews but is also replete with references, endnotes and scholarly comments, anchoring it theoretically in relevant psychological traditions. It is in effect a very good balance between the clinical approach and the theoretical. Moreover, Jayanti Basu is reflectively modest about her data. She realizes that she may not have attained the depth of psychological understanding she is used to as a practising psychoanalyst, although this book is far more psychologically sophisticated than much of the other interview data I have heard. She spells out some of her conclusions in a traditional Freudian psychoanalytic framework. Since there is now a plethora of different psychoanalytic paradigms and models, if a psychoanalyst reads this work, he or she may well interpret some of the important findings in a somewhat different theoretical way, while still valuing the extraordinarily sensitive approach of Jayanti Basu.

Lastly, I should comment on Jayanti Basu's writing style which is unusually clear and easy to read, with a poetic sensibility surfacing from time to time. This book can certainly be readily comprehended by those outside of the psychological field.

FOREWORD TO A FOREWORD

Jayanti Basu rightly suggests that there are implications in her approach and methodology for further research and interviewing of those involved in the trauma of Partition. In addition, there is a whole other body of work to be done, this one necessitated by the researcher being a psychotherapist or psychoanalyst. We now know from the work with Holocaust victims and their children that there is intergenerational trauma, where the parents who are deeply affected unconsciously pass on the effects of the trauma to their children and even to their grandchildren. In the context of Partition, this can best be assessed by the depth of psychological understanding of the person in psychotherapy. Thus, Jayanti Basu as a psychoanalyst is eminently suited to do this kind of study. Moreover, coming from this background of her family being uprooted by the soft violence of Partition in East Bengal, she must well have dealt with this in herself.

There is, however, another important aspect of the effects of the trauma that have in my observations been largely ignored in the interviewing involved in the project. Since the Western European/North American psychological approach has always been very individualistic, the focus in the project has naturally been on interviewing persons directly affected by partition experiences, whether that of the hard violence or the soft violence of the terrifying threat of harm. In South Asia, however, due to the close-knit extended family relationships, whenever one family member is affected, the rest of the family is also deeply affected. Prakash Desai, an Indian psychiatrist living in Chicago, characterized the South Asian family as being like an Alexander Caldwell mobile. When one part moves, so does every other part. All are interdependent.

This insight is confirmed by the family I interviewed where the two brothers and their parents were among the only survivors of a train massacre. Described by one of their wives, a psychologist, the mother of the family contained the grief of the family, fainting for years every time the name of one or the other of her two missing youngest children was mentioned; while the men of the family dissociated their feelings so they could work effectively in a totally new environment. However, when it surfaced through a Lahore newspaper, after the New York brother had sent a letter to the editor of their past train massacre experience some fifty years later, that the two missing youngest children might still be alive, the father upon learning this almost immediately after had a heart attack and died. The resurfacing of dissociated feelings might well have played a role in his heart attack. Further, the reactions to the trauma in the family were clearly passed on to the children and grandchildren, where communication in the family is still largely bottled up.[5] Clearly, this is a study waiting to be done but not an easy one as it will emotionally involve the therapist.

What is needed for psychoanalysts such as Jayanti Basu, who have worked in therapy with both the offspring of the refugees and their grandchildren, is to delineate the effects of the trauma on them and also to describe the effects on the entire family, which would certainly play an important role on how the individual members have been affected. Although there would obviously be other issues at stake in the therapy, this would also convey the differences between the later generations and the initial refugees.

New York, November 2012 Alan Roland

Notes

[1] U. Butalia, 2000, *The other side of silence: Voices from partition* (Durham, N. C.: Duke University Press).

[2] A. Nandy, 2009. Sarah Kailath Lecture (Berkeley: University of California), 13 March.

[3] V. Das, 1997. Language and body: Transactions in the construction of pain'. In A. Kleinman, V. Das and M. Lock, eds, *Social suffering* (Berkeley, Los Angeles, and London: University of California Press): 67-93.

[4] A. Roland, 2011. *Journeys to foreign selves: Asians and Asian Americans in a global era* (New Delhi, Oxford, New York: Oxford University Press): 106-13.

[5] Ibid.

Contents

Foreword by Alan Roland vii

Preface xviii

Introduction xxiii

1 The Perspective 1

2 A Chronicle of Emotions 30

3 A Different Kind of Trauma 98

4 The Person, the Personality and the Perception 133

5 The Self in Partition and Beyond 205

Glossary 241

Index 244

Preface

MY FATHER, UNCLES and aunts would speak of a 'true home' at Kumilla, and another 'ancestral home' at Chandpur. Chandpur was our *desh*, Kumilla our 'home'. What then is Kolkata, I wondered. We do not belong here, they would say. We are just 'staying' here. We shall have to stay here too. This is not how it should be. The sky was blue there, the water sweet, the ponds reflected the wavy shadows of the coconut trees, the fruits were juicy, the people caring. Here everything is mundane, grey, tasteless. 'Nonsense', I would say, 'Life is nice here'. '*Kisui bojhos na*,' they replied, angered. 'You understand nothing.'

My father bought his spectacles and had his eyes checked yearly from Kumilla Optic House, which was quite far from our house. Why must he go there? I thought. There are so many modern eye-clinics nearby. I have asked Father a number of times why he wasted money doing so. '*Kisui bojhos na*,' my father would say.

All of them, my father, uncles and aunts spoke official Bengali (Kolkata Bengali) inside and outside the home. Yet, when they got emotionally charged—happy or angry or afraid—they would start speaking in 'Bangal', the country dialect. 'Why don't you stick to one dialect?' I would ask. '*Kisui bojhos na*,' they would say again.

I have never seen Kumilla, nor Chandpur. I was born and brought up in Kolkata. This has been my home. I have known from my birth that I would never go to East Pakistan, the land that had become alien, today's Bangladesh. From 1971, I came to know that I might visit Bangladesh, but I would need a passport and visa. My father, uncles and aunts never needed a passport to visit Kumilla. All they had to do was to close their eyes, and magic! They were there. Not that their attitude had a deep impact on me. I led my own life with an eye to my career and family. Kumilla was nowhere within my horizon.

In 1999, I became associated with the project 'Life History Construction and Mass Violence in South East Asia', which was a part of a larger project, 'Reconstructing Lives', launched by the Centre for the Study of Developing Societies (CSDS), New Delhi, out of simple academic interest. I undertook the task of interviewing refugees with the same neutrality. Yet, I was swept off my cool certainty as I approached my very first interviewee. He was a person whom I liked a lot. I thought I understood him well. But he did not think so. 'I can tell you all, but you will not understand,' he said. He was being polite, because I was not his own daughter, because I was not a small girl, but a respectable adult professional. Nevertheless, I clearly heard his subtext: *'Kisui bojhos na'*: 'You understand nothing'.

I tried to understand him and others. Now I know that I cannot claim to have understood. I shall never understand them, because, they belong not only to a different generation, but to a different species as well. They come from another 'land'; their 'home' is foreign to me. As I journeyed into their souls, I have often felt myself to be an outsider, an insensitive 'investigator' trampling their soft sentiments. I apologize.

This book is not on the records of the experiences of the migrant Hindu population. Instead, this is on their memories. It is a product of the dialogue between many minds–theirs and mine. Their representations have two sides: one that they experienced and the other they have remembered and narrated after fifty years. I too had two approaches interacting in me: that of a daughter and that of a psychologist. These two have often been in conflict. Probably, ultimately, the academic self has overridden the daughter in me. I have tried to reconstruct from their reconstructions the very special period in history, when these elderly persons, then mere children or adolescents, were experiencing the pain of Partition, the thrashing from life as they were forced to leave their 'homes'. I was not after 'official' history. My focus was on the 'subjective history'; I wanted to peep into their inner world. It was risky and fascinating.

As I probed into their subjective space, my own subjectivity interfered. 'Interference' is probably a wrong choice of word. I sailed into their subjective space with my own subjectivity. My subjective self was my tool, the brush which I would dip into strange emotions: their emotions and my own, and paint their portraits; my very own heart was the instrument on which their music could be played.

In the process, I had to discuss the personal lives of my respondents. This was a sensitive and difficult task. I have altered the names and other personal identities of some of my respondents; for others, I have kept these intact. I had to depend on my own judgement for this compromise. Have I hurt some of my respondents for the sake of my writing? I apologize. But how else could I bring forth the 'meaning' of 'soft violence', point out how a systematic reign of terror distorted the simple sentiments of a child?

I am aware that my interpretations may not correspond to the sentiments of many of the persons whose memories I utilized. I apologize again. I do not claim to understand another person thoroughly. I am pretty well prepared to engage in a dialogue with those persons who kindly permitted me to encroach upon their lives. I am also prepared to acknowledge my error and to revise my interpretation if I understand that I traversed largely off the track.

I had faced problems writing this book. The more I read the manuscript, the more I felt that something was amiss. Sometimes, I felt it was over-simplistic, sometimes too complex. Sometimes I feared I have over- or under-interpreted. Finally, I decided to let go.

The target persons of my study were those aged Hindus who did not undergo the bloody brutalities of the partition violence, but were forced by the circumstances of Partition to migrate to

India. It is well known that corporeal violence in the east was less than in the western part of India. Does that mean that the pain was less? During the interviews, it has occurred to me that this was a different kind of trauma; I called it *soft violence*. A large portion of this treatise would be devoted to unfurling the psychological processes involved in soft violence.

I have a second thesis as well. I have seen that not all individuals I knew around me reacted in a similar fashion to the partition trauma, despite considerable similarity in their experiences. It is but common knowledge that the 'meaning' of trauma is processed through personality; the ultimate reaction is the product of experience–personality interaction. While clinical psychology traditionally emphasizes the role of personality as a moderator between event and reaction, studies of social trauma rarely do so. In the present work, I tried to integrate the two: the clinical insight and the social investigative mode.

Methodologically, I am preceded by a number of social scientists, historians as well as psychoanalysts, psycho-biographers, clinical psychologists and psycho-neurologists who recorded the subjective perception of events of famous, infamous and not-so-famous persons. Some, whose influence I consciously acknowledge, are Aaron Haas, Alan Roland, Ashis Nandy, Erik Erikson, Oliver Sacks, Robert Jay Lifton, Sudhir Kakar and Vamik Volkan. My efforts may claim a bit of adventurous spirit in integrating the clinical and the cognitive with the social-historical traditions in the scrutiny of 'soft violence'. I have commented on the way an individual's mind functions when experiencing and recapitulating less brutal but emotionally traumatic events. I have also been humbled by the spark of humanity that has shown through the fear and resentment. Simultaneously, I remained aware that society and culture, complete with the rich historical and political heritage of the land, come in the way, and participate in weaving the total pattern of the experience. Whether, with all sorts of compromises and limitations, the entire effort has been meaningful awaits the judgement of the readers.

I have many persons to thank for this book. Before anyone else, I thank my respondents whose names I cannot disclose. They revealed their personal world to me, and I in turn have introjected them into me. I have changed in the process.

The person who single-handedly pushed me into the study is Ashis Nandy, at that time Senior Fellow and Director of the Centre for Studies of Developing Societies, New Delhi. The Centre's project on 'Reconstructing Lives' focussing on 'Life History Construction and Mass Violence in South Asia' was his brainchild. On joining the project in 1999, I found it to be a cross-national endeavour, covering three countries—India, Pakistan and Bangladesh—and involving more than thirty researchers. I attended the workshops held at different times, and gained much from my fellow researchers, including Alan Roland, Ravi Kapur and Ashis Nandy. This research group taught me to see the interaction between culture and suffering.

I acknowledge my debt to those who introduced me to the refugee population in Kolkata. I have received emotional and academic support from a number of my teachers and friends. My special thanks to Amit Ranjan Basu, Debabrata Biswas, Dinabadhu Bhattacharyya, Dipankar Das, Leena Nair, Nanigopal Majumdar, Salil Gupta, Saugata Basu, Somnath Bhattacharyya. Excellent editorial help came from Rivika Israel. I am appreciative of Samya's active interest in this manuscript and the interactions with Madhuparna Banerjee and Mandira Sen.

I am grateful to Tapas and Pupai for their patience and for bearing the brunt of my edginess throughout the entire period of my work.

Introduction

A dog, a mixed breed of a cur and a fox terrier, in Ivan Petrovich Pavlov's laboratory, underwent a traumatic experience unnatural for its species. It was initially conditioned to expect food after exposure to a circular stimulus and to apprehend electric shock after an elliptical stimulus. Then the difference between the two shapes was systematically decreased to induce 'madness'. Experimental neurosis was generated in the laboratory through the conflicting responses in the dog's brain, as it failed to decipher if the given shape was a provider of food or pain.[1] The violence did not hurt the dog's body too much, but jeopardized its familiar world.

Reflecting on the kind of violence faced during the Bengal Partition by the middle-class Hindu refugees I interviewed, I came to sense that they had been up against a 'soft violence' that was relentless, insidious and disorienting. They could no longer tell with confidence whether old friends had now become new foes. Perhaps they were imagining this. Or perhaps it was a true reading of the situation. It was a confused time, and the world was turning upside down, filled with innuendo, rumour, gossip and uncertainty. Violent incidents did take place but were not on the scale witnessed in Punjab. Indeed, the refugees were the targets of a different violence, an extreme form of mental assault that chilled them with fear, and eventually led to their departure for India. The impact of this violence on their psyche was of a different nature compared to what an outright massacre would have wrought. Its consequences were lifelong for the victims, and held serious implications for the politics and social history of the new state of West Bengal.

History and psychology have a complex relationship. On the surface they seem to have divergent, even contradictory, aims and outcomes; yet underneath they are interdependent. History generally resides in the events of the outer world; psychology concerns itself with happenings in the inner world. Nevertheless, in recent scholarship, they have begun to share space judiciously. Psychology as a newer discipline, uses the word 'history' freely, as in 'case history' and 'psychohistory'; yet, because the desire to analyse one's own feelings being at least as old as the desire to document and interpret events, history too has consistently engaged with thought processes, more so in modern times in the form of emotional or sexual history.[2] Psychoanalysis has re-entered the domain of culture as another means of accessing and interpreting historical events. We shall probably not overstretch the point if we claim that recently, at least some of the major interpretations of historical events that outraged the world have stemmed primarily from psychosocial causes: the desire of the conquerors to represent themselves as not only more powerful than the conquered, but also as people who are victorious by virtue of their superior intelligence, culture and morality.

It is against this background that one must clarify the position of psychological writings on Partition—sixty-five years after the event—in historical terms. There is no dearth of historical works on Partition. Unfortunately, they leave us with a sense of incompleteness. Some of the expressions used to qualify Partition in historically inclined texts—'enigma', 'invisibility', 'riddle', 'incomprehensiveness'—are indications of the incompleteness I am talking about.[3] Indeed, there is a constant temptation in the psychologically minded to write 'another history' or a 'history of histories' of Partition.[4] Some other works on mass violence and displacement throughout the world also give the same impression—there is no satisfactory sense of closure.

There are two plausible and interrelated reasons for this. Firstly, there is perhaps a too determined search for answers in a well-researched and well-organized narration of a sequence of events. Such works end up overplaying outer history and downplaying inner history. I hasten to add that most of the works on violence today, following Robert Jay Lifton,[5] incorporate documentations of subjectivities obtained from interviews with sufferers. Yet, it is not the full story and it may not even represent the relatively untainted version of inner history; especially so, when such interviews might have begun from the presupposition that certain outer events generate specific pradictable responses in the victims. Such stereotypical generalizations about 'trauma' may end up with psychologically superficial formulations.[6] Secondly, many who have worked on the history of Partition have had personal associations with Partition. So, one can always ask if the sense of incompleteness in response to partition studies implicates the fate of their own emotions that were not properly respected within the methods and conventions of history writing.

There may be even more complex dimensions of research on violence. We know that in the deeper, 'untouchable' crevices of our fantasies, we nurture the possibility of being both perpetrators and victims of violence.[7] Does a story of violence stir such hidden swirls inside our psyche that do not follow logic? Do such stories clash with what we would like to see ourselves as and which urge us to erect defences? Groping with the memories of the victims and perpetrators, are we, the researchers, constantly negotiating with our own fears?[8]

As I am not a historian, I do not wish to comment upon or critique history.[9] I confess that I have eschewed history as understood by the mainstream discipline. The historically sensitized reader would find many significant contributions to the history of Partition missing from this book. A part of this omission must be due to my inadequate reading of history. I omitted some others despite my acquaintance with them, because I did not find the required degree of relevance to my psychological search in these works. This is not to say that I question their contribution—they simply do not relate to the domain of psychological 'meaning' of partition experience as I want to view it.

Nor is this an anthology of case histories of persons suffering violence during Partition. In the last sixty-five years, real or close to real case histories of partition victims have come up in hundreds of books, articles, and literary products, the last being occasionally more psychologically informed. My data consist of the narratives of a few persons who had left East Bengal during a stipulated time at a tender age. From their expressions, I have attempted to reconstruct the psychological nuances of a specific type of trauma. Therefore, my focus is on the memory of Partition.This book is probably the first serious attempt to conceptualize the Bengal Partition psychologically but I consider it as offering a slightly new methodology. I refer to the methodological style of eliciting total life history to put the partition experience in context of one's personality as viewed from the psychoanalytical perspective. I do not claim to proffer a complete psychological understanding of Partition or even giving a final closure. Furthermore, although a large part of my interpretative stance is psychoanalytical, it feeds mostly upon Freud and Laing, which I find more relevant to my context; and may evoke different interpretations within the psychoanalytical scholarship.

Life stories are necessarily qualitative in nature. The qualitative methodology of this work was geared to appreciate the way partition experience is retained and recollected by aged persons after many decades. Experience refers to the personal saga of passing through a series of situations in life and their individual interpretation. Thus, experience includes utilizing one's personal memory to derive meaning from new situations. Memory is a kind of record that may well be distorted dynamically, in terms of both retention and recollection, and also be reconstructed afresh. Therefore, experience works both ways; it dwells in the past to foresee the future, and hibernates to create.

Retention refers to the ability to hold experiences. While cognitive psychology and neuropsychology try to define the capacity of different 'types' of internal storages,[10] memory, especially that of personal events, remains one of the most complex phenomena. This is partly due to its brushing with personalized meaning and consequently the possibility of idiosyncratic distortion. Such distortions may be reflected in the partial and/or total forgetting of critical events, errors of memory, confabulations and dissociations in 'normal' persons, where the retained/recollected 'facts' do not corroborate objective reality. Retention, we know now, is not a simple neurological impression. The memory of the past constantly interacts with the impressions of the present and the fantasy of the future.[11] Indeed, given the constraints of empirical research, it is extremely difficult to design an adequate phenomenological technique to study such non-linear intricacies of memory.[12]

Recollection is another stage in this reconstruction of the past as recollection occurs within the scaffold of a moment that uniquely decides what may emerge and what must be suppressed. Thus the respondent's life story too is a creative production, though the respondent-creator may believe it to be the objective truth. Delving deeper into this debate makes us question the nature of reality itself. Although this is not the right place to go for this discourse, the reader may notice a tinge of scepticism about reality in my propositions, which are kept deliberately tentative. In this sense, this is not a study in oral history, since oral history, although recognizing the liabilities of memory, ultimately uses oral evidences as having some kind of retrievable truth value.[13] In other words, I embark upon the task of *understanding the memory of Partition*, not Partition per se.[14] Indeed, this is probably what Greenberg means when he claims that Partition has no one meaning.[15]

Finally, we consider chronological age, since all of my respondents were above sixty. Age in its association with decay, makes a person biologically vulnerable to the errors of memory. Age, in its association with experience, renders a richness to life. For some of my respondents, the memory of Partition has changed with age as new meanings have emerged. For others, the meaning constructed decades back had been kept intact. Others have apparently dismissed its relevance from their life.

Age is important for a second reason in this research. Psycho-neurological studies tell us that recollection of traumatic and non-traumatic memories of childhood and adolescence, although sharing some common features with adults, are subject to different brain systems.[16] During Partition, most of my respondents were pre-adolescents or in their teens, a few were in their early twenties. Given the characteristic emotions, perceptions and nature of brain functioning associated with the teens, their experiences may derive special meaning.

These considerations determine my methodology. In Chapter 1, I have detailed this methodology and situated myself within the study. I contacted a number of persons who had migrated during a stipulated time from East Bengal to West Bengal, collected their life narratives, and interpreted these in the light of psychological understanding. While this seems common sense enough, I may underscore that I have adhered to this common sense after considering the complexity of memory. Nothing but talking to my respondents would give me a chunk of their 'experience'; yet my direct questioning might motivate them to distort their memory by adopting defences. Of course, I could not claim that the respondents would not erect defences even under a free narrative condition, but I hoped that it would be weaker than under direct questions.

During my interpretation, I had to consider the unconscious distortions that would automatically shove me towards a psychoanalytically informed explanation of motives. Here I tread on shaky grounds, as I do not have adequate information to be reasonably analytic. Yet, I am grateful that there is a psychohistorical tradition that sanctions comments on the psychology of persons based on the available data of their childhood and youth.[17] I ventured a similar approach here, though my methodology was not one of clearly defined psychohistory.

In one of his writings, Ashis Nandy pointed out that there have been very few psychologically informed studies on partition violence, let alone systematic ones.[18] Yet, we do not feel that we have a dearth of comments on the psychology of partition violence–although, formally speaking, they often come from scholars from other disciplines, and also journalists, novelists, and writers of memoirs. I find the memoirs most educative; this is lay psychology at its best, and we cannot deny that often such lay interpretations ring a bell of truth in the professional's ears. Methodologically and conceptually, this has serious implications about what we mean by 'psychology'–as a subject matter and in terms of methods. But that is altogether a different issue.

That much of Partition's causes and impacts were 'psychological' has been acknowledged formally or informally by authors.[19] Since my participants were mostly Hindu *bhadralok* (the genteel, educated section of society, upper caste, middle class and above), their class characteristics showed through their responses. While some authors have tried to focus on specific groups that suffered violence of a special and sometimes spectacular kind, like women,[20] or lower castes,[21] mine were more ordinary. My respondents often did not have a dramatic tale to tell, and therefore, were often guilt-ridden both for failing to give their next generation a stable identity and for not suffering enough to justify this failure.

In this study, I have worked with the notion that although violence in terms of bloodshed, abduction, and rape was less in Bengal as compared to Punjab, the suffering, as mentioned above, was not less; this was a different kind of pain—a different quality of psychological state, claiming a distinctive methodology for study. From this perspective, violence is not only violation of the body, but also of the mind as well. We cannot simply generalize that there was more 'violence' in Punjab and less in Bengal, although we may say that there was more bloodshed in Punjab and less in Bengal. The psychological processing of this other kind of violence, though hinted upon,[22] has not been studied in depth in the context of Partition.

Although British historians liked to believe that Hindus and Muslims had never lived together amicably, this might be just another example of the outsider's prejudice or motivated folly.[23] The two-nation theory was floated strongly from 1930 onwards. The talk between Gandhi and Jinnah in 1944 was a failure. In 1945, as a strategy, the British government decided to prepare for independence of India. In 1946, the possibilities of Partition and Independence were crystallizing with the call for Direct Action Day on 16 August 1946 by the Muslim League. Subsequently, the Great Calcutta Riot was followed by the Noakhali carnage and other violent eruptions throughout East Bengal. While Gandhi's intervention brought the killings to a stop, the rift was never bridged. Migration followed like a revitalized stream, although it had probably started surreptitiously earlier. In July 1947, the British Parliament passed the Indian Independence Act that finalized the partition arrangement.[24]

After Partition and Independence on 15 August 1947, there were fresh waves of violence, though in a scattered way. A new surge of persecution and violence erupted around 1950 in East Bengal, then East Pakistan, resulting in a big influx of Hindus migrating to West Bengal. Between 1946 to 1952, the estimated number of people who perished varies between an initially claimed half a million to more than three and half million. Among those who were killed, more than three-fourths were from the western border. The number of displaced persons ranged in different estimates between ten millions to eighteen millions.[25] A proper statistics of abduction is probably more difficult to obtain.[26] That way, the killings in Bengal were fewer in number than in the Punjab. But pain may not necessarily be measured in terms of chopped heads; there exist different qualities of pain. The understanding of this other violence requires awareness about the personal interpretation of the major historical events as well as everyday incidents by the victims.

In Bengali, there have been plenty of stories on Partition, but they often do not give descriptions of gory violence, nor is the theme built around bloodshed, as may be seen in some of the famous novels concerning the events in the western border, such as in Khushwant Singh's *Train to Pakistan* (1956) or Bapsi Sidhwa's *Cracking India* (1991).[27] Of course, stories around violence in the western border, just like in the east, are not all about carnage; there are softer and humane ones also.[28] Indeed most of them, almost rhetorically talk about both bestiality and humanity. Short stories by Sadat Hasan Manto are best examples of this, and probably can serve as rich source of psychoanalytical interpretation. If we look at the stories on the eastern end of the country, in books or films,[29] we would find more pathos, a streak of sadness, mourning for the loss of an idealized life in both content and language–as in Ritwik Ghatak's films, in novellas and short stories by authors like Jyotirmoyee Devi, Narendranath

Mitra, Ramapada Chowdhury, Ashapurna Devi, in Narayan Sanyal's treatise on the refugees, in collections edited by Debesh Ray, Manabendra Bandyopadhyay, in Atin Bandyopadhyay and Sunil Gangopadhyay's stories and novels, to mention just a few. What does this difference connote?

From my interviews I felt that Bengal faced a different kind of violence, which I called 'soft violence'. Was the response to soft violence, the development of the pain, the reactions and resolutions qualitatively different? How did this pain contribute to the way the victims remembered and narrated their life stories? In my understanding, soft violence differs from brutal violence in its mode of delivery: in the shrinking difference between goodness and evil, between friend and foe, by juxtaposing contradictory emotions; like the dog in Pavlov's laboratory.

My argument develops from the analysis of the interviews of my respondents. In their life story narratives, I observed certain characteristics that I have described in Chapters 2 and 3. There was the expected eulogization of the motherland and a tone of lament. But there were other subtle clues to denote conflict. For one thing, the inability to locate the all- engulfing fear that throbbed within and around, often criss-crossed with anger and guilt. Hence neither anger nor guilt could be expressed in unambiguous terms, but peeped through innocuous statements or erupted in the form of inner contradictions.

I also wanted to understand the way the pre-existing personality disposition of the respondents might have affected their narratives. In Chapter 4, I have posited that personality characteristics render different meanings to similar experiences, and identical meaning to apparently divergent experiences. Thus, I argue that the very objectivity of the experiences can be questioned; Partition means what Partition is in one's mind's mirror.

One can see that much of this discussion refers to the confusion in identity and identification. From personal identity we move to collective self. In Chapter 5, I have suggested that the identity born through experiencing soft violence would spill over in the formation of the cultural and political identity as well. But a topic such as the formation of political identity cannot be discussed properly within such a small span. Aware of its limitations, I hope the discussion will lead other people to follow up with perhaps more success.

Why talk of Partition after so many years? Could we not just turn our backs to the misfortune and start afresh? The fact is India cannot; probably Pakistan and Bangladesh cannot either. With our globalized progression, politicized agriculture and confused industrialization, we come back repeatedly to the theme of love and hate between the neighbouring communities, enmeshed in the heralded and failed promises of prosperity and peace in this subcontinent. We witnessed intense interest and sensitivity to partition research around completion of fifty years of Independence. The attention implies that we have not resolved the partition riddle.

Psychoanalytical constructs to understand migration and uprooting also have a long history. In recent decades, psychoanalysis has got itself out of the clinic and established its position as a mode of discourse.[30] Yet, psychoanalysis has been used in the context of Partition in a small way. Some psychoanalytical concepts have been used freely by many, especially those of mourning and regression.[31] A few significant authors writing on the politics of this subcontinent, attempting to provide an answer with a psychoanalytically informed approach are Alan Roland, Ashis Nandy, Masud Khan, Salman Akhtar and Sudhir Kakar.[32]

I conclude, not unexpectedly, with a sense of dissatisfaction. Many questions continue to gnaw me. Some of them are well formed and some embryonic. My unfinished business lies in understanding how the psychology of politics of West Bengal, from 1947 through 1971, and onwards to today has been influenced, if at all, by the memory of Partition. My interviewees were Hindu; is there an identical process for the Muslims who migrated to Pakistan from India? Why does the term 'refugee' upset even those who had not seen Partition? Where lies the collective legacy? Then we have the question of perpetuation of the memory of soft violence. The generation that faced Partition is going to be extinct soon. Do they leave any impact on the next?

What about what Hirsch calls 'postmemory'?[33] How do the children and grandchildren of the partition victims look at Partition?[34] It is perhaps too early to answer these questions. Yet, I believe as we move temporally away from 1947 the memory of Partition would be painted afresh, and the new generations would continue to find meanings that the direct sufferers of Partition had found so hard to unravel.

NOTES

1 Ivan Petrovitch Pavlov.1941. *Lectures on conditioned reflexes*, vol 2: *Conditioned reflexes and psychiatry*, trans and edited by W. Horsley Gantt (London: Lawrence & Wishart). The experiment had been conducted by Shenger-Krestovnikova and first reported by Pavlov in 1927.

2 P. N. Stearns and C. Z. Stearns.1985. Emotionology: Clarifying the history of emotions and emotional standards. *American Historical Review* 90, 813-36; William M. Reddy. 2001. *The navigation of feeling: A framework for the history of emotions* (Cambridge: Cambridge University Press). Also see Michel Foucault. 1979 [1976]. *The history of sexuality*. 3 vols, trans. by Robert Hurley (London: Allen Lane). The very first line of its introduction in the first volume desires to translate fables to history: 'The aim of this series of studies is to transcribe into history the fable of *Les bijoux indiscrets*'. A new book in this genre is by F. Dhaboiwala. 2012. *The origins of sex: A history of the first sexual revolution* (London: Penguin).

3 For example, Sandip Bandyopadhyaya. 1996. The riddle of partition: Memories of the Bengali Hindus. In R. Samaddar, ed. *Reflections of the partition in the east* (Delhi: Vikas): 59-60; Ashis Nandy. 1999. The invisible holocaust and the journey as an exodus: The poisoned village and the stranger city. *Postcolonial Studies* 2, 3, 305-29; Anindita Dasgupta. 2013. Memories of a land divided. *Himal*, 18 March.

4 Gyanendra Pandey. 2001. *Remembering partition: Violence, nationalism and history in India* (Cambridge: Cambridge University Press).

5 Robert Jay Lifton is an American psychiatrist and author, famous for his writings on war and political violence. Some of his acclaimed writings

are: 1968. *Death in life: Survivors of Hiroshima* (New York: Random House); 1973. *Home from the war: Vietnam veterans–neither victims nor executioners* (New York: Simon & Schuster); with Richard A. Falk. 1982. *Indefensible weapons: The political and psychological case against nuclearism* (New York: Basic Books); 1986. *The Nazi doctors: Medical killing and the psychology of genocide* (New York: Basic Books); with Eric Markusen. 1990. *The genocidal mentality: Nazi holocaust and nuclear threat* (New York: Basic Books).

6 PTSD or Post Traumatic Stress Disorder is a category of psychiatric disorder researched upon thoroughly after the Vietnam War and included in professional psychiatric diagnosis of the day. There have been works on PTSD in relation to natural and manmade disasters as well as abuse and personal mishaps. However, the literature on trauma and PTSD has been criticized on the ground that it necessarily considers trauma reactions within a statistically defined arena of behaviours. Such categories have been critiqued for encouraging politicization of victimhood. See P. Bracken. 1998. Hidden agendas: deconstructing post-traumatic stress disorder. In P. Bracken and C. Petty, eds, *Rethinking the trauma of war* (New York: Free Association Books), 38-59; D. A. Summerfield. 1999. A critique of seven assumptions behind psychological trauma programmes in war-affected areas. *Social Science and Medicine* 48, 1449-62; D. A. Summerfield. 2001. The invention of post-traumatic stress disorder and the social usefulness of a psychiatric category. *British Medical Journal* 322, 95-98. Also see for considerations in changing the category in response to such critiques C. R. Brewin et al. 2009. Reformulating PTSD for DSM-V: Life after Criterion A. *Journal of Traumatic Stress* 22, 5, 366–73.

There are a number of direct and indirect arguments for this statement in the existing literature. Starting from the dynamics of sadomasochism, it is recognized in clinical and criminal psychology that the victim self and the perpetrator self may not be too distant. In many instances of abuse, it has been demonstrated that the victim develops a sort of identification with the perpetrator. Robert Jay Lifton had shown the psychological intermingling of victims and executioners in relation to war veterans, see 1973. *Home from the war*. Ashis Nandy says that in genocide and other violent inter-community conflicts we are actually trying to kill our hated selves; see Ashis Nandy et al. 1995. *Creating a nationality: The Ramjanmabhumi movement and fear of the self* (New Delhi: Oxford University Press). This approach is expounded eloquently in the writing of Lloyd deMause. 2002. *The emotional life of nations* (New York: Karnac). Even in smaller interpersonal contexts, victims and perpetrators seem to be bound in a dyadic relation, depending upon their pre-trauma bonding. See Jill N. Kearns and Frank D. Fincham. 2005. Victim and perpetrator accounts of interpersonal transgressions: Self-serving or relationship-serving biases? *Personality & Social Psychology Bulletin* 31, 3, 321–33; A. M. Stillwell and R. F. Baumeister. 1997. The construction of victim and perpetrator memories: Accuracy and distortion in role-based accounts. *Personality and Social Psychology Bulletin* 23, 1157-72.

8 See for subtle association between memories of violence, in patients and therapists alike, Alan Roland. 2010. Trauma and dissociation: 9/11 and the India Pakistan partition. *Contemporary Psychoanalysis* 46, 380-94; also see for similarities and contrasts between memories in violence across countries, J. D. Greenberg. 2005. Generations of memory: Remembering partition in India/Pakistan and Israel/Palestine. *Comparative Studies of South Asia, Africa and the Middle East*, 25, 1, 89-110.

9 History and historicism, as they have entered human thought, have been viewed and critiqued differently by modern scholars on different counts. One might even enumerate multiple ways of defining history. For critique of linear historicism, see Ashis Nandy. 1995. History's forgotten doubles, *History and Theory* 34, 2, Theme Issue: *World Historians and Their Critics* 44-66. The need for certainty and authenticity expounded in mainstream history has been critiqued, as in one sense it seems to lack 'ecological validity'. It has been argued that history resides largely in memory, which can be unearthed but not verified systematically to generate any singular truth. Others consider history as more inclusive. For them, history incorporates the study of society with reference to geography, archaeology, economics, anthropology and literature. Viewed that way, history contains myths and subjectivities as well. In the context of Partition, the relation between memory and history, and the role of history in violence studies have been discussed by earlier authors; see Gyanendra Pandey. 2001. *Remembering partition: Violence, nationalism and history in India* (Cambridge: Cambridge University Press). See also note 13.

10 See as a classic example, G. A. Miller. 1956. The magical number seven, plus or minus two: Some limits on our capacity for processing information, *Psychological Review* 63, 2, 81–97.

11 Ashis Nandy in his introduction to the collection *Time Warps* (2001),

expresses this as: 'If there is no "real" or immutable past, and all constructed pasts and all history are ways of coping with hopes, ambitions, fears and anxieties in the present, so are the visions and fantasies of the future. The technologies of the mind that we employ to grapple with the future are not essentially different from the ones with which we cope with the past. Only, in the case of future, our constructions regularly turn out to be self-destructive' (Introduction in *Time Warps*: p. 3).

12 Scientists have taken up the challenge of unearthing the neurological mechanisms of memory through techniques like functional magnetic resonance imaging (fMRI) that measures brain activity by detecting associated changes in blood flow. See E.A. Kensinger. 2004. Remembering emotional experiences: The contribution of valence and arousal. *Reviews in the Neurosciences* 15, 241-252; Sarah Steinvorth, Suzanne Corkin and Eric Halgren. 2006. Ecphory of autobiographical memories: An fMRI study on recent and remote memory retrieval. *Neuroimage* 30, 1, 285–98. But it is one thing to understand the underlying neurobiological mechanism and another thing to record or manipulate it behaviourally through physical or social stimuli. The former is at micro level, and the latter at macro level; each has its unique challenge.

13 Indeed, the study of remembered events through oral history and its validity form an ongoing debate. See Peter Burke. 1989. History as social memory. In Thomas Butler, ed. *Memory: history, culture and the mind* (Oxford: Basil Blackwell): 97-113; P. H. Hutton. 1993. *History as an art of memory* (Hanover, NH: University Press of New England); P. Thompson. 2000. *The voice of the past: Oral history*, 3rd ed. (Oxford: Oxford University Press); Marietjie Oelofse. 2011. Applying principles of historical critique: Authentic oral history? *2011 International Conference on Social Science and Humanity IPEDR, vol.5* (Singapore: IACSIT Press), V41-44, downloaded on 7.08.2012 from *www.ipedr.com/vol5/no2/12-H10078.pdf*; Sukeshi Karma, 2002. *Bearing witness: partition, independence, end of the Raj* (Calgary, Alberta: University of Calgary Press). In the context of Partition, in a critique of Suvir Kaul's anthology, Naunidhi Kaur remind us of the necessity to remember the limitations of memory while depending on oral history or memories of trauma. See Suvir Kaul, ed., 2001. *The partitions of memory: The afterlife of the division of India* (New Delhi: Permanent Black); Naunidhi Kaur. 2001. New perspectives on partition. *Frontline* 18, 17 Aug 18-31.

14 Earlier commentators on Partition have highlighted this diffusion of document and memory. For example Dipesh Chakrabarty writes: 'Memory is much more than what the mind can remember or what objects can help us document about the past. It is also about what we do not always consciously know that we remember until something actually, as the saying goes, jogs our memory. And there remains the question, so much discussed these days in the literature on the Indian Partition, of what people do not even wish to remember, the forgetting that comes to our aid in dealing with pain and unpleasantness in life.' See Dipesh Chakrabarty. 1996. Remembered villages: Representation of Hindu-Bengali memories in the aftermath of the partition. *Economic and Political Weekly* 31, 32, 2143. Also see in this context, Jill Didur. 2006. *Unsettling partition: Literature, gender, memory*. (Toronto: University of Toronto Press).

15 J. D. Greenberg. 2005. Generations of memory: Remembering partition in India/Pakistan and Israel/Palestine. *Comparative Studies of South Asia, Africa and the Middle East* 25, 1, 89-110.

16 Ingrid M. Cordon et al. 2004. Memory for traumatic experiences in early childhood, *Developmental Review* 24, 101–32; R. Fivush. 1998. Children's recollections of traumatic and non-traumatic events. *Development and Psychopathology* 10, 699–716.

17 Psychohistorical tradition focuses on the effects of early development on later political and social beliefs and attitudes. See Aurel Ende. 1980. Battering and neglect: Children in Germany, 1860-1978. *Journal of Psychohistory* 7, 249-79; Alan Dundes. 1984. *Life is like a chicken coop ladder: A study of German national character through folklore*. (Berkeley: University of California Press); Lloyd deMause. 2005. The childhood origins of the holocaust. *Journal of Psychohistory* 33, 204-22; Richard A. Koenigsberg. 1975. *Hitler's ideology: A study in psychoanalytic sociology* (New York: The Library of Social Science).

18 See Ashis Nandy. 2002. The death of an empire. *Sarai Reader* 2, 14-21. There were a few works earlier, and a few more have come up subsequently. Nandy mentions Stephen Keller. 1975. *Uprooting and social change* (New Delhi: Manohar). Besides: see Sudhir Kakar. 1992. Some unconscious aspects of ethnic violence in India. In Veena Das, ed., *Mirrors of violence: Communities, riots and survivors in South Asia* (Bombay: Oxford University Press): 135-45.

19 As Ayesha Jalal said, 'The psychological legacy of Partition has left a

much deeper impact on people's minds than the social, economic and political dynamics that led to the division.' (1966. Secularists, subalterns and the stigma of communalism: Partition historiography revisited: *Modern Asian Studies* 30, 3, 681).

20 See Jasodhara Bagchi and Subhoranjan Dasgupta, eds. vol 1, 2003; vol 2, 2008. *The trauma and the triumph: Gender and partition in eastern India* (Kolkata: Stree); Mushirul Hasan, ed. 2000. *Inventing boundaries: Gender, politics and the partition of India* (New Delhi: Oxford University Press); Ritu Menon and Kamla Bhasin. 1998. *Borders and boundaries: Women in India's partition* (New Delhi: Kali for Women); Uditi Sen. 2011. Spinster, prostitute or pioneer? Images of refugee women in post-partition Calcutta. EUI working paper MWP 2011/34 (Italy: European University Institute) downloaded on 20.08.2012 from http://cadmus.eui.eu/bitstream/handle/1814/19216/MWP_Sen_2011_34.pdf?sequence=1.

Indeed, partition violence had been gendered to an extent which probably has not yet been revealed in its entirety. A large number of novels and stories evince this gendered nature. In a recent article Richard Lee has commented upon how violence of Partition mingles inseparably with the violence on women: see. R. Lee. 2009. The rebirth of inherited memories, *MHRA Working Papers in the Humanities* 4, 18-24; downloaded on 20.08.2012 from http://www.shaunasinghbaldwin.com/WTBR-Article_-_Inheritance_of_Memories_-RLee.pdf. See further, Jill Didur. 2006. *Unsettling partition: literature, gender, memory* (Toronto: University of Toronto Press.). A major landmark in feminist historiography is: Shauna Singh Baldwin. 1999. *What the body remembers* (New York: Anchor Books). It is interesting to note that there are indications that even these novels and stories also reflect an androcentric bias: see Radhika Purohit. 2012. An androcentric and gynocentric perspective of women as victims in partition fiction: A comparative study. *Language in India* 12: 2 (February 2012), *www.languageinindia.com.*

21 Much of the work in this context has been done by Sekhar Bandyopadhyay. He states that the violence perpetrated on the namashudras, that is, the Scheduled Castes, in East Bengal was much more extreme in comparison to that on the middle class and upper castes. See Sekhar Bandyopadhyay. 1994. Development, differentiation and caste: The Namasudra movement in Bengal, 1872-1947. In Sekhar Bandyopadhyay, Abhijit Dasgupta and Willem Van Schendel, eds. *Bengal: Communities,*

development and states (New Delhi: Manohar): 90-119; Sekhar Bandyopadhyay. 1998. Changing Borders, Shifting Loyalties: Religion, Caste and the Partition of Bengal in 1947, *Asian Studies Institute Working Paper* 2. Retrieved 20 October 2012 from http://www.victoria.ac.nz/slc/asi/publications/02-changing-borders.pdf; Sekhar Bandhypadhyay. 2011. *Caste, Protest and Identity in Colonial India: The Namasudras of Bengal, 1872-1947* [1992] 2nd ed (Delhi: Oxford University Press).

22 Haimanti Roy. 2006. Citizenship and national identity in post-partition Bengal, 1947-65. PhD Diss. University of Connecticut. Downloaded on 21.12.2012 from http://etd.ohiolink.edu/view.cgi?acc_num=ucin1147886544.

23 See Ashish Nandy. 2002. Telling the story of communal conflicts in South Asia: Interim report on a personal search for defining myths. *Ethnic and Racial Studies* 25, 1, 1-19; Mushirul Hasan and Asim Roy, eds. 2005. *Living together separately: Cultural India in history and politics* (New Delhi: Oxford University Press); Nilanjana Chatterjee. 2005. *Interrogating victimhood: East Bengali refugee narratives of communal violence*, PhD Diss., Brown University. Retrieved 20 October 2012 from http://www.swadhinata.org.uk/document/chatterjeeEastBengal%20Refugee.pdf. Also see Tapan Raychaudhuri. 2009. *Muslims and Hindus in British India.* Barrister Syed Ishtiaq Ahmed Memorial Lecture delivered at the Asiatic Society of Bangladesh, 22 Nov 2009;.downloaded 10 May 2012 from http://www.asiaticsociety.org.bd/journals/Dec_2009/contents/1_Tapan%20R%20Choudhury.htm. Starting with the sarcasm that 'The Europeans as we all know are omniscient. Having captured the governance of India, they decided that the Hindus and Muslims are two distinct people who had been at each other's throat from time immemorial', Raychaudhuri proceeds to state the perpetuating easy flow of emotions and communication between Muslims and Hindus in this subcontinent.

24 We would miss the psychological beauty of the politics of this period if we forget that Jinnah probably never wanted two nations and also that his influence was but tentative among Bengali Muslim League politicians. See Ayesha Jalal. 1985. *The sole spokesman: Jinnah, the Muslim League, and the demand for Pakistan* (Cambridge: Cambridge University Press); Haroun or Rashid. 2003. *The foreshadowing of Bangladesh: Bengali Muslim League and Muslim politics, 1906-47* (Dhaka: Dhaka University Press); Stanley Wolpert. 1984. *Jinnah of Pakistan* (London: Oxford University

Press); and also, Jaswant Singh. 2010. *Jinnah: India, partition, independence* (New Delhi: Oxford University Press), a book that caused the author's expulsion from the BJP.

25 Volumes have been written on the history and memory of Partition–the politics, the violence, the massacre. Any list would be pathetically incomplete, but I refer to a few that contains many cross-references, some that discuss the preludes and preparatory politics of Partition and also some others that emphasize, in some way the memories of brutalities and violence in different forms. Indeed, writings on partition politics started as early as 1947, some published documents being G. D. Khosla. 1949/1999. *Stern reckoning* (New Delhi: Oxford University Press); Sir Francis Tucker. 1950. *While memory serves* (London: Cassell); A. Campbell Johnson. 1951. *Mission with Mountbatten* (London: Robert Hale); V. P. Menon. 1957. *The transfer of power in India* (Bombay: Orient Longman); Penderel Moon. 1961. *Divide and quit* (London: Chatto and Windus).

Among the relatively recent publications, see Leonard Gordon. 1978. Divided Bengal: Problems of nationalism and identity in the 1947 partition. In Mushirul Hasan, ed. *India's partition: process, strategy and mobilization* (New Delhi: Oxford University Press): 279-321; David Page. 1982. *Prelude to partition, Indian Muslims and the imperial system of control* (New Delhi: Oxford University Press); Anita Inder Singh. 1987. *The origins of partition of India* (New Delhi: Oxford University Press); Hasan, ed.1993. *India's partition: process, strategy and mobilization*; Ajit Bhattacharjea. 1997. *Countdown to partition: The final days* (New Delhi: Harper Collins); Partha Chatterjee. 1997. On religious and linguistic nationalism: The second partition of Bengal. In Peter van der Veer and Hartmut Lehmann, eds. *Nationalism and religion: Perspectives on Europe and Asia* (Princeton: Princeton University Press): 112-128. D. N. Panigrahi. 2004. *The story of imperialism in retreat* (London: Routledge); Reece Jones. 2006. *Whose homeland? Territoriality and religious nationalism in pre-partition Bengal.* (Thousand Oaks, CA: Sage). Yasmin Khan. 2007. *The great partition: The making of India and Pakistan* (New Haven: Yale University Press); Joya Chatterji, 2007. *The Spoils of Partition: Bengal and India, 1947-1967*(Cambridge: Cambridge University Press); Ian Talbot and Gurharpal Singh. 2009. *The partition of India* (Cambridge: Cambridge University Press); Ira Pande, ed. 2009. *The great divide; India and Pakistan* (New Delhi: Harper Collins); Neeti Nair. 2011. *Changing homelands: Hindu politics and the partition of India* (New Delhi: Permanent Black); Ella Moore. 2012. Partition, politics to people: A study of the high politics of partition and its impact on the everyday lives and loyalties in West Bengal, downloaded 20 October 2012 fromhttp://www.e-ir.info/2012/07/26/partition-everyday-lives-and-loyalties-in-west-bengal/.

For description and commentaries on violent massacre, see P. Moon. 1998. *Divide and quit*; Anders Bjorn Hansen. 2002. *Partition and genocide: Manifestation of violence in Punjab: 1937-1947* (New Delhi: India Research Press); Paul Brass. 2003. The partition of India and retributive genocide in the Punjab, 1946-47: Means, methods, and purposes. *Journal of Genocide Research* 5, 1, 71-101; Ishtiaq Ahmed. 2004. Forced migration and ethnic cleansing in Lahore in 1947: Some first person accounts (London: Oxford University Press), downloaded 10 October 2012 from http://www.statsvet.su.se/publikationer/ahmed/andra_artiklar/ahmed_on_the_move_dist.pdf; Ian Talbot. 2006. The 1947 violence in the Punjab. In Ian Talbot, ed. *The deadly embrace: Religion, politics and violence in India and Pakistan 1947-2002* (Karachi: Oxford University Press): 1-15; Gyanendra Pandey, 2006. *Routine violence: Nations, fragments, histories* (Paulo Alto: Stanford University Press); Jennifer Yusin. 2009. The silence of partition: Borders, trauma, and partition history, *Social Semiotics* 19, 4, 453-68.

26 See Andrew A. Major. 1995. The chief sufferers: Abduction of women during the partition of the Punjab. *South Asia XVIII, Special Issue*, 18, 57-72; Urvashi Butalia. 1997. Abducted and widowed women: Questions of sexuality and citizenship during partition. In Meenakshi Thapan, ed. *Embodiment: Essays on gender and identity* (New York: Oxford University Press): 90-106, downloaded 20 October 2012 from http://jan.ucc.nau.edu/~sj6/butaliaabductedwomen.pdf. Butalia points out how the line between abducted and widowed women is unclear in partition violence. In this context, the need for recording the partition-related suicide of women has also been highlighted; see David Lester. 2010. Suicide and the partition of India: A need for further investigation. *Suicidology Online* 1, 2-4.

27 Some other fictions placed in the backdrop of partition, mostly of the western border, are Atia Hussain. 1961,1997. *Sunlight on a Broken Column* New Delhi: Penguin), Rahi Masoom Raza. 1966, 1984. *Adha Gaon* (Delhi: Rajkamal), Bhisham Sahni. 1973, 1998. *Tamas* (Delhi: Rajkamal), Amitav Ghosh. 1988. *Shadow Lines* (Delhi: Ravi Dayal), to name just a few. Alok Bhalla. 1999. *Stories about the Partition of India* (Delhi: Harper Collins,

1994) is a rich repertoire of such literary efforts.

28 In this context, one excellent summary of the debates surrounding partition violence has been offered by Jason Fransisco while reviewing three anthologies of short stories and scholarly writings published in the mid-nineties. He noticed three phases of experience in the stories: those of rupture, protest and repair. See J. Fransisco. 1996. In the heat of fratricide: The literature of India's partition burning freshly. *The Annual of Urdu Studies* 2, 227-50. Also see Anna Bernard. 2010. Forms of memory: Partition as a literary paradigm, *Alif: Journal of Comparative Poetics* 30, 9-33; Alok Bhalla. 2006. *Partition dialogues: Memories of a lost home.* (New Delhi: Oxford University Press); Rituparna Roy. 2010. *South Asian partition fiction in English* (Manchester: Manchester University Press).

29 See Bhaskar Sarkar. 2009. *Mourning the nation: Indian cinema in the wake of partition* (Durham, NC: Duke University Press).

30 Patrick Mahony. 2001. *Psychoanalysis and discourse* (London: Routledge); S. Frosh et al. 2003. Taking a stand: Using psychoanalysis to explore the positioning of subjects in discourse. *British Journal of Social Psychology* 42, 39-53; J. A. Arlow. 1995. Stilted listening: Psychoanalysis as discourse. *Psychoanalytic Quarterly* 64, 2, 215-33.

31 David Ng and D. Kazanijan, eds. 2003. *Loss. The politics of mourning* (Berkeley: University of California Press).

32 I was intrigued to find that an early attempt to offer a psychoanalysis of Partition was made in 1947 by Arun Kumar Roy Chaudhary who tried to explain Muslim psychology on the basis of Oedipus complex and paranoia. See Arun Kumar Roy Chaudhury. 1947. Pakistan–a psychological analysis. *Journal of Abnormal and Social Psychology* 42, 4, 462-465.

33 Marianne Hirsch. 2008. The generation of postmemory. *Poetics Today* 29, 1, 103-28.

34 A few works partly deal with the way partition experience is handed over in families. See Meghna Guha Thakurta. 1997. Understanding the Bengal partition through reconstructing family histories: A case study. *Journal of Social Studies* 76, 57-65; Amrita Uttamchandani. 2012. *Crossing borders and generations: Sharing of partition stories among survivors and families of the partition of British India* (Chicago: The Chicago School of Professional Psychology), retrieved 20 October 2012 from http://gradworks.umi.com/35/15/3515281.html.

1

The Perspective

> *The past comes in many shapes and is forever eluding us. We remember it unevenly. To bring one event into focus obscures another. There is no neat chronology in it and sometimes not even a logical order.* – C.B. Strozier

THIS IS A TREATISE on memories: the memories of those who witnessed the Partition of Bengal in 1947 and migrated from East to West Bengal in its aftermath. The individuals who narrated their life-stories to me, despite their diverse personalities and experiences, share one common characteristic. They all have memories of two lands: one, their homeland in Bangladesh–East Pakistan or East Bengal, or 'Poorba Banga', as they call it–and the other, their acquired home in West Bengal, predominantly, Kolkata or its suburbs. A story of two homes: one that they inherited and lost, and the other they had to erect and accept.

This is also an account of *my* experience with the uprooted, *my* understanding of their sentiments, attitudes and behaviours, coloured by my own feelings and put into my frame of reference. This is important for two reasons. Firstly, my presence shaped the nature of the memories elicited through interviews in the form of dialogue. These were not simple sequences of spontaneous reveries on the part of the narrators, but also responses to my questions. The way I put the question was a significant determinant of the response; the results thus reflect two subjectivities, theirs and mine. Secondly, the request to talk about their lives with special reference to their experiences of Partition came from a *woman* of the *next generation* who happened to be a *psychologist*. These 'categories' carried their own subjective loads and influenced the respondents. Moreover, like all narrations, theirs too are social constructions, situated within an interactive interpersonal context.[1] All interactive transactions in turn, particularly those concerned directly with expressing oneself, are significant corollaries of one's identity, overt or covert self-definition.[2] Therefore, through their narratives, the respondents were projecting a self-identity onto the outer world with me serving as a medium. And 'medium' I was, carrying the spectre of the past, their past to our present.

In the context of constructing a sociology of knowledge, Berger and Luckmann discussed the reciprocity between the individual and society, and explained the interconnection between identity and social relations: 'Identity is formed by social processes. Once crystallized, it is maintained, modified, or even reshaped by social relations ... Conversely, the identities produced by the interplay of organism, individual consciousness and social structure react upon the given social structure.'[3] Likewise, my being a social agent with a purpose, my interaction with each of my respondents created a unique set of facilitatory and constraining vectors. Such sets of vectors in turn produced specific psychological patterns, ultimately expressed by the respondents on their part. Simultaneously, observing their efforts to organize their life-experiences into a coherent narrative, I was participating in their agony and joy, growing and changing with a renewed vision of the Partition and its impact, experiencing emotions very different from those with which I had embarked on this work. Ultimately, what I report here is an interpretation from my point of view, tinted with my own cognitive and affective biases. The identity of the respondents expressed through their narratives—the theme of this book—is thus shaped, de-shaped and re-shaped by our conjoint existence. In this sense, the book is a reconstruction of reconstructions.[4]

THE RESPONDENTS

Let us consider my research method, the nature of the available data and the perspective. The respondents come first. I interviewed only those Hindu women and men who had witnessed Partition and remembered it. All of them had been 'forced' to migrate from their homeland that had become a part of East Pakistan to a 'foreign' land in India. The interviews were taken between 1999 and 2003, more than fifty years after the event. Presumably, to remember the events associated with Partition in any credible detail, the individual had to have been at least 7 or 8 years old in 1947, and therefore born before 1940. In fact, all of my respondents were above 60, the majority above 70, and the eldest was a lady who had witnessed 92 autumns. I met most of them more than once, and the total interview time ranged between 4 and 20 hours. Some I also met on social occasions prior to or after the interview, and I tried to observe them in these 'natural' situations too. Some died before I could complete my work with them; their case files remain incomplete.

Interviewees' reactions to the research varied. Some of them greeted me with warmth, welcoming my interest in their life experiences. Some were politely suspicious: 'What exactly will you do with it? After all I am nobody big.' Some were openly unwilling; others were unwilling to show their unwillingness. Some wanted to know what they would gain from the interviews, if I had any connection with the government and was authorized to provide something materially valuable to them: maybe financial aid or a job for a grandson.

Caste was always a significant ingredient of the social and political milieu in East Bengal. Therefore, it was presumed that the reactions of the lower castes, particularly the Scheduled Castes (SC) and Scheduled Tribes (ST) would be largely divergent from those of the upper castes. In the present research, all the respondents were drawn from upper castes, to keep the purview of the study within manageable limits. However, the respondents came from a variety of social strata: labourers living in the 'basti', teachers, housewives, clerks, scholars and academicians, businessmen and a director of a multinational company. As I tried to locate their feelings in context, economic status and educational level became significant, but never so significant as to be major dividers.

India's Partition brought violence: bloodshed, abduction, arson and looting. Raw violence was, we all know, more rampant on the western frontier of the country. In the eastern part, gory violence was more localized, certain places including Noakhali, Dhaka and specific pockets of Khulna being the most affected. Somewhat lesser bloody violations were, however, prevalent across the entire face of East Bengal:[5] violation of social and personal belongings, conversion, uprooting and forced migration—and dramatic tales of brutal violence are not absent.

My focus here is on uprooting, on what I prefer to call a 'soft violence'. Almost none of the respondents whom I selected had to flee their homeland as a result of a violent attack by a mob of killers. In some cases, there were threats of killing or conversion. Most of them had heard rumours of violence, seen arson from a distance, heard war cries; some had even participated in riots. However, *none* of my respondents *migrated* to India in the wake of *direct physical assault* on themselves and *none* had *lost* their first-degree relatives. The respondents themselves or their family members apprehended violence, assessed and interpreted the gravity of the political situation, tried to deal with the problem, occasionally by migration within East Pakistan, and finally, at some point, decided to move to India. In Chapter 3, I shall discuss how these two modes of migration—one in response to direct carnage and the other out of apprehension—differ in their inner psychological meaning.

Choosing the respondents was not an impersonal or objective procedure per se; thus they did not constitute a 'proper' sample. They were largely my contacts, or contacts of contacts. Some of those I began with led me to others of similar background. It was, at least partially, a snowball technique.[6] Each of the respondents knew that I was a professional psychologist and a teacher. They were, therefore, in a position to erect their own defences against my intrusion. However, on the whole, only two persons whom I approached refused to meet me altogether. One lady refused owing to her ill health, stating that rewinding such memories would make her more unwell. Another man refused the appointment simply because he was 'not interested'. Did my age and gender matter? Some commented on my being born in post-independent India. Many told me 'You are from another time, you belong to another generation. How could you ever understand what we went through?' Some of them tried to make me 'feel' their experiences, providing me with rich details, painting verbal scenarios from the past. Sometimes I felt parented by their endeavour to make me see their past; they showed it the way one shows ancestral property to a descendant. Probably, if they had talked to someone from their own generation a somewhat different presentation would have emerged.

I am not sure about the impact of my gender. Nobody commented directly on it, though some expressed concern about my present status, enquired about my family, asked how I would go home late in the evening. Some mentioned my gender while talking about the position of women in a Muslim state ('As a woman you will understand . . .') or made an apologetic exception when expressing stereotypes about women ('You are an educated lady, so you are different, but generally women are . . .').

NARRATIVE AND THE NATURE OF MEMORY

We now turn to the relatively more complex aspect of the nature of our material. My choice was the narrative form. When approaching a subject from another historical period, it is the free narrative that makes the unknown most communicable. As Roland Barthes said, narrative is 'translatable without fundamental damage'.[7] Narratives can be analysed from numerous angles: phenomenological, historical, sociological, linguistic, and combinations of all or some of these. My focus is on psychological analysis, though I have borrowed from every other discipline that offered me anything relevant. In the psychological literature, there are many approaches to the understanding of a narrative. I would focus specifically on two. One is psychoanalytical.[8] It views the produced narration as the net expression of the dynamic interplay between the conscious and the unconscious.[9] The other approach comes from recent developments in cognitive psychology and looks upon a narrative as born out of the cognitive schema that an individual construes relating to the self and the environment. The structure, content and style of the narrative, according to this approach, depend on the processing of relevant information selected among the plethora of stimuli that act upon the organism. These two approaches emerge from two discrete schools of thought, but they are not contradictory. They can be merged into a focal point of understanding, with particular reference to understanding narratives in the context of the present study.

A narrative can be understood as a means of organizing knowledge.[10] Knowledge is both conscious and unconscious, and transcends the individual level to encompass the culture at large. The organization of knowledge is made possible by a shared communication within a given culture, and therefore comprises schema or prototypes. The psychoanalytical model probes the source of these prototypes while the cognitive psychologist explores how these templates function in individual and collective memory.

My approach in interpreting the narratives will draw heavily upon the psychoanalytical premise; however, the vast body of literature resulting from the study of memory in cognitive psychology cannot be ignored. I have resorted to the cognitive psychological approach to understand the nature and stylistic construction of the narratives and to psychoanalysis to interpret the underlying motivation. From the cognitive perspective, what we have here is *autobiographical memory* produced in the form of open narrative.[11] Such narratives are delivered consciously and with active deliberation; hence the alternative term 'declarative memory'. Autobiographical memory may be contrasted with the memories that we are unaware of, which operate involuntarily, silently, implicitly, and influence the acknowledged and the declared. There is, however, controversy about the inclusiveness of autobiographical memory. Some employ the term to encompass all forms of self-related information, while others ascribe the designation only to the recollection of significant events.[12] I have opted for the broader definition. In this sense all clinical data, including psychoanalytical free association and any other self-exposure are examples of autobiographical memory.[13]

Autobiographical memory, particularly when elicited in a relatively open form, is selective and liable to distortions. There is a tendency to recall only those events or ideas that are emotionally salient for the person. Those items too are remembered which help one in facing one's immediate problems by putting up an acceptable front. Besides, there is the interesting phenomenon of the oft-quoted 'reminiscence bump'.[14] This refers to the fact that middle aged and older adults tend to recall disproportionate number of incidents from their adolescence and early adulthood period, particularly from ten to twenty-five years of age. Studies indicate that people usually judge the political events occurring during this period of their life as more important and know more about them. This has particular relevance to our study because the majority of our respondents belonged to this specific age group at the time of Partition.

The 'represented' may be quite different from what 'really' took place. Experiments in memory have demonstrated that what is reported one day after the reception of an event is substantially altered after three years, even though the respondents are quite confident of the accuracy of their reporting. This false confidence is maintained even after providing information to the contrary. Memory of emotions is also similarly distorted. However, it is also true that the memory of directly experienced violent events is less amenable to change, presumably because of its rehearsal; one is likely to describe unusual events to other persons a greater number of times.[15] In the present research, experience of severe violence was not included and therefore distortion of memory is likely to reign relatively free.[16] Across the lifespan, with time, apparently isolated events gradually fall in a pattern, shed their rough edges, and finally a narrative is born. In this sense, an autobiographical narrative has a temporal development. This concept is evident in Polkinghorne's definition: 'Narrative is the cognitive process that gives meaning to temporal events by identifying them as part of a plot.'[17]

Like selective recall, distortion of recalled material is also related to the functional value of the distortion, that is, the distorted productions are congenial to enhancement of self-esteem.[18] During the narration of one's own life experiences, various schemas predominate in the recall. It may even be said that people have certain 'implicit theories' about particular domains of experience.[19] These 'theories' shape the nature of distortion. Another pertinent determinant of recall is the 'reception context', where the nature of recall and implicit theory depends on the circumstances in which the experience came about.[20] The ultimate content and form of the recalled material may be a resultant of all such selective and distorting elements.

After this briefing about the nature of autobiographical memory from a cognitive point of view, we come to the psychoanalytical understanding of narration. It shares with the cognitive approach the premise of selectivity and distortion of remembered material. Instead of the schema of the cognitive approach, the psychoanalytical perspective emphasizes unconscious motives for distortion. Thus, it deals more with the personal genesis of the content rather than with its form and external structure. According to the psychoanalytical approach, the prime motive of any action is the management of anxiety born out of intrinsic impulse or external threat. A large number of defensive manoeuvres and other disguising processes like displacement and condensation are devised for this purpose. The psychoanalytical approach attributes these defensive operations to a number of unconscious motivations such as narcissistic satisfaction, keeping unacceptable sexual and aggressive thoughts in abeyance, vicarious gratification of the above impulses, coordination and confrontation between impulses and super-ego.[21]

Both approaches, cognitive and psychoanalytical, emphasize and explain the distortion and selectivity of memory, in somewhat different languages. Psychological analysis of memory is essentially the analysis of the gap between an event and its representation.

Owing to selectivity and distortion, the factual validity of remembered events becomes debatable. Indeed, at this point I must underscore the fact that I have throughout remained sceptical about the 'truth' of the events as well as of the emotional and behavioural reactions reported. How this approach feeds on the huge body of literature on poststructural historicism is a separate issue. Presently, I am concerned only with the psychological truth, the truth *constructed* at the *moment* of narration: a truth *grown out* of the '*true*' experience, but by all probability, *different* from it. This truth is related more to the 'schema' or the 'script' of the individual that operates without conscious control, rather than to the historical 'facts'.

RECEPTION OF NARRATIVE

My reporting and analysis of the material I collected from the narratives are closely linked with my interviewing and interpretative stance. The intersubjective truth is as the narrator presents it and as the listener receives it. The reception module–consisting of an interactive space between the narrative and the world inhabited by the listener–is significant in the making as well as in the understanding of any narrative.[22] Each component in receiving a narration–asking, listening, and interpreting–has its own contribution to the outcome.

When I approached potential respondents over the phone or in person, and they asked me, 'What do you want to know?', I told them I was interested in understanding their entire life-experience, keeping in mind but not exclusively focusing on their witnessing of Partition, I wanted to know the impact of Partition on their lives, whether and how settling in West Bengal had changed their previous pattern of life, and the emotional transition this historical event may have caused in their lives. In most cases, I added that I also desired to understand them as persons.

Unless the interviewee was stuck at some point during the narration, I preferred not to pose many questions, at least not during the early stages of the interview. Apart from making the usual responses involved in 'reflective listening' or enquiries to clarify exactly some occasionally unfamiliar term or description, I did not interrupt the narrative. The interviews started in a relatively open and non-directional mode, allowing for a free narrative which I took down verbatim, and making note of any non-verbal cues. When the respondent had more or less completed the free narration, I asked for details or in-depth clarifications. Consequently, a large portion of the narrative was not directly associated with Partition. However, my interpretation of the case histories demonstrates that these apparently irrelevant references in fact are ad rem, pertinent; they help us recognize the total person who faced Partition.

The dynamic process of listening may be sifted at this point. Through listening, a message is received by one person from another, intact or in distorted form. Listening can take numerous modes: each individual has a habitual pattern of listening. In a conversation, various listening modes occur in succession,[23] resulting in facilitation or stunting of the exposition. As I listened to the narratives, I found the process of listening similar to that in a clinical situation: picking up on the words said, the feelings expressed and not expressed, the narrative content and cues, the silences.[24] In therapy one tries to relate personality predisposition, support systems available and coping modes to the disease; here I related the narrator's predisposition and personal contingencies to her perception and memory of Partition.

Listening opens the gateway to the understanding of the individual. There are numerous parameters. One cue is intonation. Take the statement, 'I am okay'. Apparently, it means what its content says, that is, the person is okay. Not always though. Maybe the speaker said, 'I *am* okay'. So, the speaker is okay, despite all the distress. The latter is the unsaid but not uncommunicated part. Or perhaps the speaker said 'I am *okay*', with an overdrawn '*kay*'. This means that the speaker is okay, but still pines for something else. Or, maybe it was '*I* am okay.' This has a postscript: 'Not everybody is, though'.

There are other dimensions in listening as well. One is the context of the statement. Why did the speaker choose to declare that she is okay? Did she need to tell it to us or to herself? What kind of person is she and what is her situation? How does this declaration relate to her chronic and immediate needs? For example, is the speaker generally a complaining and unhappy sort of person, who only on a rare occasion declares herself to be at ease with life? In that case, what was the occasion for her statement? Or, is she a person who is generally happy with life and was this just a casual reiteration of her overall mood? The association of the context may come in a sequential way, that is, one image preceded or succeeded by another related one. For example, the statement may have been a response to a simple casual question like 'How are you, dear?' Or it may have followed an unpleasant argument that she wanted to bring to a close. Or it may have come after a dreamy reminiscence of the good old days, an accounting of what she had had, and she was thanking her creator for the blessings. All these nuances are only revealed through listening.

Again, the associated ideas may be spatially separated, yet intrinsically bound by a similarity in imagery, language or inner meaning. Thus one task of active listening is to identify the unconscious binding theme, sometimes called the 'script', which is created by the person. The chain of association serves as a clue to the individual's untold frame, the process that operates beyond her consciousness to shape the narration.[25]

In listening to a patient in psychoanalysis, the feelings of the therapist play a major role; counter-transference is important.[26] Counter-transference is the unconscious exchange of messages between the two persons held in a bond of dialogue. It provides an indication of how the dyadic interaction is proceeding. Indeed, in a psychoanalytical paradigm the analyst is equally a part of the psychic process of treatment and equally exposed to the transforming influences. The 'reciprocal reaction of two psychic systems' paves the way to the understanding of the analysand's self by both the partners in the dyad. Although the counter-transference can, at certain points, impair the process of self-exposure, it is on the whole constructive. Keeping this in mind, in most cases I have tried to keep track of my own feelings and reactions as well.

My mode of listening was predominantly of the 'reflective' kind. Reflective listening has its roots in psychoanalysis, but is elaborated and developed in detail in Carl Rogers' 'client-centred' therapy.[27] In reflective listening, the listener adopts what Rogers called 'the therapist's hypothesis'. This is the belief that the capacity for self-insight, problem solving and growth resides primarily in the speaker. This means that the central questions for the listener are not 'What can I do for this person?' or even 'How do I see this person?', but 'How does this person see himself and the situation?' Obviously, since my object was to see through the respondent's eyes, reflective listening was the best option.[28]

Coming to the interview situation, the reflective listening mode was applied by sticking as far as possible to the following principles:

- More listening than talking. Thus the interview was simply a process of facilitating the gradual opening up of the person. In many cases, my intrusion was limited to statements like 'Would you tell me more about this?' or 'You have spoken so little about your family . . .'
- Responding to the personal rather than to the impersonal and abstract. I recall one particularly resistant person who challenged me about my knowledge of history and subsequently delivered a detailed lecture on the history and politics of India around the time of Partition. I responded first with appreciation, then prodding: 'You gave such a nice lucid introduction. All this must have been important to you, integrated somewhere in your personal approach to life . . . please tell me about your experiences, your attitudes. I want to know more about your life.' At this, his attitude changed, and with an awkward smile he plunged into his life-story.
- Restating and clarifying what the other said. This often opened other avenues for discussion.
- Trying to understand the feelings contained in what was said, not just the content. For example: 'The volunteers gave us food. Khichuri. They served it in dirty aluminium pots.' 'I suppose you felt humiliated, coming from your background' (he had described before how he was cared for at his home). 'I did. I could not take it. I felt like bursting into tears. How dare they give me food this way?'
- Responding with acceptance and empathy, neither with cold

> objectivity nor fake concern. I tried to be as 'genuine' as possible, to use a Rogerian term. This also entails being attentive to negative and ambivalent feelings and accepting them as well. I usually responded with comments like, 'I have met many others who feel the same way', or 'I suppose, under the circumstances I too would have felt the same'.

However, the reflective mode could not be maintained throughout. I was particularly interested in certain issues, and if these did not come up spontaneously, I resorted to direct enquiry. These included the declared attitude of the respondents to Muslims, the perceived impact of Partition on their subsequent lives and their political stance. In some cases where the totality of the person was missing, for example, when the family was not mentioned at all, open and non-directed questions were asked to elicit responses at the secondary level.

INTERPRETATION OF NARRATIVE

Next comes my interpretative position. My approach, at least for the greater part of this volume, emphasizes the whole person: each person's unique experience being a focus of interest. It does not imply complete absence of generalization, but essentially the orientation is idiographic rather than nomothetic,[29] whereby we look at the beauty of each single unit of humanity with self-compact interest. A tree in blossom has its condensed beauty; but this is different from our appreciation of a single flower, its curved petals, its softness, its colours of various shades merging into one another. The first is nomothetic, the individual lost in the group; the latter is idiographic, seen within context, yet analysed in minute detail. The difference between the two approaches is not only quantitative, but also qualitative.

In 1988, McAdams published a seminal paper 'Biography, Narrative and Lives: An Introduction'.[30] He commented, 'When contemporary personologists study lives, they are likely to find themselves listening to the *stories* their subjects tell, and/or trying to discern the central, underlying story that animates any particular subject's life' (p.2, italics original; see note 30). In the same article, McAdams quoted Theodore Sarbin who raised the possibility that a narrative might be considered a 'root metaphor' for understanding human experience.[31] The self-related narrative emerges as a reflection of the person as a totality, and provides cues to the way the individual has synthesized the multiple exposures to innumerable life situations in an integrated whole. Another way to understand the continuity of the individual is through the reading of the 'script' that runs across one's life span. Tomkins, in 1987, postulated the 'script theory' of personality. This theory employs the metaphor of the person as a playwright constructing one's own personal drama over years.[32] The experiencing involves an active modification of the situations; these are by no means objectively recorded or passively received. These are edited, magnified, warped and dramatized for a coherent presentation. The unit of analysis of the 'script' is the scene: an idealized, emotionally charged 'happening' that is constructed at every moment. The scenes vary in completeness, but all scenes include some kind of interpersonal interaction and affect, in other words, at least one person and one level of emotion.

Therefore, in line with my prior assertion, I repeat that my object of study is the total person within and across a loosely defined historical situation. The narration is less than the objective 'fact' and more of the subjective truth. In nutshell, we are dealing with the meaning of memory viewed from an intra-psychic perspective, rather than with the neutral events (if there can be any!).

The processing of every experience, including its registration, assimilation, distortion, recall and utilization, is related to the broader framework of the existence of the person, the developmental dynamics from childhood onwards, and the interconnection of the multiplicity of meanings ascribed to life. Dynamicity means continuous confrontation between contrasting forces and a possibility of change of the stable structure as a result of interaction. The child's impulses and her social contingencies interact in significant ways to shape the personality through various relatively predictable stages. This developmental approach views the dynamicity in a person as an intricate process comparable to, let us use our earlier metaphor, the blossoming of a flower from the first appearance of the bud; and considers all the influences, the rain, the sunlight, the insects, the manure and the soil, as it matures into a full-bloom beauty. This view of a human life considers all the genetic and environmental nuances to peruse the development and blossoming of the human psyche.

In this sense, the narrative used here has a temporal anchorage. One of the leading psychologists of the earlier generation, Henry Murray, wrote, 'The organism consists of an infinitely complex series of temporally related activities from birth to death. Because of the meaningful connection of sequences, the life cycle of a single individual should be taken as a unit, the *long unit* of psychology. It is feasible to study the organism during one episode of its existence, but it should be recognized that this is but an arbitrary selected part of the whole. The history of the organism is the organism.'[33] This temporal continuity has been observed in this project in the constant movement of some respondents from the past to the present, through the elaboration and justification of the present social and political attitudes with reference to the past ages and through open declaration that they dream of the past: 'Do you know, even after ten years of staying here I used to have disturbed sleep at night as the scenes of my birthplace came in a series of pictures before my eyes?' The growth along the temporal dimension was, of course, not uniform for each person. Some dwelt more in the past, the present pattern of life being an extension of the 'myth'; for some a smooth differentiation was obtained, though the continuity remains, and for others there was a deliberate resolution to sever the bond. One example of determined detachment: 'I do not have much concern for what happened there before my coming or after my coming. Partition or such things are not really personally important to me.'

It is impossible, here, not to bear in mind Erik Erikson, whose analyses of Martin Luther and Mahatma Gandhi are recognized as the first true psychobiographies.[34] Erikson advised looking beyond the apparent, since the words and sequence with their usual obvious meaning might not reveal the intended person. Therefore, Erikson spoke of 'triple bookkeeping' that refers to the three levels of understanding: the level of the body, the level of the ego and the level of the family and society. Erikson believed that ultimately the story of the individual is woven around the various psychosocial developmental stages of man[35] and the interpreter of the narrative should be sensitive to these stages.

My respondents are in the Eriksonian eighth stage: that of integrating their life-experiences in a meaningful whole, or struggling with despair. In one sense, therefore, I am starting from the end. I hope to demonstrate, by detailed sequential analysis of some personalities, how the flow of existence rippled over years to construct what is now being revealed in the personal narratives.

In my interpretative stance, the expressed behaviour of a person has been understood to have unconscious motives, including the motive to discharge impulses as well as the motive to stay in balance, in harmony between the self and the outside. This is the domain that Freud called 'psycho-economics'.[36] This aspect deals with the management of discharge of excitation. As there are strong impulses demanding discharge, so are there inhibitory forces to counter it. When the discharge tendency is mild and the inhibitory forces strong, there can be smooth suppression. Contrarily, when the impulses are virulent and the inhibitory forces also strong, there occurs either a rupture in the inhibitory system allowing sudden and violent discharge, or a displacement of the excitation in some other area.

In the interview with the refugees, I had encountered this kind of displacement, particularly in relation to hostility. Many respondents referred to the desperate characteristics of the refugees and their obstinate perusal of some goal once they fixed their mind on it. They were angry, they said, because they were cheated both ways. In their ancestral homeland, they were driven by fear and confusion and made to believe that they must migrate to India, an unknown homeland, nevertheless, their rightful country. When they landed in India, they were jeered at and rejected. The aggression could not be released spontaneously in either case owing to their socially marginal position. Consequently, wherever possible, they were unduly hot-headed. An interviewee said,

> 'We have been fooled there and fooled here. Now as I joined the refugee rehabilitation movement, I felt I had to get justice. Justice is what I must get, even if it comes in an unjust way [pause]. We broke in the factory gate, gagged the doorman and the other staff, hit them hard and settled inside. At least we could win at some place'.

Another respondent asserted,

> 'We can fight a lot. We are rootless and therefore struggle more. Our history has given us the power to face odd situations to a large extent ... You will not find any "Bangal" returning from the foreign countries unsuccessfully.'

In most cases, however, the displacement and similar other mechanisms are not consciously available to the individual. Not only the drives—the libidinal and aggressive ones are unconscious. In many cases the sentiments, particularly the early childhood anxieties and attachments, have been transformed into 'character traits' and have coloured the subsequent experiences unconsciously.

During analysis and interpretation of the narratives, therefore, emphasis was given not only on the manifest content, but also on the more subtle structural cues: for example, the first sentence with which the respondent opens the narrative, the non-verbal reactions, incomplete sentences and themes, the emotional expressions, and the way the respondent switches from one topic to another, the key to the associative bond.

RECONSTRUCTION OF NARRATIVE

So far, I have borrowed happily from psychoanalytic literature. Since the interviewed material came more or less in a free form of narration, one may feel tempted to compare it with the free association of psychoanalysis. Nevertheless, significant distinctions exist between the two. A major difference is that in any clinical set-up, the patient approaches the clinician for relief from distress. Here it was I, who accosted the respondents for a 'story' of their lives. So, what the person wants to reveal in these two situations is guided by two different mental sets. In a clinical context, whether one likes it or not, the discussion stems from pathology. Consequently, in the narration of the 'patient', there is less guardedness in expressing pain and vulnerability. Indeed, anticipation of getting help implies that one cannot manage one's life unaided. Despite the interplay of all sorts of defences, despite efforts to posit an acceptable self-image in denial of one's contradictory multiple selves, despite all uncertainties and antagonisms, in a clinical set-up the basic premise of pathogenesis remains.

In my interview situation, the mental set was left undefined. I did not wish to look specifically for victimization; rather my approach was to gain an understanding into the complex psychosocial processes at individual and cultural levels, generated in reaction to the event of Partition. Yet, I think, as I initially mentioned Partition and migration as reference points, a kind of presupposition of distress was implied here also; after all, Partition is rarely viewed as a natural consequence of social evolution, but is envisaged as a social trauma, a blow, a cut. I think many respondents simply took it for granted that I was after pathology and distress. That is why some were apologetic about their not suffering too much. 'Why do you ask me? I had not suffered much. After all, we had contacts here in Kolkata. We did not have to sit and lie on the pavement, never begged as some had to,' apologized a respondent. Some reacted strongly against this presupposition. An educationist retorted at my request for interview, 'Would you gain anything from interviewing me? After all, I am one person who can claim a cent percent benefit from Partition. It was a blessing for me. I don't think you would like that.'

I soon became aware of this trap, but did not really change my stance to explain on my own that I was not after pathology. I stuck to my original approach deciding to keep the stereotype playing its own role, and to keep a watch over it. I think I was rewarded for it. Some of my respondents explained the two-fold effect of Partition: material gain and emotional loss being the most common among them. One respondent expressed it in the following way:

> 'I am here. Rootless. We do not have any village, any native place to go to. No permanent address, so to say. If these events did not take place, everything would have been otherwise. The life pattern has changed . . . Well, now it is not that bad. But if there were exchange of population in a true sense, it would have been better. If they [the Muslims] are majority here we would be rootless again.'

Probably this is how feelings operate after fifty years of continuity of life. Some are good, some bad; remorse, anxiety and satisfaction merge into each other.[37]

In any study of personality, the issue of pathogenesis has been one of controversy. There is no denying the fact that much of our knowledge about the human mind (and of the human body as well) has come from the study of its deviance. Disorders, distress and abnormality create a natural laboratory to study the numerous ways of (dys)functioning. This is, of course, truer for unchartered domains. As data about functioning of the human body and mind accumulate, the focus shifts to the study of normality rather than abnormality; health is no more defined in terms of disorder, but in terms of wellness.[38] This is where psychoanalysis, concerned with reconstruction of the patient's unconscious ideas, passes on to areas like analysis of language, psychobiography and study of social issues. And this is where interpenetrations of various modes start taking place, giving the approach to a subject an eclectic flavour.

The present effort is not to be confused with the psychoanalysis of the narrations or of the persons for another reason. In psychoanalysis, the analyst and the analysand meet three to four times a week and the process continues for years. This generates an emotionally charged transference-counter-transference bond, within which the entire process of scrutiny may be held. Among many other things, this process reveals the kaleidoscopic nature of the human psyche, shuffling the thought processes and associated affects in numerous configurations, isolating and rejoining them in multiple ways and observing the various forms they can take. The defences and their vicissitudes are exposed in the process. Here, of course, no such prolonged exposure was intended. The relational bond was extremely loose and temporary and what we got was a censored and decorated version of the self. I would rather compare it to the task of a clinical psychologist administering projective tests where considerable structure is discerned within the response, and the psychologist interprets the spontaneous reactions based on a predetermined model. So far as analyses and interpretation of the narrative is concerned, I opted for the usual dynamic psychologist's techniques of interpreting non-verbal cues, silences, looking for defences and explaining a given piece of behaviour in the context of one's entire life experience. From this angle too, the similarity of my study with a testing situation is greater than it is with a therapeutic situation.[39]

The issue of pathographizing the narration needs to be reopened as we proceed to the analysis of the stream of emotions revealed in the interviewed material.[40] Although our respondents did not undergo personal physical assaults during the time of Partition, the event was a precursor to a major change in the life patterns for all of them, a change that they gradually assimilated in their beings. Thus a different self, different from the pre-Partition one, gradually emerged over years. This course of post-Partition existence was also different from their pre-Partition dreams about future life. The narration therefore contained traces of both regimes. It contained the habitual modes of responses and the defence systems from early childhood onwards, as well as the subsequent pain, its vicissitudes, the altered modes of behaviour and supporting thoughts and emotions. Above all, the narrations revealed the effort to maintain control over their lives in the wake of the historical event. Therefore, in discussing the anxieties, the fear and the hate, I have also tried to reflect the resilience, the maturity and love that carve the pathway to an individual's developmental trajectory.

I tried to understand how the nature of trauma, of fear, uncertainty, intimidation, rape and abduction, of a world becoming unrecognizable, of a way of life disappearing, generated by 'soft violence' was qualitatively different from the trauma of witnessing bloodbath, massacres and instant annihilation. The emotions, the coping techniques, the defence mechanisms elicited in this connection as well as the cognitive distortions reflected in selective attention and memory have been explored. The emotions and cognitions build the base structure of attitudes. In the present context, such intra-psychic structures of the respondents have been explored in connection with two themes, namely, attitude towards the Muslims and attitude towards the interpersonal world in general, including one's past and present social and political affiliation.

My final effort has been to locate the self of the individuals in a personal as well as collective perspective. The word 'self' here is used as an entirety of one's being: the experience of existence at micro and macro levels. Indebted to the 'social constructionist' and the 'postmodern' views of experience, the 'self' I am after is not the static description of traits, but viewed as a dynamic phenomenon continuously in search of anchorage and definition, losing the grip and plunging once again in the unabated attempt to restore some 'meaning' out of its floating existence. I consider the 'politics of memory' playing a significant part in this endeavour, so far as memory is a dialogue held in the frame of language, and language in turn is the maker of the self. Even if we refrain from the 'there is nothing outside the text' assertion,[41] the relative textuality of existence and the possibility of accessing a reality within representation and signification has to be accommodated in my journey in the search of self.

This postmodern notion of the 'real' as inseparable from the 'constructed', and the 'textual' has established its way into historiography (e.g., in the writings of Hayden White). The psychological construction of the self is also in one sense a kind of historiography, so far as it consists of relating the perceived past to the projected present. The intra-psychic politicization of the experiences in this context determines the trajectory that one's self-location (or allocation of various components of the self) takes throughout one's life. Therefore, the authentic past melts into the vivacious warmth of discovering other implicit meanings, which, as we shed our own lights on them, become explicit and dominant. Would my interpretation of the past tally with that of my respondents? Probably not. Marie Coleman Nelson in a short paper described how her own reading of the psychoanalysis of a man, her points of emphasis in mutative interpretation, her retrospection on the useful moments during analysis differed grossly from the client's own reading of the therapeutic situation.[42] She pointed out how each participant in the analytical dyad, even after prolonged 'working together', ultimately processes the interaction 'in terms of his or her evolving self-image—or as some might say—ongoing construction of the personal myth' (p. 86). In reconstructing the self, arising out of the past of my respondents, I would like to be guided by the following significant lines stated in 1963 by Frederick Wyatt in the context of historical research:

> There is no authentic past to be retrieved. We have to reconstruct it quite properly, in our own image. Reconstruction means to find a context that integrates all relevant data. Context usually derives from the historian's preferred theories and from those values and sentiments in which all theories are ultimately embedded (p.311).[43]

The epigraph is from C.B. Strozier, 1986. Historical Memory, *Psychohistory Review* 14, 5.

Notes

1 For detailed discussion, see J. Bruner. 1994. The 'remembered' self. In U. Neisser and R. Fivush, eds, *The remembering self: Construction and accuracy in the self-narrative* (New York: Cambridge University Press): 41-54. See also R. Josselson. 1995. Imaging the real: Empathy, narrative, and the

dialogic self. In R. Josselson and A. Lieblich, eds, *The narrative study of lives*, vol 3 (Thousand Oaks, CA: Sage): 27-44.

2 U. Neisser. 1988. Five kinds of self-knowledge. *Philosophical Psychology* 1, 35-39.

3 P. L. Berger and T. Luckmann. 1963. *The social construction of reality: A treatise in the sociology of knowledge* (New York: Anchor): 173.

4 The issue of subjectivity entering the space of interpretation of narratives is a much debated issue. It has been suggested that there are various levels of truth that may emerge from a narrative, depending upon the interaction of objective and subjective realities. If we proceed with this notion of multiple realities and yet intend to grasp the 'truth', we may opt for determining truth either by correspondence or by coherence. Correspondence refers to one kind of reliability by concurrence among raters; coherence takes into account the goodness of research–the extent to which the discrete items in the narration coagulate to form a consistent whole. In the latter case, the awareness of the interpreter about her own bias and attempts to check it is important. In our work, we are probably nearer to the coherence model. See for a detailed discussion of the two models, P. Moilanen. 2000. Interpretation, truth and correspondence. *Journal for the Theory of Social Behaviour* 30, 4, 377-91.

5 Ritu Menon and Kamla Bhasin report that after their initial effort to cover both Punjab and Bengal, they dropped Bengal from their study because 'the Bengal experience was so different that it merited a separate study. The migrations here took place over eight to ten years, were not accompanied by the kind of violence that Punjab experienced, and consequently the rehabilitation and resettlement of refugees were qualitatively different'. See R. Menon and K. Bhasin. 1998. *Borders and boundaries: Women in India's partition* (New Delhi: Kali for Women): 26.

6 F. Arlene. 1995. *How to sample in survey* (Thousand Oaks, CA: Sage).

7 R. Barthes. 1977. trans. by Stephen Heath. *Introduction to the structural analysis of narratives: Image, music, text,* (New York: Hill).

8 See for the treatment of memory, particularly collective memory in context of trauma, W. Bohleber. 2007. Remembrance, trauma and collective memory: The battle for memory in psychoanalysis. *International Journal of Psychoanalysis* 88, 329-52.

9 There is a love-hate relationship between mainstream qualitative research and psychoanalysis. Although both depend largely on narratives, and

emphasize intersubjective understanding, the two have remained separate in academic psychology. It is an irony that Erikson is found in the textbooks of psychology with reference to the 'stages of psychosocial development', but not with reference to psychohistory. However, there have been voices within academic psychology and within psychoanalysis in favour of appreciating, or even initiating friendship between the two. For some of the relevant readings, see, S. Kvale. 1999. The psychoanalytic interview as qualitative research. *Qualitative Inquiry* 5, 1, 87-113; R.E. Haskell. 1999. *Between the lines: Unconscious meaning in everyday conversation* (New York: Plenum Press); N. Midgley. 2006. Psychoanalysis and qualitative psychology: Complementary or contradictory paradigms? *Qualitative Research in Psychology* 3, 213-31; W. Hollway. 2006. Psychoanalysis in social psychological research. *The Psychologist* 19, 9, 544-45.

10 H. White. 1987. *The content of the form: Narrative discourse and historical representation* (Baltimore: Johns Hopkins University Press).

11 It has been observed that when people give their life-histories in the form of open narratives, these contain some common characteristics. Recall of life-experiences has attracted psychologists' attention particularly after the 1978 Cardiff Conference of Practical Aspects of Memory. See M.M. Gruneberg, P.E. Morris and R.N. Sykes, eds., 1978. *Practical aspects of memory* (London: Academic Press).

12 Support of the first viewpoint is obtained in W.F. Brewer. 1986. What is autobiographical memory? In D.C. Rubin, ed., *Autobiographical memory* (New York: Cambridge University Press): 25-49. Others have advocated the second restricted view. See K. Nelson. 1993. The psychological and social origins of autobiographical memory. *Psychological Science* 4, 7-14.

13 Mainstream academic psychology, especially that concerned with cognitive aspects of mind, rarely acknowledges its relation with psychoanalysis. However, there have always been authors who have tried to bridge the two through the common concern about interpersonal perception, memory and emotion. See P. Noy. 1979. The psychoanalytic theory of cognitive development. *Psychoanalytic Study of the Child* 34, 189-215; W. Bucci. 2000. The need for a 'psychoanalytic psychology' in the cognitive science field. *Psychoanalytic Psychology* 17, 2, 203-24.

14 See D.C. Rubin, S.E. Wetzler and R.D. Nebes. 1986. Autobiographical

memory across the lifespan. In D.C. Rubin, ed., *Autobiographical memory:* ; 202-24.

[15] See L.J. Levine. 1997. Reconstructing memory for emotions. *Journal of Experimental Psychology, General* 126, 165-77. See also U. Neisser and L.K. Libby. 2000. Remembering life experiences. In E. Tulving and F.I.M. Craik, eds, *The Oxford handbook of memory* (New York: Oxford University Press), 315-31.

[16] See F. C. Bartlett. 1932. *Remembering: A study in experimental and social psychology* (New York: Cambridge University Press). See also I. H. Paul. 1959. Studies in remembering: The reproduction of connected and extended verbal material. *Psychological Issues* 1 (monograph no.2), 1-152.

[17] D. E. Polkinghorne. 1991. Narrative and self concept. *Journal of Narrative and Life History* 1, 135-53.

[18] See M.F. Lowenthal et al. 1976. *Four stages of life* (San Francisco: Jossey Boss); M. Conway and M. Ross. 1984. Getting what you want by revising what you had. *J of Personality and Social Psychology* 47, 738-48; see also J.A. Smith. 1997. Developing theory from case studies: Self-construction and the transition to motherhood. In N. Hayes, ed., *Doing qualitative analysis in psychology* (Hove, Sussex: Psychology Press): 187-200.

[19] See M. Ross. 1989. Relation of implicit theories to the construction of personal histories. *Psychological Review* 96, 341-37.

[20] S.F. Larsen. 1992. Potential flashbulbs: Memories of ordinary news as the baseline. In E. Winograd and U. Neisser, eds., *Affect and accuracy in recall: Studies of flashbulb memories* (New York: Cambridge University Press): 32-64.

[21] The role of the superego in the formation of defences is crucial. Depending upon the punitiveness and severity of the superego, different defensive constellations and different character patterns may emerge. Helen Deutsch has described four interrelationships between the superego located internally or projected outwards, and the external object. See H. Deutsch. 1965. *Neuroses and character types: Clinical psychoanalytics studies* (New York: International Universities Press). Also see U. Hentschel, 2004. Defense mechanisms: theoretical, research and clinical perspectives. (San Diego: Elsevier).

[22] This has been endorsed by the phenomenological and the psychoanalytical models of texts. Using a phenomenological model, Katharine Young proposes a distinction between the 'tale world', where the events of the

story take place, and the other space, the realm of the narrative discourse. From a similar point of view, Genette distinguishes between the content, the text and the situation where the narrative is produced. See K. Young. 1987. *Tale world and story realms: The phenomenology of narrative* (Dordrecht: Martinus Nimhoff); G. Genette. 1980. *Narrative discourse* (New York: Cornell University Press).

Among the psychoanalysts, Melanie Klein and Donald W. Winnicott paid particular attention to the way two subjective spaces unite to make a meaning of the text–in this context, the narrative. Klein eschews any concept of epistemological truth, and considers as truth only the uncertain product growing out of the interplay of outer and inner reality. See M. Klein. 1963. *Our adult world and other essays* (London: Heinemann Medical Books). Also D. Meltzer. 1978. *The Kleinian development* (Perthshire, Scotland: Oxford Clunie Press). Winnicott conceptualizes a 'potential space' where the individual has the opportunity to test his creativity by posing challenges to himself. This is also the place of rest 'for the human individual engaged in the perpetual human task of keeping inner and outer reality separate yet interrelated'. Care-giver and infant, analyst and analysand (and also speaker and listener, author and reader) enter this space together as it is rightfully the sole domain of neither but is a shared one. Meaning is born out of this shared reality. See for reference, D.W. Winnicott. 1971. *Playing and reality* (London: Tavistock): 2.

[23] See P. Friedman. 1978. *Listening processes: Attention, understanding, evaluation* (Washington, D.C.: National Education Association); see also B. Goss. 1982. Listening and Information Processing. *Communication Quarterly* 30, 304-07.

[24] The term 'clinical' is defined as the method of studying the individual as a unique whole. For exact definition see H.B. English and A.C. English. 1958. *Dictionary of psychology and psychoanalytic terms* (New York: Mckay).

[25] See S.S. Tomkins. 1979. Script theory: Differential magnification of affects. In H.E. Howe and R.E. Dienstbier, eds, *Nebraska symposium on motivation*. vol. 26 (Lincoln: University of Nebraska Press): 201-36.

[26] For a relevant discussion on the nature of countertransference, see C.G. Jung. 1935. Principles of practical psychotherapy. *Collected works*, vol. 16 (Princeton: Princeton University Press). See also G. Adler. 1967. Methods of treatment in analytical psychology. In B. Wolman, ed., *Psychoanalytic techniques: A handbook for the practicing psychoanalysis* (New York: Basic

Books): 338-78. The Kleinian and the independent British psychoanalysts have particularly emphasized the nuances and utility of counter-transference. See for detailed discussion, P. Heimann. 1960. Counter-transference. *British Journal of Medical Psychology* 33, 9-15, and for a more recent understanding, see J. Mills. 2004. Counter-transference revisited. *The Psychoanalytic Review* 91,3, 467-515.

27 See C.R. Rogers. 1959. A theory of therapy, personality and interpersonal relationships as developed in the client-centred framework. In S. Koch, ed., *Psychology: A study of a science*, vol 3. *Formulations of the person and the social context* (New York: McGraw Hill): 184-256. See also, C.R. Rogers. 1961/1995. *On becoming a person: A therapist's view of psychotherapy* (New York: Houghton-Miffin).

28 Reflective listening has four components: *empathy, acceptance, congruence* and *concreteness. Empathy* is the listener's desire and effort to view the recipient from her own internal frame of reference rather than from some external point of view, such as a theory, a set of standards or the listener's preferences. The purpose is to obtain an emic rather than etic understanding of the situation. The listener's effort to hear the other person deeply, accurately and non-judgementally motivates the narrator to explore her 'self' more deeply.

Acceptance is closely related to empathy. Acceptance means having respect for a person for simply being a person. Acceptance should be as unconditional as possible. This means that the listener should avoid expressing agreement or disagreement with what the other person says. This attitude encourages the other person to be less defensive and to explore the hidden aspects of self and the situation.

Congruence refers to openness, frankness and genuineness on the part of the listener. The congruent listener is in touch with herself. Transparency on the part of the listener tends to elicit transparency in the speaker. In some cases however, the principle of congruence can be at odds with the principles of empathy and acceptance.

Concreteness refers to focusing on specifics rather than vague generalities. The person suffering pain or ambivalence may hide her true sentiments behind masked expressions like 'sometimes there are situations that are difficult' (which is vague and abstract), or 'most people want' (which substitutes others for oneself). The listener can encourage concreteness by asking the speaker to be more specific.

[29] See Gordon W. Allport. 1937. *Personality: A psychological interpretation* (London: Constable). The term 'idiographic' refers to the understanding of the individual personality while 'nomothetic' is the description of the measurable and generalizable features encountered in many members of the culture where the individual belongs.

[30] See D. P. McAdams. 1988. Biography, narrative and lives: An introduction. *Journal of Personality* 56, 1-18.

[31] T. R. Sarbin, ed., 1986. *Narrative psychology: The storied nature of human conduct* (New York: Praeger).

[32] See S. S. Tomkins. 1987. Script theory. In J. Arnoff, A. I. Rabin and R. A. Zucker , eds, *The emergence of personality* (New York: Springer): 147-216.

[33] H. A. Murray. 1938. *Exploration in personality* (New York: Oxford University Press): 39 (italics in the original).

[34] E. H. Erikson. 1958. *Young man Luther: A study in psychoanalysis and history* (New York: Norton). Also Erikson. 1969. *Gandhi's truth: On the origins of militant non-violence* (New York: Norton). Many later researchers have followed Eriksonian principles for psychobiographical studies; some prominent names are, Vamik Volkan, Ashis Nandy and Sudhir Kakar.

[35] According to Erikson, each individual undergoes eight developmental stages throughout the entire lifespan. These are in his words the 'eight ages' of man, namely: basic trust *vs.* mistrust, autonomy *vs.* shame and doubt, initiative *vs.* guilty, industry *vs.* inferiority, identity *vs.* role confusion, intimacy *vs.* isolation, generativity *vs.* stagnation, and ego integrity *vs.* despair. Erikson suggested that an 'epigenetic chart' can be drawn from the understanding of these stages with two basic assumptions: '*(i)* that the human personality in principle develops according to steps predetermined in the growing person's readiness to be driven towards, to be aware of, and to interact with, a widening social radius; and *(ii)* that society, in principle, tends to be so constituted as to meet and invite this succession of potentialities for interaction and attempts to safeguard and to encourage the proper rate and the proper sequence of their unfolding. This is the 'maintenance of the human world' (p.243). See E. Erikson. 1963/1977. *Childhood and society* (Frogmore, St. Albans: Triad Paladin).

[36] S. Freud. 1915. Instincts and their vicissitudes. In J. Strachey, ed. and trans., *The standard edition of the complete psychological works of Sigmund Freud*, vol14 (London: Hogarth Press): 109-40.

[37] Similar diversity of the fate of emotions and memory have been noted by

Honey Oberoi Vahali in her study of Tibetan refugees, where she noted the difficult and complex dynamics of emotions in the displaced people. See H. O. Vahali. 2009. *Lives in exile: Exploring the inner world of Tibetan refugees* (London: Routledge).

38 For the last few decades WHO is actually redefining the concept of health as a wellness of the total being including the spiritual one. See *The world health report. 1998*. Executive Summary (Geneva: World Health Organization).

39 I could even call it an experiment in the sense Hermann Rorschach used the term. H.Rorschach. 1921. *Experiment in Rorschah*. Trans as *Psychodiagnostiks* (Bern: Hans Huber Verlag, 1942). I treat the data as a response in terms of affects and ideas filtered through the censors of the mind to best befit the immediate interview situation.

40 Sigmund Freud, in his book on Leonardo da Vinci, cautioned against undue pathological interpretation of events. See S. Freud. 1910/1957. Leondaro da Vinci and a memory of his childhood. In Strachey, ed. and trans., *Standard edition of the complete psychological works of Sigmund Freud*, vol.11 London: Hogarth Press: 3-55. See also A. C. Elms. 1988. Freud as Leonardo: Why the first biography went wrong. *Journal of personality* 56, 19-40.

41 J.Derrida. 1974. *Of grammatology*. trans. Gayatri Spivak Chakravarty (Baltimore: John Hopkins University Press).

42 M.C. Nelson. 2001. On the (presumed) authority of interpretation. *Psychoanalytic Review* 88, 83-86.

43 F. Wyatt. 1963. The Reconstruction of individual and collection past. In R.W. White, ed., *The study of lives: Essays on personality in honour of Henry A Murray* (New York: Atherton Press): 305-20.

2

A Chronicle of Emotions

Who ever thought that a riot could be between people?
We saw the riot of colours on the petals of the grass-flowers spread over our meadows.

– A refugee from Noakhali

GOING THROUGH THE transcripts of my interviews, I was submerged in the emotions of my respondents. Like the ripples of a river, these emotions took different forms: with sunshine and cloud, breeze and storm. Desire, fear, frustration, anger, and guilt mellowing into sadness and self-depreciation flowed through the narratives along with an assortment of other, more positive feelings.

THE DESIRED PAST AND THE GENERATION OF LACK

Desire for the life in their former homeland emanated in its most poignant form through the childhood memories of these aged persons. How could I convey in black and white the alteration in tone when they spoke of their land of birth? Their narrations were a series of emotionally charged imageries: the people, the home, the playground, the market place and most of all, the natural beauty and serenity of life. The interviews exemplify the 'torturing memory' of a life to which they could not return.[1]

This is not unexpected.[2] An important series of writings on partition memory in Bengal was published in the Kolkata daily *Jugantar* in the early 1950s. In 1956 these were brought out in two volumes, edited by Dakshina Ranjan Basu under the title *Chherey Aasa Gram* (The Village One Has Left Behind).[3] The most prominent feature of the memories of the upper class and caste Hindu migrants from East Bengal is the idealization of nature and people in the 'homeland'. They speak of the exceptional blue of the sky, the shiny gold of the autumn leaves and the soothing touch of the cool water. Some descriptions are exquisite to the point of being poetic. The pathos of losing one's home has been creatively mingled with panegyrics on its natural beauty. For example,

> 'Even today, sometimes I dream of wild ducks. The clouds darkening the vast expanse of the sky cast their shadow on my heart. I still feel the rain in Magra that would flood the land. At daybreak, dewdrops fall on the tin roof; the leaves of the jackfruit tree fall on the ground with a murmur. I still hear these. The shop of Abhayda, Amtala, the sunset on the bank of the Dhala lake, the thronging crowd in the market place on Gudara Ghat—I still see them all. They exist on the horizon of my mind, but are lost on the border of my country' (my translation).

Undoubtedly, such romantic portrayal of nature is moving, but somewhere it misses the reality. Dipesh Chakrabarty offered an interpretation of these published narratives, and fitted the idealization into the tragic sense of displacement.[4] Similar fantasy-like descriptions of the natural beauty of their homeland were obtained from our respondents as well. Two themes recurred repeatedly in these depictions. One was water: cool flowing water, of the river, the ponds and the lakes, water flowing over the roads and the fields, being present both where it should and should not be, yet generating a sense of security. The other was the green expanse: a stretched-out lustrous 'carpet of emerald' symbolizing a sense of freedom.

When asked, 'What is it that you remember the most?' a respondent replied,. 'I remember water. Everywhere there was water.' The rainy season was particularly prominent in the memory of many respondents. They recalled the rivers overflowing into the paddy fields and the meandering paths, the reflection of the changing colours of the sky in that water and the *dinghis* that carried people through the waterlogged fields.

'It was a land of rivulets and lakes. The jute plants were as tall as full-grown men, but water flowed above them. At the end of the monsoon, the water level decreased. The sky at that time was so blue that the water adorned by the shadows of the jute plants looked like the *zari*-woven *anchal* of a blue Benarasi sari.' This poetic description was provided by Janak, a lower division clerk from Khulna.

One woman described the greenery: 'Here in Kolkata I feel suffocated. We had gardens of fruit trees. We knew exactly when they would blossom; we knew by their scent. Even today I miss the smell of nature. The scent of the soil, the scent of fruits and flowers. That was paradise. Here everything is so mundane.' Some of the other olfactory sensations remembered were those of wild flowers, rotten jute and boiling milk.

Many felt a personal oneness with nature. Manish said, 'Every single thing in our daily routine was linked to nature. Pressing of rice began according to the position of the moon . . . When it rained the whole day long, when the sun never appeared, we could tell the time not from the clock, but from other cues. For example, when the jhinga flowers bloomed,[5] we knew it was afternoon.'

The subjective meaning of intimacy with nature in the human psyche has not been adequately explored and understood. While the chemical effects of environmental pollution and its impact on the nervous system, causing fatigue and anxiety, have been 'scientifically' acknowledged, the simple visual and affective impact of nature has insinuated its way only into popular psychology, via literary works.[6] The narratives of our interviewees torn away from the security of nature call our attention to this neglected aspect. However, we can only speculate about the psychological meaning of the impact of nature, and in doing so we risk over-interpretation. We can embark upon the process of interpreting in two modes. One is by interpreting specific 'symptoms' such as emphasis on water, greenery and scents. In this mode, the emphasis would be on the particular symbolism or metaphor, although this is a controversial aspect of psycho-analytical work. For example, Jung would relate the fixation with water to birth ideations, as water is the archetype of birth;[7] Otto Rank might associate this fixation to pre-birth security.[8] The olfactory sensations that encompass a large portion of an individual's early years may be understood as a nostalgic regression to pre-verbal security.[9]

The second approach is to develop a general account of the reason for an attachment to nature. All theoretical controversies apart, the sensory images of expanse and coolness of a natural environment are obvious. One may safely claim that the self, perceived within the 'reconstructed' openness, is a secure self, contented in its acceptance and esteem, yet enjoying adequate freedom for growth. Compare it with the smallish persona in the urban environment, the suffocated, constricted self, growing hesitantly inside a closed structure! Thus, nature becomes the desired destination of the heart. Proximity with nature provides the child with a sense of mastery and control; the development of which requires a backdrop of security. Nature's smoothness and serenity, its easy submission to playful aggression without retaliation and without any fundamental damage,[10] its unlimited succour when one is in need, have led to its association with the nourishing breast, the tolerant and loving source of corporeal pleasure and emotional assurance: the primary object of human desire. The feelings associated with the descriptions I obtained, remind me of the 'holding phase' of maternal care expounded by D.W. Winnicott.[11] Nature, I submit, served this 'holding' purpose for our respondents in their childhood before migration. Nature was everywhere, in the flowing water, in the expanses of grassland and paddy fields, across the canopy of the sky, amidst the shrubs and trees, omnipresent without any violation of freedom. It was reliable without being aggressive. Its memory lingered in the hearts of those who had experienced it as the prototype of security.

Nature was more fervently recalled by those respondents who came from the village to urban localities.[12] A few, like Rekha, deliberately chose to settle in semi-urban areas where some residual greenery remained. Not everybody was this perceptive or lucky. Janak still nourishes his wish to acquire a plot of land where he can tend a garden of his own. For those who settled in areas where proximity with nature was still possible, such longing was less manifest. Could one say the 'lack' was less visible?[13] Not really; the lack was expressed through other symbols.

A theme that came up repeatedly was of food. Many recalled the fine quality of cheaply available rice and pulses, pure milk, fresh fruits, fish brought directly from the ponds, and sweets prepared on different festive occasions. One respondent recalled the fine 'Balam' rice of Barishal: 'It was so fine that girls pierced their ears with it.' A teacher remembered bori—the small decorated balls of pulse-paste, that her mother made, 'You could not decide whether to eat it or to keep it for decoration. Its taste paralleled its beauty.' A businessman said, 'Every time I pay for buying fruit, I have a feeling of uneasiness. We had so many trees around ... We plucked fruits mainly from the garden of Kuladakaka. Mango, jamun, jamrul and many others ... the taste was beyond imagination.'

'These days you contract so many diseases, because you do not get pure food. I have this pain in my joints. I tell my children, "Give me back my old home and the food I used to take, I'll be all right"', said a housewife. Surojit also mused on food: 'Do you know, the launches sailed along the Ultadanga canal? In pre-partition days, rice came from Chaulpatti. Hay, rice, cucumber and gourd were carried by boat. Have you tasted the sour soup (*ambal*) of ripe cucumber? It's delicious. During Lakshmi Puja, vegetables were brought: spinach, jhinga [a gourd], pumpkin and others.' The idealization of the taste and nourishing properties of the food was remarkable. There was a touch of eulogy in most descriptions, in expressions like 'beyond imagination' or 'superb'.

Another recurring reminiscence was of familial status in the locality. Most respondents remembered their family as being 'deeply honoured and loved' by their neighbours. Surojit reported: 'Ours was not a well-to-do family; we did not have much cash.

My father was a schoolteacher. My jetha [father's elder brother] was an MB doctor and reputed in the locality. We belonged to a respected family and had always depended on that.' Rekha Devi said, 'Our area had a Hindu majority. The Mussalmans were poor and they had deep respect for my father-in-law and husband. We were secure amidst them. We never thought of migrating.' Subhash recalled that his father, a *kaviraj* (an Ayurvedic doctor), practised in the village, and therefore a plot of land was donated to him. Manoj's father was a teacher, and the local Hindu and Muslim aristocrats begged him to teach their sons. Manoj himself was respected as *masterer pola* (Master's son). Thus, as youngsters, the respondents had been happily enshrined within the veil of honour bestowed upon their families. The sudden withdrawal of this protective shell coupled with the termination of the easy flow of food and the security of possessing a property, exacerbated the feeling of deprivation and being in a vacuum.

These numerous expressions of lack and need—of natural beauty, food, love and honour—are not discrete and different; they are psychologically connected with each other. One common thread is their positive and nourishing factor: nourishment of soul, mind and body. This nourishment contributes to the development of individual self-esteem in protected and wholesome conditions.[14] True or fantasized, the pre-migration memories, especially of the younger age group, were those of wholeness and fulfilment. The home of mud and bamboo, of bricks and cement or of logs, was enlivened by people; people who bestowed love and affection on the growing child. The neighbourhood, the school, the peers invaded the memory discretely or collectively, spontaneously or in response to specific queries. For many, the people recalled were all love and sweetness; the inevitable discipline and restrictions were acknowledged but fondly. The impression was one of care and compassion. Teachers were remembered with adoration; headmasters were honourable and understanding, fit to serve the role of ego ideal. Names of peers thronged the memory—Hindu and Muslim friends, Rashids and Nirens, Debranjans and Afjals; roaming around together in unflinching harmony.

For some respondents, however, the interpersonal world seemed to be of less significance than other things. Some had definite problems in their families and hence remained reticent. They did not want to discuss family matters with me, they said. For others, there was no such inimical decision; the human world around was simply less important to them. At least, that was the impression they made through their disregard of relationships while narrating their life histories. Some had their minds fixed elsewhere. Sudhanya, for example, was focused on his mission. As an important political figure of the neighbourhood and a devoted social worker and philanthropist, his persona, his declared self, was that of one devoted to the cause of leftist politics and bargaining with the government to procure for the refugees their proper dues. He described his involvement with freedom fighters, his decision to leave the home country, his pursuit of career in Kolkata, his righteousness on various social occasions. He offered very little about his family and friends spontaneously. All he spoke about was the structure of his family, and some basic information about his father, so that I could get an idea of the social stratum he belonged to. I waited for him to reveal something about his emotional relationships, but in vain. On the last day of my visit to him, I said, 'You have spoken so little about your family. You have never mentioned your mother.' And suddenly the floodgates of emotion was opened. 'I didn't–eh?' he said. 'Listen, Ma died when I was a student of class vi; she died during delivery. My maternal family was quite well off. I remember going there and eating hot rice with pure ghee . . . Come with me, please.' Sudhanya rose from his seat and led me to an inner room. There he showed me a photograph of a young lady with downcast eyes and one hand on her lap. The way her hand was placed looked unusual, her sari somewhat oddly positioned. 'This is my mother,' he said. 'The only photograph taken of her was after she expired. I want to remember her not as dying, but as I loved her, alive. So I asked an artist photographer friend of mine to make a sitting picture out of the lying one. He repositioned the frame (turned it 90 degrees) and changed the lines of her sari a bit. Isn't it nice?' I nodded affirmatively, though I was uncertain. I felt the situation was somewhat emotionally disturbing; but for Sudhanya this was probably a way of keeping alive the cherished memory of his mother. Though earlier he had been reticent, there was plenty of emotion in his voice now, and he started pouring out memories of his mother.

Janak showed similar initial reticence, and was keen to convey his feelings of loss and his helplessness after migration. But when I asked him about his family, his voice became choked with emotion as he spoke of his parents. 'I was fortunate to have a saintly mother. She was like a goddess. She looked like the idol of Durga. She used to read the *Ramayana* in the afternoon. I can still hear it, the humming. We were a bit afraid of our father. Even mother was [long pause]. But I saw him break down when migration became a reality. I remember wondering how this man could be so vulnerable. My mother was stable and protected us as a bird protects its fledglings. She used to sing to us very softly … I lost both of them in close succession. Father passed away six months after my mother died. I sometimes think Father was, beneath his strict appearance, too fond of my mother to bear her absence … .'

As expected, many of the respondents emphasized the status of their father and the level of his authority as the head of the family, while in describing their mother, the emotional bond was more prominent. Some, of course, spoke of decisive qualities and points of strength in their mothers too. Women, in comparison to men, more freely expressed their early relationships. They talked not only of their parents, but of their in-laws as well. Madhabi was a bit self-conscious and anxious at the onset of the interview. She might not remember all the details accurately, she apologized. Yet on the second day of the interview, she was talking happily about her family, with the enthusiasm of a young girl. 'I can go on and on like this, you know,' she said. 'Ultimately you will have to stop me.'

I asked her to go on with whatever she wanted to tell me. Her voice reflected the curiosity, naïvety and zest for life that characterized the young underexposed girl of her day. Her account had a smooth, happy and easy flowing quality as she remembered the golden days of her maidenhood and the early months after her wedding. 'What I remember most of my childhood days was the fun we had in our village house. We went there for Durga Puja. We had so many cousins there. We were all fair and plump, and I was everyone's darling. "Khuku has come"—they would shout as soon as I stepped off the boat.'

Madhabi's maternal uncle was a district magistrate, and another uncle was a film artist. Her mother had passed BA and MA; she also used to write poetry. Madhabi mourned that they had lost her poems. Madhabi's father was a good-natured and self-effacing kind of man, thoroughly honest and saintly too. He was very much dependent on his wife. If he needed anything, money or food, he used to ask her for it.

Then Madhabi talked about her marriage. Her narration reflected the happiness of a beautiful adolescent girl.

> 'I was sixteen when I got married. Do you know, I received a matrimonial proposal from S [a renowned Bengali singer], but my mother rejected it because he was of a dark complexion! [laughs] ... I got married here. My mother-in-law used to call me '*ranga bou*' (the fair, rosy red bride). It was a nice village, and we were rich. My mother-in-law loved me a lot, but the entire environment was so different from my paternal home ... They had plenty of land. Red chilly was plucked from the field and dried in the sun. It was spread all over the ground, and the rays of the sun were reflected on it. I was astonished to see such radiance.
>
> 'My elder sister-in-law was about my mother's age. When I felt lonely, she used to reassure me. Then I passed Matriculation. The way they rejoiced! My father-in-law informed the entire village and greeted me with the holy sound of the conch and *uloo* [a sound made with the palette and tongue, during auspicious occasions, particularly marriage, usually by the women]. It was 1939 ... My father-in-law invited all the villagers. One day they invited the Hindus to eat meat, and on the other day the Muslims.'

Childhood games and entertainments, strikingly simple in comparison to the present, were part of the spontaneous reveries.

Dipendu recalled the meadow beside a big lake, Pareshsagar, where they used to play all sorts of games and celebrated Kali Puja. Manish described how they caught fish and wandered about the green expanse, how they participated in various religious *bratas*. Namita recalled how she used to play hide-and-seek even after her marriage. Bikash and Subhash reminisced about how they would gossip and secretly smoke bidi with their friends beneath a tree or in a field on the outskirts of the village.

Those who had been in their late teens or early twenties at the time of migration spoke of their hopes and ambitions, their education and career schemes in pre-migration life. One group of respondents reported possession of landed property. These affluent families were not particularly concerned about the job prospects of their children. Many affirmed that nobody in their family had ever needed to take up a job. However, the attitude of such families towards education varied. Despite the assured affluence, some families wanted their children to be educated and to grow up with definite intellectual and moral values; others emphasized formal education. The less prosperous families, however, placed moderate emphasis on education and gave priority to acquiring a respectable job. An emphasis on familial dignity could be traced in most respondents, affluent or humble. Some middle class youngsters were able to continue their studies because they migrated to Kolkata, the centre of education. This was particularly true for women. Contrarily, some had to abandon studies as they started looking for jobs after sudden displacement.

A common theme was involvement with the freedom movement. Almost all respondents, who were nearing adolescence at that time, reported some connection with the freedom fighters, at least as errand boys. Others had been more deeply involved; some associated with terrorist activities as well. Sudhanya recalled how as an apprentice in underground activities he had to undergo tests of devotion and courage. He narrated with pride how he swam across the Arial Khan on a stormy day and delivered his leader's letter to a senior freedom fighter. This senior gave him a letter to carry back to his leader, which, he later learnt, expressed the senior's appreciation of Sudhanya's courage and permission to incorporate him into the core group. Kalyan proudly recalled his association with Subhas Chandra Bose, and narrated how he had persuaded Netaji to attend a function at their local club. He was associated with Anil Roy and Lila Roy (Nag) in Dhaka and used to work for them. The reflected glory was still his.

As I listened to the reveries of these senior persons about the pre-Partition 'good old days', I had the feeling that these comprised the baseline of the fables of their lives. Here we are face to face with 'desire': desire which is the prime mover of the psychic life.[15] If all other thoughts and actions–all signifiers–flow from desire, then a journey into the emotions necessitates our take-off from here. This dreamt of and desired fantasy, the ultimate wholeness, may be represented as the mother: the symbiotic omnipresence of an ever-loving and unflinching inner image. The 'desire' of my respondents therefore presumably resides in the 'absence' or 'lack' of this image on the existential plane; the absence generated by the rupture in the domain of blind trust and security. The desire is to regain this wholeness–unification with the primary state of bliss–through regression into an earlier phase where one feels comfortable.

Depending on the psychoanalytical insight about regression being an effort to connect with the earlier and inner 'I', we may look at the reveries of my respondents as a message to me, the investigator out in the environment. Their lingering on the past was probably a communication to me, offering an image of their inner reality. The relationships in East Bengal may not in reality have been that wonderful, the sky may not have been that azure, the water-logging in the fields must have caused a muddy mess! But these insufficiencies could scarcely tarnish the inner grace of the place that was the beloved shelter of these persons. This rose-tinted view is not a pathology; not a disavowal of reality; it is the inner tranquil image that they carefully painted and so graciously communicated to me.[16]

Now I can put in perspective my disquietude on seeing Sudhanya's mother's photograph. Guided only by my rationality at that moment, I wrongly emphasized the discrepancy between the truth-value of the photograph and its 'real' representation. This mode of thought disregards our 'desire'—the perseverance of our inner 'God' to fabricate a new level of 'real' that is imperishable, which increases in charm as days pass by. This urge to create a different 'real' has been exploited negatively in Hitchcock's *Psycho*, and perhaps in Wilde's *Dorian Gray*; we shiver as we are confronted with the juxtaposition of the two 'reals'. But then, psychologically speaking, each of us thrives on such fantasy: Sudhanya revived his mother by turning her photograph some ninety degrees; most of my respondents have also preserved the happiness of their childhood by turning their memories a few degrees. Like Sudhanya, they may pretty well declare about their motherland: 'I want to remember her not as dying, but as I loved her, alive.

The flow of happiness, the pearl of satiation, was punctured by the events of riot and Partition after the cessation of the Second World War. The green of the paddy fields came to be replaced by the red of blood; the coolness of the sapphire water that reflected the face of the sky by hungry flames. The love and concern of the parents, the daily predictable interactions, were substituted by uncertainty. The cherished beauty of young women became their foe, their curse. This provided the groundwork for frustration of desire: the lack was generated. Again from desire and absence, from need and frustration, emerged the differentiation between the 'me/us' and the 'them'; that is, the rudiments of perceiving the 'other' as separate from oneself were presumably born from this lack. Thus 'our community' became different from 'their community'. This perception of the 'different other' in turn was the groundwork for the socially connecting emotions; after all, love and hate, fear and remorse are but affects attached to the 'other'.

These affects are anchored in cognition, incorporated as well as expressed in language through which we can 'read' emotions. Human existence, cognitive capacity, perception and memory are brought about, Lacan posits, by mediation of human relationships and within language.[17] One may say, desire is the grain of existence against which the emotions are 'text'ured.

Language has its limitations; as a representation, it entails the inevitable gap with the represented. My data therefore include, like all expressions encased in language, a destined-to-fail attempt to represent the unpartitioned whole recreated from the desire. All the elements of narration are but efforts of the fragmented self to grab the 'imaginary', which is nonetheless unattainable forever. Hence, desire for wholeness is the 'hole in the self' on the one hand, but on the other, this itself is the mender of the hole, albeit unsuccessful; we get learned through desire alone. It is through the failure to reach out to the 'whole' in fantasy that one proceeds towards the wholeness of the self. Therefore, the narratives are also our guides to the development of the self of the respondents—a story of their making, deriving its sap from the desired past wholeness and the lack generated from the 'real'—a situation that gave birth to complex emotional vicissitudes.

FEAR, ANGER AND GUILT

The feelings of love and desire for the homeland mingled with more pungent emotions. Three qualities of negative emotions emerged in the narrations: fear,[18] anger (or hate)[19] and guilt. These three emotions are usually intricately intertwined. Ernest Jones contended that hate, fear and guilt are inseparably related. Clinically observed, fear has guilt behind it and guilt itself proceeds from a yet earlier state of fear. He further notes that hate is one of the commonest covers of guilt: 'Hatred for someone implies that the other person, through his cruelty or unkindness is the cause of one's sufferings, that the latter are not self-imposed or in any way one's own fault. All the responsibility for the misery produced by the unconscious guilt is thus displaced onto the other supposedly cruel person, who is therefore heartily hated.'[20]

Regarding fear, Jones notes, the first layer is of primal pre-lingual dread arising from the intolerable tension of unrelieved excitation. At the second layer, after the separate identity of the external object has been established in the mind of the child, the privation becomes identified with frustration, or deprivation. Then, the 'signal' dread of danger outside oneself comes into existence, and with the privation being identified with deprivation, there arises the anger at frustration, and consequently hate.[21] Regarding the feeling of guilt, there is firstly the 'pre-nefarious'[22] inhibition arising out of the primal fear reaction, and secondly the stage of guilt proper, whereby the subject denigrates herself.

In any emotion expressed by an adult, we observe the secondary defensive layers that cover the attitudes of fear, hate and guilt. 'Any one of the primary attitudes may prove to be unendurable, and so the secondary defensive reactions are in turn developed, these being derived, as was just indicated, from one of the other attributes. Thus a secondary hate may be developed as a means of coping with either fear or guilt, a secondary fear attitude (signal anxiety) as a means of coping with guilty hate or rather the dangers that this brings, and occasionally even a secondary guilt as a means of coping with the other two. These secondary reactions are therefore of a regressive nature that subserve the same defensive functions as all other regressions'.[23]

Although Jones eschewed the special significance of any one of the three emotions, in a good number of clinical cases fear or anxiety seems to be the primary channellizing force.[24] Indeed the neurotic conflict has rendered its typical complexity when anxiety is substituted by guilt. Feelings of guilt represent a 'topically defined anxiety, the anxiety of the ego toward the super-ego'.[25] From a psychodynamic outlook, anxiety changes in part into guilt as the super-ego develops and becomes strongly functional. The guilt signifies a fear (of loss of love or of castration) not from an external agent but from the introjected representations of the danger, the internalized parents. The super-ego thus becomes the monitor for self-appraisal and self-esteem, since it is being regulated by the feelings of having done the wrong or not having done the right thing.

Later psychoanalytical literature has added substantially to the understanding of these three emotions. Pertinent among them are Melanie Klein's treatment of schizoid and depressive positions[26] arising out of the interplay of these three emotions, Winnicott's analysis of guilt[27] and Lacan's exposition of aggressivity.[28] I shall not elaborate on these views here, but refer to them as and when required. In the following sections, I use the narrations of my respondents at various phases of their lives before and after migration to try and shed light on the interplay of various emotions in these phases.

UNCERTAINTY AND THE VEIL OF FEAR

Fear took a very special form in the young victims of Partition. The major fearful feeling reported by the respondents was a pervasive sense of impending doom, rather than any specific directed locus of fear. This feeling became so intense that it resulted in a kind of terror: a socially reinforced state of panic. The terror had sensory accompaniments, particularly auditory and visual. A recurrent memory was of the call 'Allah Ho Akbar', used as a war cry. A respondent described this cry as 'freezing: it seemed all our faculties were benumbed when we heard the cry.' Namita said, 'Our hearts literally thumped inside our breasts at every cry.' Another woman reported a different auditory sensation, or rather the lack of it. 'Those days there was a kind of strange silence all around. No usual chatter of human habitation. You could hear the drop of a needle. It pressed heavy on our hearts. One cannot bear this silence for long. We knew we had to go.'

Among the visual accompaniments of terror, the sight of fire was the most prominent. 'In the evening we went to the rooftop and saw flames on the Noakhali border. We knew that the Mussalmans were setting fire to Hindu houses. We would stand silent and terror-stricken.' Indeed, the sight of flames in adjoining areas generated such unbearable tension and apprehension in the onlookers, it was one of the decisive factors for migration. Bikash from Sudhara, Noakhali, recollected, 'I came back home in 1946. Immediately after that, we heard of looting, rape and arson. We came to know that many houses nearby were being reduced to ashes. We could see the flames from our village ... We were panic-stricken. I was wondering what to do! We had a gun for killing birds. We cleaned it, put larger bullets for killing animals like pigs or crocodiles in it, and started for Noakhali town. From our steamer on the Meghna we saw fire and smoke. People said that Hindu mahallas were being burnt.'

Trying to relate to the respondents' experience of fear on seeing fires nearby, I was reminded of Laing's description of the reaction of engulfment after terrible insecurity.[29] Laing observed that many of his psychotic patients reported having experienced the feeling and imagery of fire as a reaction to fear. Fire, Laing found, had two connotations. One, it could be the uncertain flicker of the person's own inner aliveness: one's effort to stick to reality. The other was its conceptualization as an alien power, a destructive force determined to engulf one. Thus, fire has an ambivalence ingrained within its imagery. It is fascinating, warm and devastating at the same time. One is engulfed by it and devoured by its licking, sucking flames. Our respondents reported how they could not take their eyes off the fire; they continued to watch it from a safe distance, at the same time feeling terrified and helpless. The sight of fire around, not yet touching them, but waiting to reach them at its will, left them numb, in a state of paralysing psychotic silence.

The fear escalated with news of increasing violence and brutality, Bikash had further reason to be terrified. 'The President of Hindu Mahasabha lived in our locality. The Muslims came and killed him with a ramda (a sword-like weapon) thrust into his neck. His son climbed up a tree to save himself. He was pushed to the ground with a bamboo stick, and killed. The two daughters were abducted. The day I heard this I came home and told everybody that we should leave immediately. We did try to stay and resist. The local blacksmith manufactured swords for us. We fired blank shots throughout the night. But how long can you take this kind of tension? We left everything behind.'

News of violence was the decisive factor for Namita's family too, in Dhaka. She recalled how a young girl, a relative of their family, was widowed at Noakhali. They were attacked by a band of Muslims, probably known to the family. The girl was wounded but somehow saved; her husband and husband's brother were brutally killed before her very eyes. Her father-in-law climbed up a coconut tree, but the killers got him too. The young girl and her mother-in-law, violently widowed, came to Dhaka and took shelter with Namita's family. This made Namita hate and mistrust the Muslims. 'We were in a state of mourning and panic after the event. Although we were relatively safe within the high boundary walls of our area, we literally jumped every time we heard a shout outside.'

Dipendu's narration poignantly expressed the gradual process of increasing terror. In 1950, Dipendu was eleven. He lived with his parents at their house in Barishal town. I shall quote from his narrative at length (with some names and details changed) and then analyse it.

> 'During 1948-49 the scenario started to change. Even in 1948, we, the Hindus and Mussalmans together, arranged the Kali Puja on the bank of Pareshsagar. We also enacted a drama. The local DM, or may be the SDO, was a nice man; his wife sent fruits and sweets for us. We shared it, Hindus and Mussalmans together.
>
> 'Now I am coming to 1950. Gradually the atmosphere changed. After Partition, a few Hindu families had migrated to West Bengal for no apparent reason. Initially, there was no impact. Nevertheless, the fact was, all the families that occupied their houses were Mussalman. Not that they were unfriendly, but we noted and remembered it.
>
> 'I recall the day I got a jolt for the first time. Our Headmaster was an influential Mussalman. He came to join the *adda* [regular meeting of friends to chat and gossip] at our father's place. I do not know what he told my father, but I heard my father say, "I think we cannot live in this country any longer." With passage of time, this became an oft-repeated statement everywhere. This was a cruel statement. Somewhere something was not right, even we children knew that.
>
> 'We had a Mussalman neighbour. A nice person, a widower with two children. Mother used to take care of these children; the younger one was her special pet. He was so good—this man [pause]. These Mussalmans had two types of reactions. The upper or enlightened class gradually became helpless; they understood that they would not be able to protect us. The relatively lower class was still confident. '*Kaan je jay?Amra to achhi*' [Why do these people migrate? We are still here], they used to say.

'I remember the migration of one family was decisive for us. Anita Sengupta, the famous sportswoman, belonged to this family. We were close to them . . . . I heard the word "riot" first in their house when they migrated because of the violence all around. That day we knew we too would have to leave [long pause]. Violence is not only bloodshed you know. To a child, a sensitive child, any abrupt unpleasant change is violence.

'The person who came to occupy our beloved Senguptas' house was a maulavi. He was an evil man. We children looked at him and knew it at once. He never laughed, did not entertain Hindus in his house and was always in an agitated mood—we really hated him.

'Will you believe me if I tell you that I did not know that the trouble was between the Hindus and the Mussalmans? I thought it was some kind of trouble somewhere else about something else. There was a boy in our class; I think he was in such a group [anti-Hindu group]. One day we were standing together, the boy uttered the word *malaun* [faithless]. Another boy reprieved him, "Hey, stop. Ravida [not his real name] is standing over there." This Ravida was a school hero—a Hindu boy. I thought it funny that this second guy was concerned about Ravida who was standing at some distance, but did not notice or care to consider that I was standing even nearer [pause]. Maybe he was not conscious that I was a Hindu, that I was different. We were very close, you know.

'I recall how small incidents added to the gradual dawning of terror. Our cricket captain was Rashid—he was an excellent player. I used to play cricket very well. Perhaps if I had stayed in Barishal I would have played test cricket [pause]. One day Rashidda suddenly called me aside and said, "Dipendu, tell your family not to be afraid. We are still alive." I recall that I wondered why he had to tell me this so firmly—there was something unnatural in his insistence.

'By this time riots had spread all over East Bengal. There was arson and looting nearby. We could see the fires from our house. There were rumours, exaggerations and fear; along with it the inevitable depression all around. Nobody was happy.

'Then there was the "Ansar Bahini". Even today, I am not sure if it is a military or paramilitary troop. They paraded in front of Pareshsagar. There was apprehension and gloom everywhere. I vividly remember this atmosphere. Our Mussalman friends were depressed; they felt so helpless. They never wanted us to go. That was very evident.

'On our part, the Hindus started telling each other, "We have to go, today or tomorrow." I hated those words. Whenever I heard them I wanted to shriek, [long pause] deny it.

'My elder brother was in Kolkata. He was studying at Presidency College. My maternal aunt had been married in Kolkata. At this time, this aunt and our maternal uncle were staying with us. Father went to Kolkata to visit my elder brother. Mother sent my aunt and uncle with him. My mother was afraid that something bad might befall her siblings.

'Now at our home we were five—Mother, we three minor brothers, and my blind grandmother. It was a time of complete chaos. Father had not returned yet. Usually he came back from Kolkata within two or three days, this time he did not return for 15 days. We felt helpless, afraid, terror-stricken. We did not know what had happened to him.

'One thing I am sure, our Mussalman neighbours were never happy with the state of affairs. At night, they formed groups and protected the town from external dangers. However, they were becoming increasingly nervous. One night they came and told us that they were not sure of our safety. We fled our home and took shelter in a Mussalman mason's house nearby. We still had no news of our father.

'Later we heard that the local hooligans of the Mussalman mahalla just behind our house planned to set fire to our house. Influential and well-disposed Mussalman police officers had already been posted out of town; it was being done systematically. The friendly DM was also transferred. Afterwards we came to know that the DM's wife drove the police jeep herself and reached DM's office to bring in the security force. I do not know if the threat of our house being set on fire was a rumour or not, but my father always remembered this lady with gratitude. "Exceptional lady," he used to say of her. "I owe your lives to her."

'In the meantime, the horrors were increasing. The entire system had collapsed. All connections, conveyance, everything was cut off. Barishal is full of waterways; steamer was the main transport. Every service had stopped. We were hearing news of violent riots in Kolkata and elsewhere. And Father was in Kolkata. We were terrified. I remember one small thing. At this time I had just been promoted to the next class. I had been bought the new books. They smelt so good. When they talked of leaving, I thought I couldn't leave because of these new books. Ultimately, I had to leave my new books behind.

'Amidst all this confusion, one morning Father arrived. What a relief! He said he had not come earlier as all means of transport were being attacked. From him we came to know of the condition in Kolkata. Refugees were pouring in. Our father frequented Sealdah railway station in search of us. Trains arrived occasionally, empty trains, washed with water, in which you would see at places a broken *shankha* [conch bangle worn by Hindu married women in Bengal] or bloodstains. And there were of course rumours of further violence. Finally, he could take it no more and returned despite severe risks. Some Mussalman men on the steamer had recognized him as their doctor and given him a lungi [cloth tied at the waist, dropping to the ankles] so that he might pass for a Mussalman.

'Now it was decided. We packed up. But the steamer was not leaving regularly. Day after day we went to the jetty and had to come back. What did I feel then? Adventure —I can tell you. I was young, you know. Once decided, I thought the journey was fun.

'Finally we boarded a steamer [pause]. At this point, I learnt that Father was not migrating with us. I still do not know the reason, perhaps he decided to stay back and try to arrange some property matters. Or maybe he was not allowed on the steamer; there was very little space on it. But I was afraid.'

Through the above account, the 'process of terror' unfolds gradually before our eyes. The boy of eleven did not understand the meaning of riot. Nevertheless, he could understand when the family members were uncertain, when they felt unsafe or terrified. In fact, the feelings of the children about the environment were initially secondary to those of the adults. Once sensitized, the child had his own perception, his own clues. In Dipendu's account, the gradual change in his feeling of belonging was palpable. I find three clear phases. In the first phase, he became sensitive to communal tension and confusion. Starting by remembering small changes like the increase in the number of Muslim residents, Dipendu in his narration passed on to registering the change in the environment. He spoke of the altered feeling in the adults (for example, his father's reaction to the Headmaster's remark), the repetition of the 'cruel' statement that they might have to leave, the migration of the Sengupta family being decisive in the context, his enhanced sensitivity to the behaviour of his Muslim friends, the playground being trampled by the parade of the Ansar Bahini, and finally the clear recognition of depression, helplessness and gloom. In this phase, Dipendu also repeatedly recollected the goodness of his Muslim friends, their assistance, resistance to communal attack, confusion and sadness. He narrated how he felt hurt when the Muslim boy who rebuked his friend for uttering the word *malaun* disregarded his presence, and then almost forced a justification for this negligence by adding that perhaps this boy was so close a friend that he simply forgot that Dipendu too was a Hindu!

In the second phase, the tone changed from one of sadness to fear: Dipendu described his mother's concern for the safety of her sister and brother, the scenes of fire nearby, the father's absence and rumours of persecution followed by total confusion and temporary flight following the information of probable attack. Here also we find reference to good Muslims; those who were active in their support (e.g., the guards). If the first phase was of preparation at the emotional level, the second phase was one of activity and enactment of the emotion. Also, the process of denial had already begun when Dipendu said, 'I hated those words. I wanted to shriek, deny them.'

In the third phase, starting after the return of Dipendu's father from Kolkata, there was little mention of his Muslim friends. The decision had been taken and the bond had already been severed. At this crucial phase, Dipendu had the sense of going on an adventure. This shifted back to fear when he realized his father was staying behind.

Dipendu's account demonstrates how apparently positive gestures can add to the feeling of despair under conditions of terror. Rashid's assurance and the other Muslim boy's reaction to the word *malaun* were both humane efforts to maintain communal harmony. Not that Dipendu missed it entirely; he repeatedly spoke of 'good Mussalman friends'. Nevertheless, even positive events were interpreted in a way that strengthened negative feelings, once the suspicion was generated. The narrative also shows how children read hostility in human faces, Dipendu's description of the maulavi who in their eyes usurped the Sengupta house being one illustrative example. All these gestures and situations, spread over months, fell into a single pattern, as pieces in a puzzle, ultimately leading to the decision to migrate.

EMOTIONS UNDER THE SHADOW OF VIOLENCE

Although our respondents had not experienced direct brutality, they had lived under the shadow of violence. For some of them there was the direct threat of violence, particularly loss of religion, property and life. Others witnessed violence inflicted on others. Anger would have been their most natural reaction. Often, however, direct expression of anger in response to violence and threat was mellowed by the inhibitory emotions of fear and guilt. Anger, although present in the form of indignation and resentment, was not consciously emphasized. Bikash was afraid of the rioting and violence he witnessed at Noakhali and migrated with his entire family. 'The bastards ultimately succeeded in driving us out of our home,' he said. In his narration characterized predominantly by fear, anger was given vent to only through such abusive words.

Subhash too was from Noakhali. He described how the threat of conversion loomed large upon them.

> 'The riots had started, I told you. There was a station at Chowmani ... Violence erupted at various places on the Tripura border. We heard that a neighbouring village had been attacked and people forcibly converted. Such pressurization began at our village as well. A number of Mussalman people approached us. They were preparing lists of Hindus, and told us to sign on the list ... We were instructed to go to the Masjid on Friday. There we would be forced to sit for

Namaj with the Mussalmans and afterward they would feed us pulao [with beef in it]. They threatened to kill us, cut us in two, if we dared disobey. Most of these Mussalmans were from other villages. Those who belonged to our village did not exactly support them and told us later, "Don't go, we are with you." But we were panic-stricken. The neighbouring Hindus came to me and asked me "Dada, what should we do?" I was a kind of *matabbar* [leader] in the locality. I went to the aged Mussalmans of our village; many of them were fond of us. I folded my hands and told them "I am younger than all of you. You know better than me, you are our shelter. If you decide to kill us, you can do that. Still, I entreat you, kill us by your own hand. Let the tigers of our own land kill and devour us; please do not allow us to die at the hand of foreign tigers. The outsiders are threatening us. If you support them on principle, kill us yourselves, don't let us fall in their hands." I was weeping—everybody was standing silently, even the matabbar Mussalmans of our village were silent.

'I can still see it. It was a rainy day, raining all day long; the sky was overcast. We were supposed to go to the Masjid. I was talking with the two maulavis, I went to their place by a boat made of the trunk of a palm tree. We were standing on a vast field, it was so vast and green you would think that a green carpet had been spread over it. One of the maulavis asked, "Why this delay? Let us go to the Masjid." The other one interrupted. "You read the Koran, don't you? Tell me where is it written in the Koran that a Hindu should be forcibly converted, forced to sit for Namaj and eat beef?" "Don't you belong to us?" snapped the first one. The second one said, "Yes, both of us are Mussalman. We both wear fez." The first maulavi said, "What then?" The other replied, "Nobody in this village will be forced to go to the Masjid unwillingly."

'You see, it was I who fooled them, the idiots. After that we arranged to keep watch on every border of the village. Ten men on each of the four sides. They were equipped with weapons as well as bells, *kansi* and conch [all sounded during worship and thus available in most Hindu homes]. If a Mussalman from any other village was spied, the guards were supposed to sound these. Each house was equipped with weapons. I too kept guard. I was very strong. We gossiped the whole night [laughs], we also had arrangements for

> hookah and salted tea. We saw fire and heard shrieks and sounds of violence from other villages nearby. But nothing happened in our village after that.'

The narrative was one of fear, tears and efforts at self-defence in the face of imminent danger. It is apparent that the more knowledgeable and humanitarian maulavi of the village spoke against forced conversion and saved the Hindus from violation of personal religion. Nevertheless, near the end of the story, Subhash changed his tone and spoke as if it was he who had 'fooled the idiots'. Probably this is an ad hoc effort to maintain self-esteem by belittling not only the powerful oppressor, but also the powerful saviour.

Others witnessed serious and hard-core violence. In such cases, a complex emotional trajectory could be discerned. Witnessing violence has two different consequences. In a typical violent situation, there are two parties: perpetrator and victim. One represents the aggression and the other the fear. Here, from the data I obtained, I think a complex problem of identification emerged. In a typical violent situation, with whom would the observer identify? The question has no simple answer; indeed, it is possible that he identifies with both. In the first place, at the conscious level, the observer may identify with those with whom he shares the obvious characteristics of a physical or social category, for example, a man with a man, a Hindu with a Hindu. Of course, this is not the ultimate criterion. Identification is not skin-deep. We do not necessarily identify on the basis of observable physical and social categories, but often on the basis of characteristics that strike our sentiments in subtle ways. Most observers of violence readily identify with the victim. Among other things, one important reason for this is the self-preservative impulse: what has happened to the victim may happen to oneself as well. Thus, the automatic orientation towards the victim generates tendencies of altruistic action. For instance, if a Hindu witnesses the murder of a Muslim by another Hindu, the observer Hindu might have a double identification: one with the murderer, as his co-religionist, and the other with the victim who provides warning of probable hazard to himself. But while it is true that identification with the victim is a natural impulse of human beings, there is also a contradictory process at play—identification with the aggressor.

This is a particularly suitable defence mechanism for those who suffer from low self-esteem, or are at the receiving end of persecution and/or mercy alike. Through identification with the aggressor,[30] the observer can shed some of his inadequacies, and assure himself of his ability to act out effectively. Identification with the aggressor, coupled with rationalization, can also at least temporarily minimize the admonition from the super-ego, as the super-ego itself takes up the role of the aggressor. On certain occasions, all these variants of identification may operate simultaneously, especially if the situation has strong emotional impact. The resultant cross-identification leads to conscious and unconscious contradictions. Thus, in our previous example, a Hindu observer of the murder of a Muslim by another Hindu might empathize with the murderer who shared his religion, condemn the same person for the crime, feel the pain of the victim, and again draw some sap from the violent triumph of the perpetrator. One consequence of this complex identification is guilt: that of mentally being the perpetrator through identification, even for a moment; hence the oft-heard lamentation of not being able to do anything to prevent violence. Even if, for example, the witness is a Hindu, the victim is Hindu and the perpetrator Muslim, identification with the perpetrator may take place if the scene of violence serves the purpose of boosting the observer's weak ego for a while (best exemplified in the appeal of violent movies). Most of these identifications are unconscious. At the conscious level, the person will feel dumbstruck or confused because each spontaneous feeling is criss-crossed by others. The usual numbness of the observer of violence may be a result of these quickly shifting conflicting emotions rather than the simple sight of the violence itself.[31]

How is the above theoretical argument applicable to the reactions to witnessed violence as narrated by my respondents? Among those who spontaneously provided detailed accounts of violence and angry reactions to it were Kalyan and Barun.

Kalyan witnessed and participated in the violence in Dhaka in 1946. All through the night, there were shouts of 'Allah Ho Akbar' near their residence. Kalyan and his group were able to keep the town free from riot for 48 hours. Then it went out of control. There was the nawab's house beside the Buriganga, he recollected. The Muslims used to light a red lamp at the top of this house before anything unusual took place. The Hindus used to light green lamps as a message of counter-attack. It was like 'regular warfare'. One evening they heard shouts of 'Allah Ho Akbar' for one hour. Kalyan and his friends could tell that the Muslims were attacking the Hindus. They decided not to light the green lamps but spread the message by word of mouth. All able-bodied Hindus including some women came out of their houses.

Kalyan described the 'battle' in detail.

> 'We were at the frontline. We saw fire and murder and stabbing by the Muslims. Then we decided to attack. There was a Muslim locality nearby, a poor one. We attacked them and the entire basti was pulled down, shredded to bits. We had weapons with us: kripan, bhojali and daggers. These could be obtained from the Nepalis. We had revolvers too, as we were associated with the terrorists [pause]. Some men were murdered. Mostly the poor ones [pause].
>
> 'I recall one event [long pause]. I will tell you about it. Our group had attacked a Mussalman basti. I was at the back of the group. I must tell you that I was never involved in direct killing. There was a little Mussalman girl, seven or eight years old. One man caught hold of her arm and chopped it off. She was wearing a bangle. This man took up the arm that had fallen on the ground and pulled off the bangle. It was a child's hand. I was so shocked. We came home silently. We could not speak [silence]. From that day I stopped joining in the attacks.'

Kalyan had already identified with the Hindu aggressors; he was in the group. The identification was satisfying to him. It implied affiliation with a powerful and righteous representation of the self. This righteousness of aggression is explicit in his description of the preparatory phase of the riot, the sequencing of the events and the assertion that their attack was a strategic response to the Muslim attack. However, when the child's hand was chopped off and the inhuman greed of his friend came out blatantly, the identification acquired a different meaning. The fight for a right cause became torture of the weak for a selfish material reason. This generated strong guilt. The guilt was of course expressed in the narrative by way of silence and hesitation, by the declaration that he had never killed and that he was at the back of the group. Thus, he was dissociating himself psychologically from the persons who killed. Another interesting defensive manoeuvre was manifested in his sudden change from singular to the plural number. He was shocked, but 'they' went home silently. They could not utter a word. This sudden shift from 'I' to 'we' can be read as another attempt to dilute his guilt through the sharing of its content among many. The altered pronoun is like an appeal to the listener to note that it was not only he who had committed the wrong; his friends were equally guilty.[32]

In other cases, anger came as a reaction to guilt. Of all my respondents, anger was most prominently expressed in the narration of Barun, an ardent supporter of Hindu activism. He talked freely of the violence he had witnessed in Dhaka. He recalled how as a young boy engaged in social work, he witnessed a truck full of dead bodies escorted by the Muslim police to a spot near the Rail bridge and simply left there to rot. Barun, along with his friends, cleared the truck. He saw mutilated naked bodies of Hindu men and women, headless bodies of children with signs of brutality on the bodies. He cannot forget the scene even today. Indeed, the memory of a mutilated female corpse was a turning point in his life. Barun assured me that his conscience would not rest in peace until he could compensate for the trauma inflicted on such women. He is so set on his mission that in the last 50 years he had not read anything but matters relevant to the communal issue. Apparently, Barun considers it his personal duty to undo what was inflicted by Muslims on Hindus. His involvement in the tragic incident, his long-standing desire to take into his own hands the responsibility of avenging the brutalities he had seen, made me wonder whether he felt some kind of guilt associated with the violent acts that he definitely had not committed (see also Chapter 4).

For many others, however, the reaction to observed violence was rendered innocuous or its impact mitigated through the use of various defence mechanisms. Violent scenes were described by some respondents, usually in response to my enquiry, in a matter of fact way, almost as if such brutalities were part of ordinary occurrences. Surojit provided one such seemingly dispassionate account of the riot in Kolkata in 1946.

> 'A number of murders took place near Chatubabur Bazar . . . They travelled with open swords . . . . I have witnessed a number of such killings in the area. People of the two communities used to attack each other in the evening in front of our very eyes. The dead bodies were removed in the morning by a garbage car. A few of the bodies still moved, they still had breath in them. Nobody cared.
>
> 'I noted one thing, you know. The Mussalman killers used daggers and stuck these into the belly of the enemy, injuring the liver and other organs. The Hindus used ramda, the wound was on the neck or head, or if on the belly it was in a different place.'

Achintya's narration was also apparently conflict-free and devoid of any intense emotion. He described his own involvement in rioting in Kolkata:

> 'At that time, I was staying at Maniktala. The Mussalmans had taken out a procession. We were walking alongside. Suddenly a battle ensued and there was complete chaos. We ran into the lane and stayed indoors until our friends were prepared. In each house, they kept water heated to pour over the assaulters. We were eleven altogether, ready with weapons. There was a real fight. One of us died. All of us were wounded to some extent, as were many of them. A hand grenade hit my leg and my foot was burnt.'

Achintya's mode of narration was straightforward and he showed me the burn marks on his ankle with a casual smile.

Debendra narrated how he saw an Afghan lying in a pool of

blood near Deshapriya Park in Kolkata. Somebody had stabbed him. The Afghan was strikingly sturdy and fair. He still had his last breath in him. People passed by casually. Some kicked him, and others poked at his wounds. Debendra remembered the blood trickling down from the wounds. One woman described how she and others were confined in their hostel at that time. If they secretly opened the windows they could see and smell blood and death outside. These persons seem to have come to terms with the violence they witnessed and have resolved any conflict surrounding it in their own way.

Such dispassionate narration of violence is not unexpected. The major defences enabling transformation of emotionally loaded traumatic experiences to innocuous ones are isolation[33] and rationalization,[34] which often go hand in hand. Violent scenes were remembered by the respondents, sometimes in minute detail, but the cognitive component had been dissociated from the affect of repugnance and horror that naturally cohabit such experience. Such dissociation, when challenged, was justified using historical and philosophical clichés (e.g., 'such has been India's fate—always', or 'what is so meaningful in life, after all?').

Violence was given less conscious importance except by a very few, for whom it had some symbolic personal meaning. Few respondents mentioned violence spontaneously. Nevertheless, when they did so after my probing, the narrations were quite elaborate. That is, for most of the respondents the memory of violence did not form a crucial part of their reminiscences; probably, fifty years after the event, the salience of witnessing violence is reduced, unless it forms the background of one's self-definition or is integrated in one's life scheme. It remains a part of the myriad of experiences of one's life and is exposed only when asked about. But it was not repressed either, as it came up with an enquiry. [35]

PARTITION AND THE EXPERIENCE OF MIGRATION

I had anticipated a strong upsurge of emotions in my respondents when they spoke of two significant experiences in their lives:

the day of Partition and the actual migration. It did not turn out to be so. While most of my respondents spent hours talking about the pleasure of their pre-migration days and then of their post-migration efforts to resettle themselves, their feelings on the day of Partition and during migration were usually dismissed in one sentence: 'Then Partition took place', or, 'It was not possible to stay any longer, so we came here to West Bengal ... .'

Many had blurred memories of 14 August 1947, of processions and festivities. A number of respondents recalled that they had participated, willingly or unwillingly, in functions to celebrate the creation of Pakistan. Probably, as youngsters, most of them were not aware of the implications of Partition. The atmosphere was festive, with fireworks in the streets and premises decorated with flags and garlands. Arun recalled how he enjoyed participating in the celebrations and shouted out gleefully 'Pakistan Jindabad'. Dipendu could not recollect the events of that day but remembered the assassination of Gandhi some months later. The older respondents, particularly those who were politically conscious, were more watchful and often harboured feelings of resentment. Of course, as long as they had not planned migration they had to consider themselves residents of Pakistan and submit to reality. Some recalled how, over the year preceding Partition, the division of India had been accepted as the 'only option' by the common folk.

As I asked the respondents about the feelings they had about Partition, many of them did not refer to any specific affect. Rather, they skirted the issue, discussing the politics of the pre-Partition negotiations, but not their emotions. Let me give an example. When asked how he felt on the day of Partition, Sudhanya replied, 'Problems cropped up because the National Congress and the Muslim League had conflicting interests. They both said they wanted freedom. Ultimately, however, we did not win freedom. We received it like beggars, as a favour from the British. Sarat Bose, Suhrawardy, Fazlul Haque wished for undivided Bengal. But the other leaders were not in favour of it. They recommended Partition and assured proper rehabilitation and compensation. It turned out to be a hoax.' Kalyan responded to the same question with a cursory 'Bad'. Then he spoke about how he had always detested the concept of Partition as political folly; he had had a premonition that all assurances would turn out to be elaborate lies. I had enquired about their personal feelings, but in neither case emerged any direct acknowledge-ment of emotion; what I got instead was political opinion.

Some of the respondents were already in West Bengal in 1947. Many came here after the riots in 1946, while others had come for jobs or studies and were considering settling here. They viewed their ancestral home in East Bengal as an abode for the older generation, to be visited during vacations. Their responses too were confined to brief mentions of the Independence Day celebrations on 15 August in Kolkata. It does not seem that they internalized the emotional significance of Partition at that moment.

A similar mellow response was observed when questioned about how they felt during migration. Some said, 'We were but children'; some replied, 'Just like everybody else'. One lady said, 'It was so sudden that I do not remember much.' Yet, she had vivid memories of earlier periods.

For some, of course, migration was a process rather than an event. Even years after they had migrated, many had family members still living in East Pakistan. For some, transportation of the entire family took about ten years. Therefore, the break was not clean. Some links remained, diluting the feeling of forced separation. Many of my respondents provided details of when each member of their family had come to West Bengal. Janak's family of fourteen members migrated over five years, from 1948 to 1952. Dipendu's father, who had stayed back when they came to Kolkata with their mother, joined them two years later. Sudhanya had been working in Kolkata since 1942, and used to go home to Faridpur on leave. His brother was already trying to procure some land in West Bengal. After 1946, events had caused the family to consider migration. In 1948, the Pakistan government seized the gun of his uncle. Sudhanya's family feared that this was a prelude to a planned attack. In fact, a gang of dacoits did attack and loot their house a week after. This was a deciding event for them, and by 1950 every member of the large family had migrated.

In the narrations of Arun and Subhash, one moment they were in East Bengal, the next they were in Kolkata. Pre-migration and post-migration periods were enthusiastically elaborated upon, with a sort of emotional jump in between, as in Ritwik Ghatak's films. Arun who provided an exceptionally detailed description of the glory of Kumilla, was quite restrained about his feelings of separation from it. 'When in 1950 there was a big riot, our family decided to move. The Mussalmans helped us to cross into Tripura from where we took a flight to Kolkata. The Tripura border was just a few kilometres from our place.' He virtually provided a road map of directions from Kumilla to Tripura, but he did not say a single word about how he had felt during the journey. Subhash described at length the fear, the threat to their village and the resistance they put up against the Muslim invaders. And then he simply added, 'Nothing happened in our village after that ... A few days later my brothers came to Kolkata. I also came. Within a few days, my entire family migrated here. We are religious people, Vaishnavas. Gosai [the human incarnation of Lord Krishna] has looked after us.'

Some respondents spoke of the feelings of others rather than their own. Girish was apparently a sentimental man. He wept a number of times as he narrated the events. 'Serious rioting took place in Noakhali. We were afraid ... Everybody said the riots would spread; there was widespread violence, rumours of violence. Everybody was panicky. And I had already got some land here. So you see ... We had land there. Also a mallai dinghy [boat with limited capacity]. We fled with all the belongings we could carry. We came to Patharhat on the Meghna. The Mussalman boatman wept like a child [weeps]. But we had to stay here [weeps].' Though visibly emotional at the recollection of migration, Girish actually described the feelings of the boatman, and not his own. Similarly, after describing the pervasive fear, Bipul spoke of the depression of the Muslim neighbours, but not his own. 'When we decided to leave, the Mussalmans of our locality were depressed. They asked us to stay back, but their assurance was not enough. We packed up.' When categorically asked about his feelings, he was philosophical. 'We had no option.'

The most elaborate sentiment about leaving one's home came from Madhabi, a retired school teacher. Madhabi described the fear that 'lay like a sheet of cloth' over the entire locality of Durgapur in Chittagong.

> 'My husband finally said that we had to go. He had learnt that people were planning to attack the neighbourhood. My son was one year old; my daughter was five. We still did not take the threat seriously; how can you simply tear yourself away from what is your home? But one evening he came and told us that we had to leave that very night. Or else there might be serious problems. It was all so sudden. We went out that very night in whatever clothes we were in. We just put on a few extra clothes. We also took some money. I had my son pressed to my bosom and my daughter was walking with us. I felt so bad leaving the entire household behind. Small, small things that a person collects, arranges in her house [pause]. That is home. We had an old servant; he was so close to us that I hated calling him a servant. He came along with us with a lamp in his hand. The light of the lamp was reduced to a bare flicker for fear of being detected. We reached the railway station from where we took a train to Chandpur. There we boarded a steamer to Goalondo and then came to Kolkata by train.'

Here, some feelings were expressed, but these few sentences were all she said in her long interview over days. In common with our other respondents, Madhabi did not give full vent to her emotions during the nightmare and agony of migration.

POST-MIGRATION: CONTROLLING THE OUTER AND INNER LIFE

Anger and guilt obtained a new platform in post-migration life. A recurrent theme here was the struggle of settling in a new land. Some already held jobs on the western side of the border; others had to go through various degrees of readjustment and humiliation. Bearing small and major insults, feeling cheated, persevering in the face of odds and finally settling down to a career was the common story. In contrast to their lives in East Bengal, they suffered from the humiliation of taking stale food and a feeling of dishonour. They were served khichuri by the volunteers, and some cannot bear to eat khichuri even today. The refugees were perceived by the inhabitants of West Bengal as usurpers of their lands and jobs. They were unwelcome to their 'own people', and looked down upon as permanent liabilities of the government. The harshness of the new life was expressed, amongst other things, in the unacceptability of the Bangal dialect.

In common parlance, the inhabitants of East Bengal were called 'Bangal' and those of West Bengal 'Ghoti'. It was always understood that the two cultures differed, and stereotypes prevailed on both sides. Even before Partition, differences were palpable, in terms of weather and nature of land, agrarian rural naivety versus urban sophistry, and variations in culture and dialect. If language reflects the cultural identity of a race, the migrants were robbed of their treasure at a very early stage. They were jeered at by their peers; sarcastic comments were passed if they failed to understand the idiom of the 'civilized' people of Kolkata. One respondent recalled his Ghoti schoolmates reciting a scathing rhyme: 'Bangals are not human beings, they are like animals. They have no tails, yet they jump up the tree.' (*Bangal manushya noy, jeno ek jantu / Laf diye gachhe othhe, lej nai kintu.*) Another respondent narrated how he took pains to change the 'defects' of his pronunciation, requesting a school friend to 'correct' him if he mispronounced any word. Janak, who at the time of migration was studying in class vii, recounted the harassment he faced at his new school in Shyambazar. 'They always taunted me for my pronunciation, and sang out slang songs to tease me. Fortunately, I was not the only boy of my kind there. There were a few more among whom Ratan was very strong. He gradually fought his way into the peer group. We followed suit.'

Most gave detailed accounts of their education and the nature of jobs they held in West Bengal; and expressed the usual pride and frustrations in that regard. Manish recalled how the principal of a famous college in Kolkata denied him admission because he had not been able to bring his school certificates from Barishal. Some others fared better. Many asserted that as the Hindus of East Bengal were generally cultured and brilliant in studies, they were soon appreciated for their merit in class. However, given that they had left the security of landed property behind, the urgency of earning and looking after the family was given precedence over higher education. Achintya went in for a profession, studied chartered accountancy and became successful in life. Those with lower levels of education went for blue-collar jobs.

A few were strongly influenced by the socio-political demands of the day and got involved in refugee rehabilitation. Bikash procured a job in the Refugee Rehabilitation department of the government while Sudhanya, working as a clerk in a suburban locality of Kolkata, devoted all his free time to solving the problems of refugees. Anupam too spent his entire life in refugee welfare. He was the founder president of a housing colony and is now a respected leader in his locality.

> 'I came here in 1950 and erected a cottage. There was jungle all around. I organized the local people here and went to the SDO. We wanted to get some land here. The terms and conditions that he laid down did not suit us. We began a hunger strike. In the meantime, Bidhan Roy took oppressive action and I was arrested and taken to Barasat Jail. I was always with the socialist movement, and worked for the refugees. They were pouring in . . . wretched people. I was released soon and joined the movement again. Bidhan Roy was trying to send the refugees to some odd places by train. We stopped the train at this station. Bidhanbabu called me for discussion. Ultimately he consented to our demands.'

The inclination to work for the refugees probably reflected the unprocessed aggression that lurked in the hearts of the youngsters taking a constructive channel. The expectation of being welcome in the 'land for Hindus' had been shattered like glass as soon as they had disembarked from the train at Sealdah. The labels of 'Bangal' and 'refugee' pursued many of them for the next few decades. All the anger which had remained diffused in the pre-migration period now found a definite enemy in the rulers of India. It would be interesting to explore the psycho-political domain to understand how the consolidation of the Left movement in West Bengal fed upon this volatile aggression of this doubly deprived population and shaped it into an electorate. I cursorily touch upon this in Chapter 5.

Some respondents recounted how in their new home in West Bengal they participated in rescuing Muslims from Hindu hooligans and assisted in spreading intercommunal harmony. Girish recalled 1949. 'What those days were like! There was a Mussalman mahalla nearby. In the middle of the night, we heard shouts from there. The Hindus were attacking them. We had resisted the Hindu assault on the Mussalmans quite a few times.' Barun was one of the most ardent Muslim haters, but he saved the lives of many Muslims. I asked him why he did this. He said, when a man is in danger it is one's duty to help him out, whoever he is.

Such efforts exemplify some of the mature defences an individual takes to deal with the internal sense of loss of self-esteem. Two defences used here were 'sublimation' and 'altruism'.[36] Through these defences, negative affects are turned into socially and personally meaningful sentiments and actions.

During the narration of this phase, the pre-Partition affluence and peace was often juxtaposed against the post-migration atrocities. I had the impression that the respondents were occasionally taking refuge in the cool water of their lost peace while traversing the painful hot desert of their journey into subsequent reality. This regressive mode was more prominent for those who most deeply lamented the past; for others who were stronger, it was just an oasis.

Psycholanalytically, the migration from the homeland to the foreign country may be compared to the forced weaning of a child. The weaning of the child has two messages: deprivation and the recognition of growing up. It is only with the acceptance of weaning that the infant enters the fascinating and challenging complexity of the social world. Hence the ambivalence towards growing up towards life itself; hence Lacan's conceptualization of 'object a': the substitute which can never really touch the original 'real', yet forms the very essence of our growing into the world. Indeed, realization of complexity is associated with the generation of substitutive objects; the fantasy of a sole supplier—immutable and perennial—is but a simplistic notion. It is with the frustration that the object world, characterized by eternal lack and never-ending attempts at substitution, is opened before our eyes: the search itself is the motivation for living life to the fullest.

As the respondents were weaned from their motherland, whether abruptly or gradually over years, a plethora of emotions also come into play: apprehension, frustration, expectation, partial success, joy, anger and remorse. The associated negative ideations were of failure, loss of self-esteem, feeling lost in the 'outer world' and attribution of blame onto self and others. The positive ones were of being independent, growing up, taking responsibility and attaining new meaning in life. All these affects and ideas were expressed in their fullest during the delineation of the post-migration days.

THE PRESENT PSYCHOLOGICAL STATE: LAMENTATION VS. CONSTRUCTIVE COPING

The respondents described their present position in terms of physical, economic and psychosocial status. Not all of them, however, related it to the partition experience. For some, the experience of Partition was not significant in the context of their entire life. 'I witnessed Partition,' said one respondent, 'but I have no reason to believe that it shaped my life. Whatever I did, I did on my own.' For others, the deprivation they experienced was knit into their fate. 'We were penniless there. Fate had denied us affluence. Here too I have little to bank upon. Even at this age, I have to think of my daily livelihood. Partition or no Partition

I am the same poor fellow.' Bipul did not blame Partition as much as he did the political leaders of this country. He was indignant about other people having enhanced salaries. 'My status has not changed. I was poor and am still poor. But the leaders have not been able to develop a proper structure for the country. Uneven development ... See, for example, why should the salary of school teachers increase? They don't teach much ... do they? Then look at the Khadim case [a case of kidnapping that was very much in the news at the time of the interview] ... There is a lack of moral values everywhere. Imbalance pervades ... Now at this age I am frustrated. The government at the Centre is useless. I don't know if even my sons will ever get good jobs. Girish's family lost their land property in Barishal and he did not fare well in West Bengal. He is involved with an organization as a social worker, but somehow following the ideal of serving others has not been enough to fulfil him. 'I am a very wretched fellow. I was tricked by my fate. Fate was cruel to me. Partition robbed me of the smooth and secure life we enjoyed at Barishal, of the property and the political values we shared. But I have lived an honest life and have tried to do good.'

Some passed through difficult times, but are now faring better. Not all of them have been able to sail out of the emotional loss, however. Manish and Arun made the point that all said and done the homeland was far better than anything else and Partition had done great damage to their emotional wellness. Surojit thought that the feeling of being uprooted would never leave him. For these people the lamentation was perpetual. They have never come out of mourning.

For others the sigh for the past was moderated by the challenges thrown by their new life. Subhash was very poor, but had a strong sense of pride. He also held that he had remained as poor as he would have been in East Bengal and, therefore, Partition had not affected him in any way. He had accepted his fate without a grudge. Indeed, he discerned some benefits in the change. 'I think it has done me no harm. After Father died, we were already in trouble. Financially we would have lost everything even there. Our lands were also gone. Here at least we have been exposed to urban culture and my children have fared well. I do not have any remorse.'

In starker contrast are those who consider their entire lifestyle, their goals and understanding of human interaction as having been altered in a positive way by the event of Partition. Usually such individuals look at the impact of Partition from a balanced perspective, recognizing positive as well as negative outcomes. An example is Achintya, who has vowed to take on any responsibility given to him by the India government without charging any fee. When asked what impact Partition had had on him, he described how after Partition the family had passed though financial crisis. Achintya belonged to a landed upper-middle class family in East Bengal and therefore did not have much liquid cash on migration. 'We had to sell the gold ornaments of our mother and aunts to survive. That would have been unthinkable for us at one time. Therefore, I grew up to be responsible and I have been able to look after my family and to continue with the works I wanted to do as well. This was thanks to Partition.' Although Achintya mourned the separation from the homeland and still dreams of pre-Partition days, he has been able to turn the pain of Partition to his favour by engaging in a successful career in tandem with his altruistic work.

Sudhanya was also balanced in his evaluation. 'Partition had both positive and negative impacts,' he judged. 'The course of events gave me a sense of values and direction in life. Refugee rehabilitation became my goal. It makes my life meaningful. But we also lost substantially. Look, I am not very sure. We were not very well off as such. And even before Partition we sometimes thought of coming to Kolkata. Maybe we would have come anyway. However, I can tell you one thing for sure. Now my life has got its significance owing to the pain I received. This is, I consider, the positive contribution of Partition.'

Dipendu and Manoj offered their distinct viewpoints. Dipendu said, 'Partition has been extremely painful to me. But now at this age, I can tell you, Partition has enriched my world of experience. There [in Barishal] it was a protected environment. The event of Partition shattered the protection. I had to go through all kinds of hazards. You may say it has taught me to face life.' Manoj was more introspective. 'In East Bengal we were in a narrow environment. It was beautiful no doubt, but it was sheltered. With Partition, all the known paradigms were broken. At that time, it was shattering ... But I can tell you, now I think it did me a lot of good, as a person. At one time, I had the feeling that I had been robbed of what was mine. I could not think of the dreams I had. It bled. But now I can delve in the old memories and dreams. They would never come true, but they have a beauty of their own ... We were witness to a crucial event in history. I realize now that one should never be too sure of anything, yet one has much to enjoy in life.'

Indeed, human resilience is such that at least for some it can turn pain to stability, it can extract meaning from chaos. The ability to integrate and synthesize experiences, to accept reality and to withstand delay of gratification are signs of maturity that can be obtained only through accommodating pain and frustration. Frustration can promote or deter maturity depending on one simple thing: perception of one's relation to the frustrating event. More categorically, maturity means an inner assurance that one has been able to assimilate the external painful event and use it as a resource. Here we again launch upon the issue of mastery and control over oneself and one's surroundings. This endeavour may take different forms.[37]

One kind of adjustment is assuring oneself that something can be done to bring about change in the environment. This is what Freud means when he says that the passive infant develops its ego by actively crying for milk and believing that its cry brought the mother and produced the milk.[38] This gives the child a sense of mastery over the environment, a power, a kind of control. Control or power has a positive and a negative connotation. It is with control that one defines oneself, gains self-esteem, and it is with the same control that one turns aggressive and exploits others. With the development and active intervention of the super-ego, the attempt to control the environment may take an altruistic bent, in which case the person works for change in the environment with the purpose of doing good to others. An altruistic man is rewarded by an elevation in self-esteem owing to his control over the environment, and procures the approval of the super-ego by doing the right thing. Achintya and Sudhanya adopted this mode of accommodating the frustration of uprooting. They channellized their actions at least partly toward the welfare of others: in case of Achintya in his solemn promise to respond to any call of the country as well as in his social work; and for Sudhanya in his devoted efforts for refugee rehabilitation and local welfare. These efforts earned both of them socio-political appreciation and high position. Both Achintya and Sudhanya have been politically active since their youth, Achintya more inclined towards Congress ideology and Sudhanya towards Marxism.

The narratives of Dipendu and Manoj exemplify another kind of positive adjustment to trauma that comes not from external activities but from an attempt to resolve the trauma within oneself. In this kind of accommodation, the individual does not try to change the environment, but alters his or her perception of the external world. At one level this might be mistaken for a passive response, but it is not necessarily so. The dynamicity of change in such cases lies within the personality rather than outside. Dipendu and Manoj attempted to defend their hurt ego through the mechanism of understanding. Not all interviewees could reach the same level of understanding. Nevertheless, a positive mode of defence, even if partially successful, mitigates the pain and enriches one's internal repertoire.

It was interesting to note that the impact of Partition was seen as positive more often by middle-class educated women than by men. Many women, particularly those who were to establish some kind of career in later life, saw Partition as helpful to themselves. Karuna became a renowned professor of philosophy and Pro-Vice Chancellor of Calcutta University. She felt that it was only because of Partition that she was able to continue her studies. Madhabi believed this was true for her too. 'If I hadn't come here, I would not have studied or worked ... Partition liberated me personally.'

During the 1920s and 1930s, the status of women, particularly in Bengali Hindu middle-class families, was undergoing changes. The education of women was being recognized as important, yet the traditional practice of getting them married off early was equally prevalent. Thus, it was a period of conflict and confusion about what a woman's role should be. At this juncture, Partition and its consequent atrocities provided practical reasons for women to pursue education and careers.

Even women who had not been eager or equipped to build a career were more accepting of the Partition than men. 'We, as women, in any case, were to be married off and were destined to leave our homes. You never know what is going to be your fate. This was also a change—after all, we did not fare too badly', said Namita. Rekha expressed the same sentiment. 'After all, what really matters? I would have stayed happily wherever my husband and family were. This place is not bad, only I have lost my husband to share it with.'

It is this reaction to Partition among women victims of soft violence that contrasts with the women victims of brutal violence. The former's generally disadvantaged position on the one hand, and their social sensitivity on the other, rendered them a different kind of coping strategy during Partition. In the first place, in the families encountering only uprooting and migration, the women were much more protected than men. At the same time, they were not allowed to participate in the decisions. Rarely did they exert any kind of judgement in the matters of migration. They were but passive recipients of the patriarchal order. The lack of control over external factors owing to Partition was just an extension of their usual powerlessness. Unless particularly traumatic events took place, they could remain more or less placid during the changes. For the same reason, the women who gained some power after Partition counted the positive gain greater than any financial loss.

Among my respondents some have flourished in West Bengal. They revealed a certain degree of discomfort about this; a trace of guilt about what they felt was their undue privilege compared with others. Dipendu reported that his elder brother had had to give up studies to support the family, while he, being the second one, got the opportunity of higher education. Manish also considered himself fortunate, as his brother bore the major brunt of the financial struggle. Many expressed guilt for having survived at all, and wondered where the less fortunate ones were. Namita felt a pang for the young girl who had lost her husband in rioting, yet had to stay in Dhaka, immersed in mourning and misfortune. Manish often thinks of his ayah who looked after him. 'I am lucky sitting here in my living room and engrossed in reminiscence. But where is Kailasidi? Nobody knows where and how she died.' However, survivor's guilt was definitely not the major characteristic among these victims of soft violence.

THE CONSTRUCTION OF THE OTHER: ATTITUDE TOWARDS MUSLIMS

In the process of experiencing uprooting and persecution, the 'other' was constructed. Among my respondents, this perception of the other community was by no means linear. It contained a streak of ambivalence: reflecting the love-hate relationship between the communities, as well as the self-contradictions in judging the Muslims in terms of their actions and intentions. Such ambiguity and conflicts in attitude and judgement were probably born out of the pain of soft violence, of its uncertainties, and the rapid alteration in perception before any hardening could take place in the judgement of the person. These were reflected not only in the expressed opinions of the respondents, but also in their cherished life-views and philosophies as well as in their political perceptions. Here we find a clue to how the 'enemy' was defined and personalized as a result of painful experience.[39]

In the respondents' social and communal relationship with Muslims, both idealization and contradiction were apparent. They were unanimous in perceiving pre-Partition communal relations as harmonious. 'There were no distinctions between Hindus and Mussalmans. We were like two flowers on the same branch', or 'We never knew that the communities had any disparity.' Yet, contradictory statements of almost equal strength were made simultaneously or in quick succession. They exemplify the respondents' inner conflicting attitudes about Muslims. Often the respondents were not aware of the conflict; it emerged from their language, juxtaposition of content and non-verbal expressions.

Manish was a bit hesitant when I asked him about his sentiments towards Muslims, and how he interpreted the issue of Partition. 'As children, we did not think; when they said that the Hindus and the Mussalmans are different, we did not bother. But personal experience is important. The violent cry "Allah Ho Akbar" ... these are meant to be benevolent words, but they have been defiled ... they still haunt me. That cry made me hate them. I still get the nightmare.'

He was thoughtful for a while.

> 'The Partition did no good. The total economy collapsed. Hindus were better off than Mussalmans, even poor people like us were. India has gained nothing. The Mussalmans, yes, they have [flourished], some of them have. We were the privileged class. Therefore, if we had stayed on I would have been at the top; not, say, Mozammel Haque. They, the Mussalmans, were mostly peasants. They were perhaps exploited. We never heard of the idea that soil should go to the tiller.
>
> 'But my point is, have they followed the path of prosperity now? Have we followed it? Maqbur worked for us. Maybe he gained something. He set fire to our house. Now he is even poorer. Yes, some Mussalmans, some opportunity grabbers, have prospered. It would have been tougher for them if we had stayed on. Nevertheless, the exploited remain exploited, now by their own people.
>
> 'Hate, you think? We were not politically conscious. But Mussalmans were not allowed inside our house. If they touched our pots, we discarded them. Like if a dog touches something. This is hate, you may think. But then my mother loved Ajij like her son. From her paltry savings, she used to give him money. He was invited to our house if some delicacy was being cooked. Of course, he never crossed the threshold of the house. These contradictions existed.
>
> 'Initially we Hindus were in higher positions than the Mussalmans. But we did not hate them. Then there was news of killing, stabbing;

> we learnt that the Mussalmans were the cause of violence; yes, gradually we started hating them.
>
> 'Now I may accommodate a Mussalman girl at my home. But I cannot allow my daughter to stay with a Mussalman family in Pakistan, I mean Bangladesh. I don't trust them [hesitation]. Mussalmans are ferocious, racial, they eat differently. They take ginger, onion. They are polygamous and violent. They are eager to dominate by sheer number, quantity rather than quality ... No, I would never trust them.'

Is Manish simply a blind Muslim hater, as one may think after his declared mistrust? If so, then why did he demonstrate clarity and empathy when asked about the cause of Partition?

> 'Neither the Hindus nor the Mussalmans did it. It was the last kick of the British. I may dislike the Mussalmans, but I know they did not do it. A few Hindus and a few Mussalmans may have been involved; their religion was not important, their greed was. They exploited the illiterate, half-educated, simpleton rural people and then there were pervasive rumours, intentional and unintentional, misguiding, instigating all of them towards prejudice and violence. Otherwise why would Maqbur burn down our house?'

The above paragraphs evince a juxtaposition of rejection of the other community with rationalized and humanitarian acceptance of them. Manish was ostensibly uncomfortable in explaining his attitude. The piece of narrative is a striking combination of anger and guilt. Manish started by claiming innocence, that in his childhood discrimination on the basis of religion never came up. He highlighted the fact that owing to his exposure to Muslim violence, the war cry and persecution, he had come to hate the community. Thus, the process of rationalization is apparent here.

Next, the speaker's feelings about the loss of privileged position came to the fore. His sense that his prospect of holding a position of honour in his own land had been thwarted came out in raw form as he envied the fictitious Mozammel Haque. Immediately after, he recognized that the Hindus had been exploiting the

Muslims. Presumably, his wish to arrogate the heightened position of the Muslims in his former homeland evoked rebuke from his super-ego, and consequently generated guilt. By admitting the exploitation of the Muslims by the Hindus in general, the guilt was expressed, simultaneously attributing the responsibility to the entire Hindu community and thus reducing his personal involvement. Similarly, by the assertion that he had never thought that the 'soil should go to the tiller', he implied that they were not consciously exploiting the other community. His further attempt to mitigate the guilt was evident in his statement that exploitation of the poor Muslims had not stopped after Partition; now their own people are exploiting them.

Then he spoke of how they had discriminated against Muslims. The expression 'like a dog' revealed a sentiment that he denied in his very next utterance, that it was not hate. But neither did he condemn practices against ritual pollution. He simply added that his mother loved Ajij like her own son, though this 'son' was not allowed to come inside the house. It is probable that neither Manish, nor his mother, nor even Ajij, was conscious of the drama of social prejudice they were playing out every day. Manish did admit that this entailed some contradiction, but was not seriously bothered about it. In fact, this is a striking example of the coexistence of humanitarian and prejudiced selves. Hateful and sympathetic statements came rushing out one after the other. And they coexisted in surprising harmony disregarding all contradictions as did the Hindu and Muslim communities in pre-partition Bengal.

After these deliberations, however, Manish's anger came up vibrantly. The declaration that one could never trust a Muslim was an expression of the concentrated antagonism he harboured against those who had shattered his dreams. Yet, again, hatred was not the last word. Manish was confident in his perception when he categorically denied the role of common Muslims in the disaster. He traced the issue to the political manipulation of the British and a handful of selfish political leaders. It took me a bit by surprise that he identified not only with the poor Muslim community at large, but also at the individual level. Near the end of the narration, Manish commented that the Muslims too were victims, misled by prejudice and greed. So far, Manish had spoken bitterly about Maqbur burning their house. At the end, suddenly his tone changed and he identified with Maqbur and other ordinary Muslims.

What was the precise nature of Manish's perception of the Muslim community? It was not painted in a single colour. Contradictory processes of identification and distancing, the memory of acceptance and spontaneous reaction of rejection, and finally a guilt born out of the hatred, coexisted despite his intellectual excellence and knowledge. Manish seemed only perfunctorily aware of this contradiction, if at all.

What makes two ideas contradictory? The logical rational contrast is operative only at the conscious level; the psychological contradiction entails an unconscious appreciation of two emotions that cancel each other. When an intelligent individual fails to appreciate an apparent logical contradiction, we may infer the play of overlapping unconscious emotions involving merging of cognitions. In the case of Manish, the overlapping emotions were hatred toward Muslims, followed by a fear of his feelings of aggression (owing to the disapproval of the super-ego), thus producing guilt. The ultimate inconsistency of alternating positive and negative statements in Manish's narration may be understood as an expression of his hate, fear and guilt.

The hate was facilitated by the mechanism of projection. This was apparent as generalized negative qualities were thrust on the entire Muslim community. Immediately afterwards, the aggression was inhibited, owing to super-ego intervention. There was a second factor inimical to uninterrupted projection. Some members of the Muslim community, living in close vicinity from childhood, had been identified with and hence introjected. This existence of the 'other' within himself also interfered with the projection of the 'other'. The result was guilt and discomfort, the attempt to redraw a picture from another angle where the self, or those akin to self (e.g., the Hindus) were the exploitative aggressors. Then the ego detected too big a loss in self-esteem, and again the feeling of anger was fomented. The two tones of feeling, when coming in close succession, produced the kind of contradiction that Manish revealed. However, to maintain the undulating pattern, another modification of the cognitive system was necessary, that is, his not being aware of the contradiction.

Manish used two tools to enable the simultaneous accommodation of opposite sentiments. Firstly, although both projection and introjection were used, his overall attitude was dominated by projection, where a kind of mistrust and bitterness pervaded his mind. In the course of his narration, he once summarized his life-view. 'Life has treated me badly. Our own life was snatched away from us and we lived on snatching other people's property. And then I had difficulty in getting admission to college, in pursuing my higher degrees, people were jealous ... Write down what I have learnt from life: The basis of all private property is unethical, illegal, based on exploitation and violence. Ultimately it is legalized for political purposes.' Thus, Manish had kept busy counting the hurts he had received from outside and this effort served a secondary purpose by protecting him from being hurt by his own aggression.[40]

Secondly, Manish used the mechanism of denial to remain relatively unconcerned about the other side of his narrative, his self-derogatory comments about his prejudices. The negative or 'not-it' defined other areas of his personality as well. When asked about his political beliefs, Manish described himself negatively, as *not* a communist. He adored Gandhi for his 'satvik' life, but was doubtful about the application of his principles. The *not* was here too.

Manish was not the only one who revealed contradictions. Rather, I was struck by the number of respondents who made frantic efforts to integrate the contradictory emotions and cognitions of this critical period. Another example was Arun. 'My friend was studying at City College. I accompanied him and was put up in my elder brother's mess at College Street. One day, at midday, when the mess members were gone and only the servants and cooks were in, rioting broke out. The servants forbade me to go out but I ventured just beyond the gate on hearing the cries. Then the paanwala told me, 'Hey Bangal, don't go out.' I came back and stood at the window. I saw a young boy of twelve or thirteen running towards the Eden Hospital gate. A big burly Hindu Kalwar was pursuing him and caught hold of him near the hospital, turned his head in a peculiar angle and slit his throat. Next day unfortunately I saw the same scene. This time it was a man, he jumped up the rails of the hospital to save himself, but his lungi got caught in the rails. The same Kalwar pulled him down and cut his throat in the same fashion. He must have been a professional. All these were so upsetting.

'There was Rakhal.[41] He was behind many killings. There was a big Muslim slum in Eden Hospital Road. One evening we saw Rakhal going that way, a few minutes later there were cries from that direction. Then Rakhal and his group came back with the looted things; those were all sorts of goods from the shops.

'We were but helpless spectators, not able to do anything.

'After two or three days there was a *shanti michil* [peace march]. Dada had come back. We also joined in. There were leaders like Vijay Singh Nahar, Prafulla Ghosh, and student leaders like Purabi Mukherjee, Geeta Mukherjee, etc. There was a rumour that the Muslims are spraying acid from the rooftops of Rajabazar. Then we discovered that it was rose water.'

I asked, 'Considering your experience, what is your attitude to the Muslims?'

'They engage in riots very easily. Aggressive lot. Temperamentally cruel. Maybe it is in their culture, their belief. Every Muslim family keeps arms; the Hindu families do not. Only professional killers among the Hindus keep arms. During the riots, the Muslims were most brutally beaten up by the Sikhs at Bhawanipur, because theirs is also a fighting community.

'We were afraid to cross the Gas Street. Our local Hindu friend ... boasted of how many Muslims he had cut. Gopichandra [again, not the real name] was another killer in the notorious Muslim slum area called Peshwari busti.'

Arun had witnessed killing only by Hindu hooligans. He had not witnessed any direct act of violence by Muslims. He had instinctively felt for the victims, the boy running for his life and the man trying desperately to climb over the railings of the hospital. He had felt guilty as a 'helpless spectator' not having the courage to do anything. Based on this, one would expect that he would condemn the Hindu killers or at least have a balanced opinion. Nonetheless, he categorically labelled the Muslims as aggressive and cruel. By asserting that the Hindu killers were hired men, he distanced himself from them and avoided any identification with them. Yet, at the end of the discussion, he again recalled a few Hindu names who boasted of killing.

I consider this inconsistency of labelling the Muslims as violent while recounting events of violence by the Hindus as an eloquent example of the defence of 'isolation'. Arun was in a state of conflict between what he saw and what he believed in. He already had strong negative feelings about the Muslims owing to the prior stereotypes and the threats faced in East Bengal. Therefore, a palpable aggression was already present in him and that was probably stimulated by the scenes of killing. However, witnessing direct murder of ordinary people, especially of a boy, was too strong for his intent. This probably generated strong rebuke from his super-ego. Consequently, a compromise was struck: any identification on his part with the Hindu killer was shoved aside by the perception that he was a professional killer, killing not out of hatred, but for money, signifying an instrumental role of the person rather than an emotional one.

As I asked Arun about his feelings towards Muslims, he wanted to tell me that they were dangerous. Yet, time and again his perception of the Muslims as cruel was not corroborated by the schema he had developed from his experience, first in the killing episodes, and second at the peace procession, where they expected acid, but received rose water instead! These challenges to pre-existing prejudice had however not been so intense as to really alter his perception. With my enquiry, the contradictory imagery appeared at the forefront and some integration of facts and ideas needed to be made. The defence of isolation was called upon. The scenes of violence committed by Hindus were reported, but only at the cognitive level, isolated from feeling. The negative affect was retained for the Muslims, or even transported from the Hindus, while the contradiction of this affect with actual events was mitigated; hence the apparent inconsistency of Arun's narrative.

Namita spoke of the Muslim friends she had in Kumilla and how the Muslims loved their families. However, when I asked her about her attitude towards the Muslims, she retorted aggressively, 'Me? Why, now I get irritated even if you name a Mussalman. They caused the tension. Though I must admit I am no worse off here, the entire problem was due to them. I will not trust them at all. It is for them that the young girl was widowed. It was not proper, was it? ... We were saved, but the fear that reigned at that time was intense. The Mussalmans were its cause.'

Sandip Bandyopadhyaya has commented upon such feelings of animosity, despite contradictions, among respondents in his interviews. 'They emphatically hold that it was impossible to get along with those people whom "you can never trust". But in the course of interview all of them would admit that some members of the "other" community had tried to protect them and had entreated them not to leave for West Bengal.'[42] The negative sentiments were remembered as affect-laden, the positive were only rational presentation of theory. Ranabir Samaddar in one of his articles, elaborates on the nature of the multiplicity of selves developed in the context of such disaster and attributes this kind of contradiction to the simultaneous operation of such selves.[43] When one part of the self is activated, the others are silenced, thus maintaining a semblance of inner consistency when in reality there is none.

Some respondents, of course, were aware of their inconsistencies. When asked about his attitude towards the Muslims, Surojit initially reported the harmony and the social balance that prevailed.

> 'We lived in a village where the majority were Mussalman. There was communal harmony. The Mussalman people were generally uneducated. In the entire village there was only one educated Mussalman man . . . who later became a doctor. Their family did not mix with other Mussalman families, but only with us. It was an

agrarian village; there were 24-25 ploughs [indicating the number of peasant families who could afford to till their lands].

'There was a kind of local but fair judgement system. The matabbar of our panchayat was a Mussalman. He was a strong man; everybody obeyed him. He was very proud of his religion. He declared: "I am a Mussalman, so I will talk in favour of Mussalmans." He spoke like that, but ultimately his judgement would be fair. Again, he knew that among the Hindus wearing *tilak* [the Vaishnava sandal-paste mark on the forehead] implied a kind of status. If a *tilakdhari* committed any offence, he would say, "You are being punished lightly, because you are wearing tilak." He decided that one such offender would be kicked in the ass, but ordered him to rub off his tilak first. This is social judgement. We were satisfied with these small judgements and arrangements.'

After sometime he said, 'I understand this is not right, but one thing I can tell you ... I do not know how to explain it. We did not feel any difference with the Mussalmans we knew, but—as a community—I am not sure. When we heard rumours about Hindus attacking the Mussalmans I recall thinking, "All right, fine, they deserve it; they also have tortured Hindus at other places." The pain and reproach that we should have ideally felt as sensitive human beings was not present, at least not in me.' Surojit was ashamed of his anger, but he did not deny it.

Girish also acknowledged his ambivalent perception. Asked about his attitude to the Muslims he said, 'I have my reservations, but no hostility. A Mussalman donated this land. He used to come here on the occasion of Lakshmi Puja each year. We also saved Mussalman people. Nevertheless, they are different, culturally, socially. I cannot think of being very close to them. Not personally, or at a familial level, I mean.'

Many respondents like Surojit expressed antipathy towards the Muslims as a community, but not as individuals. All these persons had spent considerable time with Muslims as neighbours, friends and faithful servants, and were not able to obliterate the memories completely. Yet, with the human tendency to categorize and to form stereotypes, over-generalizations occurred for many.

A split in attitude was achieved: towards the group and towards the person. It became possible to hate Muslims as a community and to love Ajij or Nur Chacha; it was also possible to 'avenge the death of hundreds of Hindus after indescribable torture', yet keep in close touch with one's Muslim friends in Bangladesh who had bestowed love on one as a child.

Shades of guilt were apparent in many responses. I have discerned three types. The first is the guilt for one's personal activity or inactivity. Kalyan's guilt for being in the group of rioters and Arun's guilt for being a helpless spectator were typical examples. The second is the guilt for one's extended self in the form of wrongs done by one's family. Finally, there is the third kind of guilt for an even greater extended self: the Hindus as a community.

Madhabi gave a detailed account of her pain as her paternal as well as her in-laws' family discriminated against the Muslims even without understanding that they were doing so.

> 'My grandmother had serious reservations about the Mussalmans. We used to play with the Mussalman girls till the age of ten or twelve. Yet we did not usually bring them home. They also did not want to come. I will tell you about an embarrassing episode. We were playing hide-and-seek outside our house. A Mussalman girl, in her excitement, hid inside one of our rooms, and my grandmother was there. She cried out, "All is lost! Get out, I say, get out!" Then she started cleaning the room. She used to keep drinking water in a pitcher in that room. She poured it away. She used to chew betel leaves, and for that she kept lime soaked in water. I noticed that she poured out the water in which the lime was soaked, but did not discard the lime! I remember noting the incongruence.
>
> 'You know, I cannot blame the Mussalmans when I think of the way we had treated them.
>
> 'I had a very close friend, Fatema. I used to go to her house. One day her Amma said, "I want to invite you and some other friends of Fatema. Will you come? But then you must not tell your parents." I agreed. She cooked meat; it was so delicious. Another Hindu girl was with us too. Fatema's brothers were sitting near the gate, lest anybody

> came in suddenly. They knew it was socially prohibited. However, I did not keep it as a secret. I was a small girl. I told my grandmother that I had eaten meat with Fatema. She called my father and said, "Everything is lost; this girl will never be married off properly, she has eaten meat with a Mussalman family." Father was much more rational. "We will see about it in time, Ma," he said, "after all, Fatema is her friend." My father was the only person who was somewhat free from this prejudice. Probably that was because he was a teacher and a humanitarian as well as an intellectual kind of man.
>
> 'The condition of the Mussalmans was wretched. They were often employed only for menial jobs. Their children remained uneducated. Their connection with the upper class Hindu families naturally withered away as there was so much difference in status and orientation.
>
> 'I always resented the way they were treated at my in-law's house too. In my in-laws' house there were separate sitting arrangements for the Hindus and the Mussalmans. The Mussalmans were not offered chairs, but tree trunks cut to size.
>
> Isn't it interesting that ultimately we were afraid of those whom we did not count at all?'

While Kalyan's personal guilt was expressed in his narration, he also exemplified the third type of guilt. He posited his own view of Muslim hatred of the Hindus based on Hindu cultural domination.

> 'A student from Dhaka University participated in the debate in 1944. The subject matter was Independence of India. This Mussalman student attributed the entire responsibility of the downtrodden Mussalmans to the Hindu community, and not to the British government.
>
> 'Now that we look back and think, I have this feeling that the middle-class Mussalman society could not express themselves owing to the domination of the Hindus.'

Kalyan illustrated how the Hindus had occupied the prime position in all areas of achievement including sports, music and cultural activities, though in school, college and university education, they were given relatively equal opportunity. Kalyan explained the cause of this disparity.

> 'Do you know the difference between Hindu and Mussalman society? The Mussalmans were mostly labour class. They worked with their bodies. The masons, the tailors, the labourers and porters were Mussalman. There were of course high class Mussalmans ... But they were almost separate from the common poor Mussalman folks.
>
> 'The way the Hindus tortured the Mussalmans was pathetic. The Mussalmans drove the horse carts. The Hindus used to lash them with the same whip they used for the horse. These drivers were very witty, known as "Kutti". They pleased people with humour and jokes. Bhanu Bandyopadhyay [a famous Bengali comedy actor] has made a record of such jokes. There were many downtrodden Hindus as well. They were not so witty. When, later on, I went to Dhaka, I have tried to find these Kuttis. I never found them.'

While reviewing these excerpts, I wondered about the psychological function of these statements. In the latter two kinds of guilt, that is, blaming one's family like Madhabi, and blaming the Hindu community like Kalyan, the rejection by the super-ego was not directed towards the individual but towards the family or the entire Hindu community. What happened in such cases was that blame and guilt merged; some personal guilt was experienced, but its sting was minimized as it was experienced by the self as part of a community. The first category of guilt had, of course, a personal reference and had to be resolved within oneself.

The context was, indeed, a dyadic situation, and we are dealing with verbal narration of one's life; a kind of memoir. Guilt comes here as a sort of confession to a person from another generation. Some conveyed this directly. 'Talking with you I feel relieved. You know after your first visit, I was reviewing so many things that we had done and not done. You are documenting these. Maybe the future will judge us Bengalis in the light of these right and wrong decisions.' Many used the word 'confess' while talking about their aggressive thoughts and actions.

Indeed, the institution of confession is a very old one in human society. Guilt, when confessed, bears the promise of absolution. While guilt can be gnawing, it can be cooling too; it puts an end to the incessant power game by deciding once and forever who rules whom. And through absolution the offender is once again on the same plane as before; she can start life anew.[44]

I view the guilt expressed by my respondents as a coping mode; one not used very frequently, but having its own niche in the individual's intra-psychic arrangement. Thus, guilt has more than one function. Firstly, it is a reaction, a defence against aggression, a punishment inflicted upon oneself as opposed to on the other, specifically the powerful other. Secondly, it often entails absolution in itself, particularly when it is shared by a group or community. That is, if a person is guilty of doing what fellow group members also did, she claims a superior position through her understanding of the guilt, thus slightly separating herself from the group. After all, one who repents is better than one who does not, and hence has greater chance of obtaining forgiveness. Guilt is also an excellent way of handling inappropriate and unmanageable desire for power. It mitigates the sense of defeat as it implies that one is responsible for one's plight and is not simply a passive recipient of disaster. 'I did not do this' also means 'I had the capacity to do this'. Therefore, guilt also is a subtle mechanism for experiencing some degree of mastery over situations.

Before I finish with instances of contradiction, I must mention another category of respondents. They professed secular attitudes, and declared that they did not have any bias against the Muslims. Nevertheless, the declaration was not necessarily the sole truth for all of them. The contradiction was most prominent for those who used rationalization as a basis for secularism. Some of these persons were involved in a political philosophy that explicitly supported secularism and therefore felt a compulsion to stick to the flexible and the rational mode of perception. But not all of them genuinely succeeded. The contradictions showed in their faltering rationality and hesitant personal decisions.

Bipul had been in the Congress for a while and in 1951 joined the 'Red party'. He proudly declared that he had never done anything for himself, but had simply obeyed party orders. He emphatically stated, 'I am completely secular. I do not believe in God. Religion is the opium for people. One must be materialistic, rational and scientific.' But then he hesitated, 'However the Muslims are often more fundamentalist than the Hindus, at least in greater number. But I have no bias so far as the Muslims are concerned.'

I felt his statements a bit overdrawn and asked if he would get his son married to a Muslim girl. Bipul hesitated. 'That's different,' he said. 'What I wanted to tell you was that I do not believe in communalism. I believe in only what is scientific. It has little to do with my personal decisions.' With a striking use of denial and isolation, Bipul separated his personal and public stances.

Another committed political worker with a declared rational stance also started with the statement that he had no prejudice at all against the Muslims. Then he himself qualified the idea and said, 'I have no bias. The well-off Mussalmans initiated the conflict. They were not attentive to the welfare of the total Mussalman community. Jinnah introduced this feeling. One exception was Fazlul Haq . . . we had Mussalman friends. I remember Nur Chacha. But Hindus used to mix only with rich Mussalmans and vice versa.

'Write it down: I never hate Mussalmans. I am a non-believer and a completely rational person. But sometimes they hate us. When I went back to East Pakistan after 1947 the local Mussalmans threatened me. They would kill me, they said, if I stayed any longer. They have looted our house, though they never tortured us. They did not save us either, though they were our neighbours.'

Before ending the session on the last day, he expressed his attitude to life. 'I have never believed in God, destiny or superstition. None at all. Science and rationality are the only truths. I have learnt that we have to struggle with whatever comes up. We must carry on.'

I noticed a few rings set with stones on his fingers and asked him why he wore these if he did not believe in superstition and destiny, which the stones are supposed to influence. He smiled in embarrassment and explained that somebody had presented these to him and he wore them to respect the giver. Then once again, he asserted his sincere belief in science as the only true discipline.

This man's attitude towards the Muslims fluctuated between what he thought he should believe and what was generated by the persecution he had experienced. That is why his answer was hazy and faltering. Again, his over-emphasis on rationality that immediately followed was probably more a defence of rationality rather than a genuinely rational mode of thinking. The tendency of a guarded response was evident from the contradiction in his behaviour and belief, in his embarrassment at his stones being remarked upon. He was neither able to integrate emotion and rationality, nor accept this failure with a brave face; hence the hesitation and compromise.

I would like to give some justification of my attempt to interpret people's behaviour in this manner. The episode of the stones, for example, was unrelated to this man's communal attitude, yet I brought it up in the context. I did so deliberately, because I believe that to understand the emotions of a person, the totality of all emotions with all the inconsistencies must be taken into account. This respondent's confused exposition of his communal attitude and the contradiction between his rational belief in science and irrational practice are intra-psychically bound in the same string, in his idealization of rationality and his emotional block against it. This must not be interpreted as a denouncement of the person. It is, indeed, imprudent and childish to anticipate that any person will have an entirely integrated and rational existence; if we do find one, it is possible that we have not probed deep enough. The wearing of the stones along with the declaration of indisputable belief in rationality does not imply my respondent's duplicity; it is but an expression of human vulnerability under certain overbearing emotions. Although I am looking at the processing of the partition experience of these persons, these tangential characteristics do lend completeness to the understanding of the person as a whole.

Russell once said, 'Man is not yet, he will be.' The idealism of the modernist era being dissolved in the postmodern notion of fluidity and unpredictability, may I be permitted to say, 'Man is not, and may never be'. We are rational only in portions of our emotions and actions, with pockets of irrationality and inconsistencies. As I had the opportunity to probe into the hearts of these seniors through this Partition project, the marvel of the intricacies of the human mind intrigued me. We strive to push each piece of thought and attitude into its appropriate slot, as if life were a puzzle that had a solution. We frantically try to tie up all loose ends, so that a semblance of integration is suggested. Sometimes it appears we succeed in putting up an illusion of consistency, but one pull at a loose knot and the tie is undone. Here is the human tragicomedy, so far as one can laugh at our quixotic attempts to set up a front, yet immersed in the pain of confusion, of vague anxieties and uncertainties, of uncontrollable passions. Human history has consistently been one of failure to organize itself.

Finally, there were some respondents who expressed a relatively conflict-free and spontaneous broadness, at least, so far as their attitude towards Muslims was concerned. Usually their statements were not over-emphatic; they did not try to give any theoretical reasons for their broadmindedness. Neither Marx, nor Vivekananda, nor the sacred scriptures of India had to be associated with their declaration of their non-prejudicial existence. Status and money too made little difference in this regard. Subhash with all his poverty, simply said, 'They have their own way. It is an issue of what you believe from your childhood. I rely on Radha Govinda; they rely on Allah. What's the difference? But some are bad and some are good everywhere.' Another respondent said, 'I might have been immature at that time, but now I know the entire issue of religion is bogus, an eye-wash for simple exploitation. You psychologists might know better, but I think there is more difference within the Hindus and within the Mussalmans than between the Hindus and the Mussalmans.'

These then are some of the glimpses of love, fear, wrath and guilt within a population, its response to the shattering of a dream. Here we have a simple narration of emotions, but this is not to forget that an individual's emotions have two definite roots. One is in the individual's history, predisposition and typical constellation of personality and behavioural tendencies in the character traits as crystallized at a given time. The second root is in the culture, where the fear experienced at an individual level turns into collective sensitivity, the anger turns to rebelliousness, the separation and pain turns into collective symbolic mourning and guilt turns into collective confusion and hesitancy. These need to be explored to understand how the emotions are processed.

Notes

1 E.W. Said. 1994. *Representation of the intellectual* (London: Vintage): 46.

2 Many articles as well as poems, memoirs, films, stories and novels in Bengali reveal the same yearning for the lost paradise. See A. Basu Raychaudhury. 2004. Nostalgia of 'Desh', Memories of Partition. *Economic and Political Weekly* (Dec 25): 5653-60. There are a number of intensely emotional poems by Sunil Gangopadhyay, Shankha Ghosh, Birendra Chattopadhyay and others. A few of the many important memoirs are Mihir Sengupta. 2004. *Bishadbriksha* (Kolkata: Subarnarekha), Tapan Raychaudhuri. 2007. *Bangalnama* (Kolkata, Ananda Publishers), Jayantanuj Bandyopadhyay. 2005. *Oparer Chelebela* (Kolkata: Subarnarekha). Ritwik Ghatak's films represent a genre of its kind in cinema. Numerous short stories and novels include the sentiment as their central theme or part. Yearning for 'desh' has never really left Bengali sentiment.

3 D. R. Basu. 1956. *Chherey aasa gram*, vols 1 and 2 (Kolkata: Bengal Publishers).

4 Dipesh Chakrabarty. 1996. Remembered villages: Representation of Hindu Bengali memories in the aftermath of partition. *Economic and Political Weekly* 31, 2143-51.

5 Plant of the gourd family, termed 'cucurbitaceous', also known as ridged gourd, a creeper; a common vegetable in Bengal. The white flowers

bloom in the afternoon. This creeper has featured in Bengali literature, as in some writings of Bibhuti Bhushan Bandyopadhyay.

6 I recall in this context a novel by Mahasweta Devi: *Kabi Bandyoghati gainir jeeban o mrityu*. In this novel, a tribal youth, born and brought up amidst the myths and realities of the forest, comes out secretly into 'civilized' society, and demonstrating his superior merit and cre vity, gains the post of royal bard. When, however, his identity is disclosed, he is persecuted by the king and the aristocrats. To save himself, he tries to go back to the forest. But the forest now rejects him: he has lost his sense of oneness with nature. In the exposition of his agony immediately before civilization crushes him, the symbolism of being and not being within nature's womb comes up repeatedly.

7 See C.G. Jung. 1911-12/1952. Symbols of transformation. *Collected works*, vol 5 (New York: Routledge and Kegan Paul).

8 See O. Rank. 1952. *The trauma of birth* (New York: Robert Brunner).

9 Under stressful conditions, sensory regression is facilitated, whereby the visual mode is abandoned in favour of smell, taste or hearing. The sensation of smell may have its root in anal eroticism, one of the earlier phases in psychosexual development, and thus entails regressive defences. See O. Fenichel. 1946. *The psychoanalytic theory of neurosis* (London: Routledge and Kegan Paul): 73; see also, J. Breuer and S. Freud. [1893-95]1955. Studies in hysteria. In J. Strachey, ed. and trans., *The standard edition of the complete psychological works of Sigmund Freud*, vol 2 (London: Hogarth Press).

10 I refer to the mild torture every child loves to hurl upon the surrounding elements–tearing leaves, throwing pebbles in the stream, digging into the ground–small acts of symbolic aggression that can be pacified through the acting out and assimilated in the expansive acceptance of nature. It gives shelter to the uncertain child; it accepts the infringements on its system and assures nurturance. Probably, this is why nature is a 'she': Mother Nature.

11 D.W. Winnicott. 1960/1965. The theory of the parent-infant relationship. In D.W. Winnicott, ed., 1965. *The maturational processes and the facilitating environment: Studies in the theory of emotional development* (New York: International Universities Press): 37-55.

12 Chakrabarty, in Remembered villages (see note 4), notes how the village became the 'true spiritual home' for urban Bengalis.

[13] I refer here to the concept of 'lack' (manqué), as in Jacques Lacan. In his elucidation of the four fundamental concepts of psychoanalysis in Freud, Lacan formulated that in the post-mirror phase of individuation, the early images of the mother as a 'whole form' is repressed. Consequently, 'desire' derived from unconscious fantasies comes to connote a lost sense of union. It is the fate of the 'moi' (the Lacanian concept of subjectivity) not ever to be assimilated in any final, conscious integration. A human being is destined to search for ever–search for its Other. See the chapter on 'Lacan's four fundamental concepts of psychoanalysis' in E. Ragland-Sullivan. 1986. *Jacques Lacan and the philosophy of psychoanalysis* (London: Croom Helm).

[14] Self-esteem has one of its major sources in the feeling of omnipotence. The initial sense of omnipotence comes through the infant's delusional sense of control over the external world, when through incorporating satiating objects, that is, food, the child develops a sense of mastery over regulation of nourishment and hence, a sense of esteem. Thus, in the terms of the unconscious, food and love are equivalent; nourishment and honour are symbolic substitutes at the level of infantile perception. See S. Rado. 1928. The problem of melancholia. *International Journal of Psychoanalysis* 9; also O. Fenichel. 1934. *Outline of clinical psychoanalysis* (New York: Norton).

[15] Of course, I use the term 'desire' here in the Lacanian sense: as a fantasy caught up in the culture, and contained in language. See J. Lacan. 1992. *The seminar of Jacques Lacan*, Book V11, *The ethics of psychoanalysis*, Jacques-Alain Miller, ed. D. Porter, trans. (London: Routledge).

[16] In this sense, regression for my subjects was both a form of coping and an essential element of the construction of their narratives. Indeed, in normal life, regression may be precipitated by significant changes, both beneficial and impeding. It can serve as a temporary shelter while the individual accommodates the changes that disrupt one's habitual lifestyle. See for discussion, R.W. Firestone. 1990. The bipolar causality of regression. *American Journal of Psychoanalysis* 50, 121-35. Indeed, regression can even be creative. Ernst Kris conceptualized 'Regression in the service of the ego', which is an essential part of any creative process. See for reference, E. Kris. 1936/1958. *Psychoanalytic explorations in art* (New York: International Universities Press).

[17] See the chapter on 'The agency of the letter in the unconscious or reason since Freud' in J. Lacan. 1966/1977. *Écrits*, Alan Sheridan trans. (London:

Routledge). In this article, Lacan asserts that 'the unconscious of the subject is the discourse of the other' (p. 61). However, it is not a simple two-way process of conscious communication; it is a resonance. To quote Lacan, 'The *omnipresence of human discourse* will perhaps one day be embraced under the open sky of an omni-communication of its text. This is not to say that human discourse will be any more harmonious than now. But this is the field that our experience polarizes in a relation that is only *apparently two-way*, for any positing of its structure in merely dual terms is as inadequate to it in theory as it is ruinous for its technique' (p. 61, my italics).

18 I was initially hesitant about the use of the term 'fear' as I thought the term 'anxiety' would be technically more accurate. Fear stems from a real threat; anxiety from the apprehension of a threat, which was more common among my respondents. Yet, somehow, as I delved deeper into their narratives and participated in their feelings, I found the term 'fear' appropriate. In Bengali, the synonym for 'fear' is *bhoy*, and for 'anxiety' it is *dushchinta*, *udbeg* or *utkanthha*. My respondents always used the term *bhoy* in the context of Partition.

19 The concept of anger is confounded by a number of terms: aggression; hostility; destructiveness; animosity; hatred; and so on. The most familiar word in psychological literature, however, is 'aggression', which literally means 'advancing towards'. Aggression implies an overt observable behaviour, that of intentionally hurting somebody. Anger is the emotion accompanying aggression, and has, like all emotions, its cognitive and affective components. Blame is a frequent accompaniment of anger.

20 See the article on 'Fear, guilt and hate' in E. Jones. 1968. *Papers on psychoanalysis* (London: Baillière, Timball and Cox): 304-19.

21 A corollary of hate is the sadism resulting from the sexualizing of the aggressive impulse. In the early stages of his theorization, Freud considered aggression as serving as a reaction to the blocking of libidinal impulses. In this sense, anger and aggression is secondary to desire. This view is a reflection of the ancient dictum of the Bhagavad Gita: '*kamat krodha-vijayate*'. Later the situation was modified and made complicated by the introduction of the concept of the death instinct. S. Freud. 1923/1961. The Ego and the id. In Strachey, ed. and trans., *The Standard edition of the complete psychological works of sigmund Freud*, vol 19 (London: Hogarth Press): 3-63.

Freud's writings imply that aggressive tendencies constitute a considerable proportion of 'human drives and are reflected in a plethora of human endeavours. Partly, they have a reactive character, that is, reactive to situational thwarting. Partly again they are connected to libidinal drives, particularly pre-genital sexuality. A third group of aggressive behaviour appears to arise quite independent of sexuality and has an existence in its own right. This is aggression emanating spontaneously from within: an urge to destroy self or other with an intention to get back to the formless origin. This is Freud's 'destrudo', the death instinct, on the basis of which the Nirvana principle was formulated.

[22] Jones used this term to mean the period in development when the infant has not yet identified any external agent as evil.

[23] Jones. 1968. Fear, guilt and hate. In *Papers on psychoanalysis,* 317.

[24] S.Freud, 1926/1959. Inhibitions, symptoms and anxiety. In Strachey, ed. and trans., *Standard edition of the complete psychological works,* vol 20: 77-175.

[25] See for discussion, Fenichel. 1946. *The psychoanalytic theory of neurosis:* 134-38. Fenichel also draws an excellent comparison between the various stages of anxiety and guilt. He identifies a triple stratification for both: the three stages of trauma, danger and panic, showing how the unspecific ideation in anxiety becomes the specific anxiety of guilt. The end product is anxiety hysteria *vs.* melancholia.

[26] M. Klein. 1975. *Love, guilt and reparation and other works,* edited by M. Masud and R. Khan (London: Hogarth Press).

[27] D. W. Winnicott. 1958/1965. Psychoanalysis and the sense of guilt. In D. W. Winnicott, ed., 1965. *The Maturational processes and facilitating environment.* (London: Hogarth Press): 15-28.

[28] See the chapter on Aggressivity in psychoanalysis, in Lacan. 1966/1977. *Écrits: A selection,* 9-32.

[29] See R.D. Laing. 1959. *The divided self* (Harmondsworth: Penguin).

[30] For a detailed discussion on identification with the aggressor and case illustration, see A. Freud. 1937. *The ego and the mechanisms of defence* (London: Hogarth Press): 117-31.

[31] Indeed, that is why the training for systematic violence, be it approved by the state or anti-state terrorism, is directed towards reducing sensitivity towards the victim and promotes unambiguous identification with one specific ideology.

[32] The severity of a guilt feeling is lessened if it is shared by many. This sharing serves two purposes. Firstly, the super-ego can be pacified as the decision was not entirely of the person in question; so far as the action is concerned, an anonymity can be feigned. Secondly, the punishment, if any, becomes relatively bearable when shared by many. Fenichel calls this sharing a 'quasi-projection' of guilt feelings. See Fenichel. 1946. *Psychoanalytic theory of neurosis*: 165.

[33] In case of the defence of *isolation*, the individual loses track of the connections and emotional significance of the traumatic event. Sometimes the individual, in employing isolation, interpolates real spatial or temporal intervals between the two domains meant to be kept separate. Many solve conflicts by isolating different spheres of their life from one another: one of the two isolated spheres usually represents instinctual freedom and the other stands for controlled and approved behaviour: bad *vs.* good is the result. Some even split their personality and act like two separate persons. Another variety of isolation is represented by attempts to solve conflicts around ambivalence, that is, conflicts between love and hatred of the same person by splitting the contradictory feelings, so that at one time the person is only loved, at another only hated, a counter-cathexis preventing the two feelings from having contact with each other.

[34] Through the mechanism of *rationalization*, 'emotional attitudes' become permissible on condition that they are justified as reasonable. The individual finds one reason or another why he must behave in this way or that, and thus avoids becoming aware that he is driven by instinctual impulse. One type of rationalization is idealization. The realization that an ideal requirement is going to be fulfilled brings to the ego an increase in self-esteem. This may delude it into ignoring the fact that through the idealized actions there is an expression of instincts that ordinarily would have been repressed. Each time an ideal requirement is fulfilled, the ego regains some of its early sense of omnipotence. In this sense of elation, the ego neglects its ordinary testing of reality and of impulses so that instinctual impulses may emerge relatively uncensored. See for discussion, Fenichel. 1946. *The psychoanalytic theory of neurosis*: 486. See also, A. Freud. 1937. *The ego and the mechanisms of defence*.

[35] In the early stage of psychoanalytical movement, 'repression' was the queen of defences. Although, as Anna Freud rightly pointed out, Sigmund Freud, in his 1926 book *Inhibitions, symptoms and anxiety*, robbed this defence of

the special position it had so long enjoyed, it still retains a special place, because in all practical situations, some degree of repression is combined with every other defence mechanism employed; A. Freud. 1937. *The ego and the mechanisms of defence*. Repression is expressed by the absence of content. 'It consists of an unconsciously purposeful forgetting or not becoming aware of internal impulses or external events which, as a rule, represent possible temptations or punishments for, or mere allusions to, objectionable instinctual demands'; Fenichel. 1946. *The psychoanalytic theory of neurosis*: 148. In my respondents, a lack of awareness of feelings was observed in relation to the memory of the day of Partition and the experience of migration.

36 The defence of *sublimation* may be called 'mature' for two reasons. Firstly, in sublimation, under the influence of the ego, the aim or object (or both) of instincts is changed without blocking an adequate discharge. Thus, it does not impair human productivity. Sublimation is to be differentiated from immature defences that use counter-cathexes. In sublimation, as in many other defences, the impulses find their outlet through an artificial route. Sometimes the defensive aim is completely opposite of the original aim. In such cases, one may confuse sublimation with reaction formation. However, the difference between the mature defence of sublimation and the immature defence of reaction-formation lies in the pathogenecity and functional inefficiency of the latter. Secondly, sublimation may positively promote creativity. Indeed, it has been closely related to the creative function of the ego, namely, 'adaptive regression in the service of the ego'. The unconscious material is temporarily accessed and processed, often using the mechanism of sublimation, to contribute to a new object of aesthetic or literary or humanitarian beauty.

Through *altruism* the individual undergoes a vicarious experience by means of constructive and instinctually gratifying service to others. It includes benign and constructive reaction formation, and therefore can be included under mature defences. Altruism of this kind has to be distinguished from altruistic surrender, where surrender of direct gratification or of instinctual needs takes place in favour of fulfilling the needs of others and the detriment of the self, and the satisfaction can only be enjoyed vicariously through introjection.

37 Leopold Bellak has enumerated a number of ego functions as potential modes of coping with the conflict between reality and desire. One of them

is the 'sense of mastery and competence'. This entails a perception that one can control one's own fate and can manipulate the environment at least to some extent upon one's desire. This sense may not always adhere to reality; it may be an illusion, an over-statement or an underrating. However, it is essential for the development of self-respect and self-esteem. See L. Bellak, M. Hurvich, and H. Gediman. 1973. *Ego function in schizophrenics, neurotics and normals* (New York: John Wiley).

38 S. Freud. 1915/1959. Instincts and their vicissitudes. In Strachey, ed. and trans, *The standard edition of the complete psychological works of Sigmund Freud*, vol 14. 108-40.

39 This idea of predominant ambivalence between communities is somewhat different from what some other comentators of intercommunity strife would suggest. The ambiguity in relationship may not be apparent in all instances of such rift. For example, Valkan stated that when fundamentalist communities define themselves, they draw a rigid boundary between self and other, often defining themselves in terms of food, clothes, geographical location, and so on. The split between good and evil becomes a part of collective identity. See V. Valkan. 2004. *Blind trust* (Virginia: Pitchstone Publishing). The respondents in the study did mention such demarcation criteria, but on the whole the tone was more of ambiguity than of a clearly defined enemy.

40 This indeed is the function of the defence of *projection*, which is utilized at the early stage of ego, that is, the purified pleasure ego; see S. Freud. 1915. Instincts and their vicissitudes. In J. Strachey, ed. and trans., *The standard edition of the complete psychological works of Sigmund Freud,* vol 14: 108-40, when there is a clear split between the good and the bad, that belonging to the ego *vs.* the non-ego. Although with maturity, greater tolerance of ambiguity is expected, this primitive mechanism is retained and used extensively under critical situations. In general, the organism prefers to feel dangers as threats from without rather than from within. Usually projection in an adult is not random, but directed towards some point in reality where it is met halfway. Often a semblance of reality orientation is maintained, and some kind of justification is offered. Thereby rationalization is a frequent companion of projection.

The internally dangerous object is a product of *introjection*. It involves incorporation of objects, in a psychological sense, that is, incorporation of images of objects. Introjection is originally a means of identification. Thus, it is an essential tool for early ego development. In later life however any object relationship, when in difficulty, may regress to identification. The instinctual aim associated with the relationship may regress to introjection. Thus both libidinal and aggressive instinctual aims may be incorporated; see Fenichel. 1946. *The psychoanalytic theory of neurosis*: 148. Projection and introjection together often make the ideal backdrop for ambivalence, as was seen in Manish's case.

41 Not his real name, not his real nickname even. Historian Tapan Raychaudhuri has used the pseudonym 'Rakhal' to refer to this notorious man in his memoirs *Romanthan athaba bhimratipraptar paracharitcharcha* (Kolkata: Ananda Publishers, 1993). I have followed suit. Arun, of course, used both the real name and nickname.

42 Sandip Bandyopadhyaya. 1997. The riddle of partition: Memories of the Bengali Hindus. In R. Samaddar, ed., *Reflections on the partition in the east* (Delhi: Vikas): 59-72.

43 R. Samaddar. 1997. The history that partition creates. In R. Samaddar, ed., *Reflections on the partition in the east*: 1-34.

44 The issue of guilt is closely associated with the idea of morality and the amount of distress and salvation derived from it. Thus, guilt may be utilized as a coping endeavour as well. Guntrip disagrees with O. Hobart Mowrer's concept of guilt as core psychological distress. Guntrip looks upon guilt as a struggle to maintain object relations; a defence against ego disintegration. See for detailed discussion H. Guntrip. 1977. *Schizoid phenomena, object relations and the self* (London: Hogarth Press).

Theodore Reik comments on the unconscious sense of guilt, the need for punishment, and the unconscious compulsion to confess. T. Reik. 1925. *The compulsion to confess* (New York: Farrar, Straus and Cudahy). Nunberg holds that although the sense of guilt and the need for punishment both arise during super-ego formation and are intertwined, they should not be seen as identical. The sense of guilt involves an attempt to cancel the deed, while in the need for punishment the deed is carried on in relation to the subject's own person, that is, the 'talion principle'. Nunberg also recognizes the healing function of guilt and resultant punishment. See H. Nunberg. 1926. The sense of guilt and the need for punishment. *International Journal of Psychoanalysis* 7, 420-33.

3

A Different Kind of Trauma

THE WORD 'PAIN' has multiple meanings. Pain is generated when one is dismembered in a physical or psychological sense, and is thus a response to forced separation: severance of a part from the whole. Two factors are crucial to the feeling of pain: one, the sense of a once-upon-a-time completeness which has been torn apart, and the other, the ability to feel, the possession of a functional and receptive physiological and psychological apparatus. The subjectivity of pain is closely linked to the identity of the individual, which in turn encompasses memory.

Partition was the vivisection of the country. The pain that the individuals felt would depend on their personal interpretation of the experienced event. Thus two factors, external and internal, would influence this interpretation: the content of experience and the individual's personality. I begin with the experience. The reminiscences collected from the western border of India consist predominantly of descriptions of violence and horror, gory accounts of slaughter, rape, abduction and looting. Gyanendra Pandey states: 'The truth of the partition of the Indian sub-continent in 1947 lay, at least for its victims, in the violence done to them'.[1] Pandey notes how the trauma experienced and remembered by oneself or those close to one served as the basis for the self-other/we-they division.

Bengal had a different story to tell.[2] In a symposium in Kolkata (February 2002) on 'Porous Border, Divided Self', Jasodhara Bagchi and Subharanjan Dasgupta highlighted the difference between the experiences of Punjab and Bengal. They held that the intercommunity division—political, administrative and cultural—was much more definitive and rigid on the western border, but diffused and porous in the east. Even remembering Noakhali and Kolkata in 1946, keeping in mind the riots in Dhaka, Khulna and Narayangunj, violence, at least in terms of sheer slaughter, was significantly less in Bengal than in Punjab.[3] For those who did encounter such violence in Bengal, the impact would presumably be the same as for the sufferers in Punjab, or the 2002 carnage in Gujarat, in the European Holocaust, ethnic cleansing in Bosnia, or any other genocidal project elsewhere in the world. To what extent do the feelings of the rest, the majority of Bengali refugees who did not encounter such horrors directly, but suffered the paralysing 'fear',[4] correspond with their violently victimized fellow compatriots?

Some studies of the victims of the Bengal Partition report violence as a major theme in their reminiscences too. Sandip Bandyopadhyaya, for example, found violence as a predominant theme in their retrospection,[5] although their statements about the role of the other community were often contradictory. My interviews, as I have detailed in Chapter 2, did reveal contradictions, un-emotions; however, violence was not the prominent theme in the narratives; though present in some. Additionally, I found confusion in the respondents' identity formation, followed by a defensive attempt to maintain the continuity of the selves, challenged not so much from outside as from their own entangled emotions. My interviewees had not been exposed to direct carnage or corporeal persecution, nor had their immediate family members been harmed. Of course, they had witnessed violence and some had faced serious threat or persecution. It is expected that the nature of the intra-psychic injury here would be different from that in victims of direct physical assault.

My proposition is that there is a categorical difference between the psychological impact of brutal violence and that of 'soft violence'. Direct experience of violence leaves a lasting scar on the personality and identity of the individual; at the same time, it provides a clear marker, a sort of binary distinction between the 'we' and the 'they', between the good and the bad, between the 'before' and the 'after'. When there is no such event of demarcation, but only suggestion of events, the certainty of evil is lost, though negative feelings persist. The absence of a defined boundary can sometimes be worse than its presence, even if that boundary is drawn with a brush of suffering. Under anchorless and ambiguous conditions, pain becomes relatively indefinable, difficult to locate, yet it remains incessantly throbbing within.

REGRESSION TO THE HOMELAND

Sandip Bandyopadhyaya reported that all the individuals he talked to 'started with the horrible descriptions of the violence unleashed by the other community whom they would brand as enemy: the rival community'.[6] In contrast, most of my subjects opened their narration with a description of their homeland. Many started with the exact address and location as well as with some information about the status of their family. Typical beginning statements were:

'We lived in Jessore, Parameswarpur, Haritala Post Office. Our family had plenty of land. Selling fruits, vegetable and bamboo were our major source of income.'

'I am from Kumilla, Baburhat. I was Chaudhuri before my marriage, my husband's family was known as the "Nandy barhi" in the locality of Milodia. I was married when I was seventeen years old. I remember both places.'

The difference in starting themes may partially be attributed to the researcher's approach. From the very outset, I was interested in knowing the person, in exploring the entire identity, though with special reference to Partition. If the interviewer expresses interest only in knowing about the interviewee's partition experience, this is likely to point the narrative exclusively towards issues relating to Partition. There may even be an implication that the interviewer wants to know specifically about violence. In fact, despite my approach to the contrary, some of my respondents themselves harboured such a notion and were apologetic that they had not experienced much violence.

Did my 'life-reconstruction' approach predispose the interviewees towards a chronological narration, their birthplace being the natural point of take-off? It is a strong possibility. However, the near universality of the opening theme deserves further comment.

There were some respondents who started in what I can call an evasive mode, an attempt to deny or bypass the sentiments associated with the pain of separation. I asked one such respondent, 'Will you tell me about your childhood, youth, your experiences during Partition, your past and present feelings about the event, and what happened after that till now?' He responded with the denial of emotion. 'You want to know about Partition. Partition is a major historical event, you know, but on the day of Partition we felt nothing. It was like any other day.' Immediately after, he continued in a contrasting mood, 'Barishal is a beautiful town, a very enlightened one, not a high-profile and posh locality, not very sophisticated, but many upper classes learned families settled there [pause]. Partition is not an event; it is an experience, a segment of life separating me from Barishal [pensive]. What was I saying? Yes, Barishal–how beautiful!'

Despite my emphasis on the person as a whole, he considered me interested only in Partition, and started with it, but repeatedly drifted back to Barishal. It seemed that my request had generated two fragments of demand in him: one, to talk about Partition, and the other, to talk about his childhood and later life.

Sudhanya also read my approach as being related to Partition alone. He spent an entire session of almost three hours instructing me about the major markers of historical change in British India. Indeed, I learnt a lot from him. He was a cautious and aware person, conscious of each word he said. After his neatly organized and illuminating exposition, he declared in a conclusive tone that he had finished whatever there was to tell me about Partition. I thanked him for clarifying many vague notions I had had about the politics of Partition, and added that though I was interested in his ideas and opinions about the event, I also wanted to know about his life-experiences and attitudes centring on Partition, before and after. He paused, as if he was not prepared for so personal a conversation. Then he smiled awkwardly and said, 'My life? What is there in it? Okay, listen if you must. I am from Faridpur, Madaripur Subdivision. We had two houses, one at the town and the other at the village–some 4 miles away from the town at Dhulagaon. My father was a businessman in the town. We lived with him ...'

However, such roundabout modes were rare. Most respondents started straight off from their homeland.

From the psychoanalytic viewpoint, the opening theme of a narration, particularly if self-related, is of special significance, as it reveals an important clue to the unconscious preoccupation of the person. The first sentence usually comes out before any systematic resistance can operate. Often the opening statement is an innocuous one, without much apparent significance, one that easily passes across the barrier of the super-ego, yet contains valuable information. Therefore, I consider the opening theme of my respondents as revealing the best-garbed reflection of the predominant preoccupation in the psychic life.

I reckon that the homeland is the major preoccupation in my respondents since it constitutes the marker of their identity. They still define themselves in terms of their past abode. In response to my attempt to get a glimpse of their inner selves, they start with exposing that part of the 'self' which is defined in terms of their homeland.

Homeland was not only the opening theme; it was also the most repeated. In Chapter 2, I have tried to project the respondents' fantasized depictions of the wholeness of their pre-partition life: the glorification of the homeland in terms of natural beauty, food, honour and communal harmony. I also tentatively formulated how this 'imaginary real' was constructed. However, considering the priority, intensity and repetition of this theme, I propose that the clinging to the internal 'real' may not be the only reason for repeated regression to the homeland; its importance is probably overdetermined.[7] The further intra-psychic functions served by this fixation to the homeland may be better understood in the context of the nature of the violence experienced.

THE BACKDROP OF FEAR

In connecting these people's fixation with and regression to the homeland with the experience of soft violence, I need to address a few other pertinent questions. One is the precise reason for migration from the paradise that had been their abode for generations. What exactly happened to force the difficult decision? I submit that here is one major point of departure from the victims of hardcore violence. When there is a physical attack on a person or on his immediate family, there is the presumption that they would have to leave and take shelter elsewhere. Leaving home, or migration, becomes a 'realistic' necessity, both for the migrant and in the eye of the researcher. While it is possible that even in such cases, the feelings associated with migration and the attribution of cause may vary widely from case to case, the priority of violence as a 'cause' of displacement remains an accepted fact. The experience of soft violence defies such a simplified schema.

Many of my interviewees could not specifically pinpoint the actual 'cause' of their decision to migrate. We saw in Chapter 2 how the prevailing fear altered their mind state towards the 'never dreamt of' decision. The most common expression was, 'It was not possible to stay on.' Some left because they apprehended 'Muslim torture', some because they heard stories of arson, rape and looting, others because the neighbouring upper-caste and well-to-do Hindu families were leaving, and some because the local Muslims advised them to. Apparently, each of these precipitators, viewed in isolation, does not justify the enormity of the decision. One has to place these apparently inadequate 'causes' against the backdrop of the omnipresent fear mentioned by all of them. One might say that the immediate persecutor was their mental state rather than an event. Typical phrases used were: 'We left because we were confused', 'We were really afraid', or 'We could not endure the pressure of fear any longer'. The internal feeling rather than the event was emphasized in many narrations.

Tarapada recalled that theirs was a brahmin-majority locality.

The brahmins were affluent; they left first, and next went the kayasthas. There was pervasive fear. Everybody said it was not safe to stay back any longer, particularly when the rich and the educated had decided to leave. 'We thought: "they know best",' said Tarapada.

Girish, a retired schoolteacher, cited a different cause. He was proud of his participation in the freedom movement and his present involvement in social work. He described an incident of 'dishonour' as the cause of his decision to migrate. 'At that time, we did not care for life,' he declared. As he was involved in the freedom movement, the British police interrogated him in connection with guns being looted in the locality. Girish denied any knowledge of a hidden arsenal. The police threatened him, beat him, he never divulged the secret. Then he was put to jail. When he came out, Independence had been declared. He found everything altered. The younger generation had changed a lot. Then the 'crucial event' took place. They had a milkman called Rahaman. One day Girish asked him, 'Rahaman, is your milk good?' A Muslim lad passing by overheard this. He came forward and insulted Girish for calling such an elderly man by name. Girish dared not assert himself. 'That day I understood that we would not be able to live here any more', he said. He had been undaunted by the beating of the police, but could not stand the insult and challenge to his position from a member of the other community.

What was this fear, I wondered, that was worse than the boots and the batons of the British police? Some reported personal and social threats from the Muslim community, but the actual probability of the threats being carried out was often not adequately evaluated. This is not to say that the threat would not have been enacted, but the question was simply never asked. At that moment, the person took the threat at face value, was panic-stricken, and acted accordingly; that is understandable. But what strikes me as strange is that the reality of the threat was never questioned even within their mind, not in the fifty long years after the event. Such is the case of Surojit, a retired officer who at the time of migration was an adult.

Surojit asserted that all was well in Faridpur till 1948. In 1949, he was in Kolkata and his mother wrote to tell him that there were 'problems with the Mussalmans'. His sister was eighteen years old. Some Muslims who earlier never dared to 'look up straight at her face', now started 'teasing', harassing her and threatening the family. At this point, they came to Kolkata, leaving everything behind.

I asked, 'It was pretty sudden, wasn't it? Do you think the threat to your sister was real?'

'See, I was not there,' replied Surojit. 'Ours was a joint family. What they decided was a joint decision. I never thought of asking if it could be otherwise.'

Indeed, the facts might be right or wrong, the threat real or imagined, but there was not a thread of doubt about the urgency of the sentiment. The feeling was so real that one never thought of questioning it.

Most of the respondents spoke of an atmosphere that was created all over East Bengal/Pakistan between 1946 and 1952: a changed and charged feeling of hostility and suspicion, a lingering bitter taste, in stark contrast with the idealized peace and love of former days. So intense was this feeling of animosity that it became 'unbearable'. This 'atmosphere' could be defined only hesitantly in terms of discrete events; for most, it was simply there 'in the sky, the water and the air'. Listening to the descriptions, I could feel the claustrophobic bleakness; I could almost hear the thumping of panic-stricken hearts. The fear was all the more disconcerting, because it followed decades of relative peace, with the advantages tilted on the side of the Hindus. I find it remarkable that what was executed by brutality in so many places was accomplished in Bengal primarily by threat. In the *Mahabharata* Yaksha asked Yudhisthira, 'What is the most powerful force on earth?' 'Fear,' replied Yudhisthira. The same fear-terror, fuelled through rumour, drove these families away from their ancestral homes.[8]

But who or what was responsible for the terror? Walter in a threadbare analysis of terror discerns two types: siege of terror and regime of terror. The former is directed towards overthrowing a system of authority, as in a rebel. The other is initiated and maintained by those who are already in power, as in a totalitarian society.[9] Noam Chomsky's elucidation of the culture of terrorism falls in this second category.[10] All sorts of terror include violence, not only in the sense of corporeal damage, but any kind of 'destructive harm'[11] caused deliberately or unwittingly. It includes physical assault as well as mental or emotional harm. Terror cannot be generated without violence, though the specific act or threat of violence may be involuntary or intentional. In the process of terror, there are various elements: the source, the agent, the victim and the target of violence. The source or agent may or may not be the same; for example, one may plan to kill and execute the killing oneself, or may employ somebody else, an agent. Usually, the planners of the riot are distinct from the hooligans and killers: the agents. The victim and target of terror also are distinct. The victim of terror perishes; the target does not. But the target is terrified by the action. In this sense, the target consists of those who witness the violence and react spontaneously to the news or the spectacle of destruction with some kind of submission or accommodation, by withdrawing or inhibiting potential resistance. So the utility of terror is control. As Walter said, 'Thus in civil terror we are dealing with two processes, one dependent on the other: the processes of violence in the service of terror, and the process of terror in the service of power.'[12]

In the context of Partition, this distinction between the victim and the target of terror is exemplified in the two categories of sufferers of Partition: those who underwent carnage and those who were driven away by fear. In this sense, the majority of the refugees on the western border were victims and many of the migrants in the east were targets.

THE PAIN OF SEPARATION

This fact of being overwhelmed by terror released a number of defensive operations in the sufferers. This explains why during narrating the relocation from East Bengal to West Bengal, very few respondents clearly described any gross sense of trauma, any painful sentiment at the moment, or any immediate pangs of separation. We have seen that while the terror and the confusion were almost universally reported, the emotions during preparation for migration and separation from their home were virtually absent from these narrations.

Yet, it was not that these persons were emotionally blunt. Their attachment to their homeland and the pain of lost security were prominent in their descriptions of post-migration adjustment. For most of the interviewees the pain of separation still throbs hard. It seems that sensitivity to this pain was absent during migration, but developed gradually later. The realization of loss came late, and when it came it was agonizing. Surojit said, 'The feeling of being uprooted has never left me. Not in my entire life.' Achintya happened to go to Bangladesh on an auditing assignment. The director of the host organization offered to arrange for him to visit Barishal, but Achintya refused. 'I felt that my dreams, my memories would be tarnished if I saw it now,' he said. Manish articulated his sentiment for his motherland in a different manner: 'This November, I went to my homeland with my wife. ... I picked up the soil of the place. It was my desh. It was a pilgrimage for me. I took the soil from the bank of the river where my father had been cremated.'

How then does one explain the 'lack' of feeling at the time of migration, while earlier and later feelings remain intact and intense? I attribute this gap to the various contradictions that lay in the situation itself. I have already mentioned that many respondents did not understand that they were leaving for good. 'We were sure that once the problems were over we would come back and resettle.' Bandyopadhyaya also mentions that at the time of departure some migrants did not believe that they were leaving for good.[13] Many, like Janak of Khulna, recalled requesting their neighbours to look after their house and property until they came back, only to hear later that their houses had been occupied by others. Why, I ask, did they not foresee the permanent separation? After all, they had been under the veil of fear for long before they decided to leave. Why did they expect, against all odds, that their properties would remain safe? Bandyopadhyaya has interpreted this as a kind of denial, the inability to believe that the country and the identity of the citizens could be split in this way. I agree. The process of denial is particularly apparent in those who, like Girish, were already buying land in West Bengal, yet reported that the migration was not premeditated. A doctor had tried to build up a practice in Kolkata, to provide for the possibility of migration there. Yet, he claimed that they had decided to migrate 'all on a sudden' after some stray incident. Probably, while the rational component of their minds led them to try and establish some security in West Bengal, the emotional part remained oblivious. Thus, there was dissociation between the self-referent affective information and the sequence of events that took place.[14] The respondents reported one kind of emotion, and simultaneously enacted a specific behaviour that contradicted this emotion.

The respondents talked a great deal about their post-migration adjustment. One may wonder why, if repression takes place with unpalatable events, the struggle in West Bengal, which involved considerable pain and insults for many, was not denied or repressed, as was the pain associated with the events of Partition and migration. I submit that there are intra-psychic differences among the experiences of the three consecutive and distinct phases: pre-migration, migration and post-migration. The distinctive criterion that separates the migration phase from the other two is one of psychological control, control over one's life and the surrounding environment. In the wake of Partition and during subsequent migration, the individual, as a child or adolescent, was like a single leaf caught in a storm; he was carried by the circumstances, the political twists and the decision of the elders of the family. This lack of control was initiated by the pervasive terror itself; one did not know what to think, where to look for help and act. There was no time for introspection. Blind flight was the only option. This lack of control over one's life is so disruptive that one would probably prefer to deny it at that moment, only to retrieve its reality when some kind of stability is regained afterwards. On the other hand, the post-Partition life was one of rebuilding, where activity, control and constructive endeavour could be registered. The struggle was rewarding, particularly for those who succeeded in later life. Hence, unpleasant and troublesome as it might have been, the defences of repression and denial were not required when recalling the post-migration strife.

I further propose that the confusion and inconsistencies in the narrations of the victims were a result of their efforts to survive in the face of terror, their urgent actions and the frantic alteration in defensive modes: from denial to projection to rationalization. The confusion was undoubtedly present in their surroundings, but more so within themselves. There was this blind and wishful belief in one day being able to come back 'home', the sense of still belonging to a land that had been politically deemed 'foreign'. At the same time, there was the implicit, or even explicit, understanding that one had lost the happy abode for good; that terror would be part and parcel of life if one stayed back. All these created an inner perplexity, a sense of bewilderment, adding to the unpredictability already generated by the political conundrum of the period.[15]

UNCERTAINTY AND LACK OF CLOSURE

As pointed out above, the major difference between brutal bloodshed and soft violence lies in the presence or absence of events that are universally accepted as 'traumatic'. In the case of the former, one is able to define one's life prior to and after the 'incident', marking a clear boundary between the good and the bad period. Of course, no event is a sharply defined one in a time-space zone, not in any absolute sense. Usually for any political or social disaster and for many personal ones too, there are prior indications and building up of tension. Confusion, anxiety, vagueness and contradictory emotions prevail as well. But once the disastrous event takes place, it assumes a special significance in memory, particularly with the passage of time. A violent event generates strong emotional reactions, renders oneself momentarily helpless and the impact of the emotion colours the subsequent recollection of the flow of life before and after the event. The shock, the impact, the helplessness results either in succumbing to the disaster–depression or even death–or else provides a kind of coping strength, a rationalization, a cause to fight for.[16]

For many Hindus of East Bengal, the absence of a palpable disastrous event created a problem of attributing blame. Blaming the persecutor is a mode of counter-violence; even the worst rogues can be humiliated in one's mind by labelling them 'morally weak'. Somehow, such direct blame was absent in most of my respondents. In the absence of any direct enemy, the responsibility for any decision fell upon themselves. In taking the colossal decision to uproot themselves in the absence of clear outer violence, some inner violence must have been executed. This process was not one of simple guilt, not aggression as in depression, but one with a semblance of rationality and judgement. It was a decision taken with the utmost indecisiveness. This is a different kind of trauma, what many of our respondents tried to express through the term 'chaotic feelings'. If we compare it to physical trauma, it is not a sharp cut, or a forceful blow, but a gnawing pain within, a chronic but silent bleeding that makes one dysfunctional.

'Trauma' is a Greek word, used in English for centuries in its literal meaning of an external wound. Towards the end of the nineteenth century, it was extended figuratively to also mean a psychic wound, a stressor that can cause dysfunctional psychic reaction. In 1893, Freud described how 'an apparently trivial circumstance ... attains the dignity of trauma' by summated effects with other stressful events.[17] For our respondents, too, the summated terror topped by a single incident suddenly acquired the 'dignity of trauma' and goaded them to the decision. For example, when I asked Janak why he left, his immediate reply was, 'Because Badru Chacha told us to.' Then he elaborated the background.

> 'Over more than a year we slowly came to realize that we were being cornered, the gradual building up of tension was getting beyond our

> tolerance. Around 1946, news poured in from everywhere, we heard that Hindus were being forcibly converted, the girls raped and tortured to death. We saw fires in nearby localities . . . I remember how sometimes we sat awake throughout the night [pause], every sound was a source of fear. My eldest uncle possessed a gun. He polished it every day. I don't think my words alone can describe the feeling to you. Every single incident added to our tension, incidents we could otherwise have ignored.
>
> . . . We went through it for a year and half, the land was partitioned; we joined the procession and shouted 'Pakistan Jindabad'. But deep inside we knew we did not belong. By 1949-50, the situation worsened. We had a neighbour, a Muslim lawyer. We called him Badru Chacha. He was my father's friend. He told us that things might worsen. He was depressed. Father was afraid, because this man was one of our supports. I still recall my father's face, his fear that he might not be able to save us. He said, 'If Badruddin is afraid, we must not delay any more. We left with whatever we could.'

That chronic uncertainty is a different kind of trauma and is not only true for the victims of soft violence, it has been recognized in the victims of carnage as well, when they lacked defining events or dates. The difference in psychic reaction depended upon the availability of anchoring events to provide an organized picture of the situation to oneself. A number of Holocaust studies have shown that those who have not been able to trace the death of their near ones suffered a different kind of tension. Aaron Haas discusses how lack of confrontation with a family member's death makes it difficult for survivors to fully appreciate the finality. Haas describes one Joseph Simon who never knew when his mother was killed. He therefore settled one particular day for saying *yahrzeit*, the prayer on a death anniversary, for his mother: the day she was arrested and therefore ceased to exist for him.[18] Veena Das, working on the women victims of Punjab, narrated the fate of Shanti. Her family was dragged out of the house and killed. Shanti learnt of the destruction of her entire family, but never found the bodies. Probably they were burnt by the killers. On the cognitive level, Shanti knew that something beyond her control had taken place, yet, as Das highlights, it was not a simple kind of hatred and mourning that she experienced. The absence of the dead bodies, which could have borne direct witness to the catastrophe, was disturbing to her and impaired her process of mourning. She developed an obsessive ritualized behaviour to ascribe some meaning to her existence.[19]

The trauma generated in the absence of definite events is probably associated with the question of identity, closure and meaning. As we define ourselves to ourselves, we need to find an underlying thread of meaningfulness, in our modes of thought, our values and idealism, our perceptual integrity, organization and categorization. What Simon and Shanti failed to attain was this meaningful continuity of life. Tragedy is in one sense meaningful; death is the point of closure, even if a tragic closure. But for Simon and Shanti, such closures were missing; so their life-narratives remained incomplete to themselves, creating a preoccupation with the identity they could not stabilize. Hence the forced and rationalized closure by Simon and the obsessive behaviour by Shanti.

The lack of certainty and meaning produces anxiety, and when the specific cause of a disturbing emotion cannot be pinpointed, the person remains in a generalized and protracted anxious condition. At one point of existence, this free-floating anxiety can turn to acute anxiety, to panic. At first we feel a constant threat at the subjective plane, but cannot anchor it with certainty to its source. Then there comes a stage when the unbounded anxiety cannot be contained by the ego anymore, and it grows out of proportion; panic is created. In one sense, panic is the premonition of danger in the absence of realistically assessable danger.[20]

THE FACELESS ENEMY

I find a similarity between the fear reported by my respondents and that of a litttle girl I had seen in the clinic. She was a child of six, brought to the clinic for her panic reaction to a horror story and subsequent refusal to go to the toilet or to any other place alone. The girl was mature and intelligent, and she herself recounted the event that had precipitated the fear. Her parents were doctors in a district hospital and they lived in the hospital quarters near the children's wards. Some of the nurses used to visit the family and they would tell the child stories. One day a nurse told her about a strange animal that looked like a weasel but had wings like a vulture, which lived in a hole in the ground of the cemetery and flew and sat on a tree near the children's ward on the days when a child was to die. The girl repeatedly asked the nurse whether it was a weasel or a vulture, because if it were a weasel it would not sit on a tree, and if it were a vulture it would not live in a hole in the ground. The nurse insisted it had features of both, and that is why it was the messenger of death. After listening to this story, the girl became extremely fearful, started crying and refused food. Consoled by her concerned parents as well as the apologetic nurse, she recovered a bit and started eating from the next day. But she absolutely refused to go anywhere alone, particularly to the toilet since its window opened towards the children's ward.

When asked what exactly she was afraid of, since she feared neither a weasel nor a vulture, and she had been exposed to stories of deaths in the hospital from an early age, she seemed at a loss to explain. 'Why should she [the nurse] tell me of an animal which is neither a weasel nor a vulture? I won't be able to recognize it if it comes,' she said.

I think the child was afraid of the unfamiliar animal, since it defied any control or prior preparation on her part to prevent a catastrophe. One may not be afraid of the enemy one knows, but if the face of a friend suddenly turns into that of an enemy, this stimulates the strongest fear and horror in our heart, giving the threat of violence a kind of magical power. One becomes as vulnerable as a child in the darkness who apprehends attacks from bizarre creatures any moment from any side. This indeed is the inner torture of a paranoid schizophrenic: in the drawings by William Blake in his psychosis; the faces of persons one trusts become unpredictably the faces of persecutors. This releases the most desperate defensive systems in the individual.

Listening to the narratives, I had this feeling of the bizarre, when the panic described was not adequately supported by the events said to have caused it, leaving a gap to be explained. This gap can be filled, from the psychological perspective, only by the violence created within by the fantasy that follows strong anxiety.

In my opinion, the 'psychological atmosphere' of pre-partition Bengal was one of free-floating anxiety, because the situation could not easily be assessed; there was chaos and confusion. At a certain point, the uncertainty grew to an extent where the anxiety crossed the limits of the subjective space and was acted out in the form of panic and flight.

One important source of uncertainty and undefined fear for this category of migrants was the facelessness of the enemy, the confusion between the benefactor and the harm-doer. My interviewees did not have a clear-cut enemy whom they could blame. They did not have the Gestapo or even the big-built Pathans with naked swords. They had only an indefinable environment to fear, the smell of hostility transmitted through news and rumours of slaughter and arson. Their experiences seem innocuous in comparison to what happened in the Punjab border or closer to home in Noakhali. Nevertheless, when I asked them, 'Was there any option? Do you think you could have stayed?' most of them replied that at the moment there was none, they had to run for their lives. They ran, but chased by whom? Their pursuers were the army people and the hoodlums, of course, particularly those attacking and looting at the borders, but the greatest pursuer was fear itself. The feeling of being cornered, having no option, is characteristic of a panic reaction.

If they fled in fear of the Muslims, why is there a hesitation to blame this community? The fact is that in Bengal mass violence was not often enacted directly, and ordinary Hindus and Muslims were not split forcibly into opposing groups. Thus the categorization was not complete. Usually under extreme conditions, one can partially overcome one's vulnerability by hating the enemy wholeheartedly and thus regain self-esteem to some extent. This is indeed a rudimentary healing process of the psyche that protects one from confusion and uncertainty. However, in certain situations this automatic therapeutic process is disrupted. To compare it with a physical phenomenon: if a foreign substance is introduced in the body, a number of antibodies are automatically formed to deal with it. However, if for some reason the body cannot recognize whether the element is a damaging or beneficial one, then some good ones may be rejected and some bad ones accepted, ultimately resulting in physiological chaos. For our respondents, also, the distinction between friend and enemy was confounded. Indeed, owing to the complexity of the social situation and limitations of human cognition, it was difficult to assess people's motives properly at that time. When an upper-class Hindu left his homeland and advised his neighbour to do the same, when a Muslim expressed his sadness at the political situation and his inability to protect his Hindu friend any longer, the feelings were genuine at one level, intended to help or console the person. On another level it served the very opposite purpose; it enhanced the fear lurking within and made the target person more vulnerable. In addition, there is the fact that in some cases there may have been ulterior motives not altogether unconscious; many reported that the same people who had advised them to leave, later usurped their house and property. Namita said, 'When we left, our Muslim neighbours over there were so sad, but when we tried to get back we found that they had grabbed our house and property and we were denied entry.' Manish recalled that their peasant employee, who had apparently been loyal and submissive, looted whatever they had left, set fire to their house and took over their land. Janak has never gone back to his home at Khulna. 'Apparently the local Muslims took over our property. But we heard something else too. This Muslim chacha, Badruddin, was our favourite. He was influential and a lawyer. We respected him a lot. He called my father "dada". But we heard that after we migrated, he took command of our house and distributed our property among the Muslims. Of course, not without taking his own share.' Janak laughed bitterly and continued, 'We used to go to Badru Chacha's house to play. He would seat us on a high revolving chair and whiz us around. He loved us a lot. I don't know how he could do such a thing.'

We shall never know if such reports were true or false; some Badruddins were treacherous and others well meaning yet helpless. But this is of less importance to us. We are concerned here with intra-psychic truth. If this is the way the respondent felt, then it must have its own subjectively real existence. Now what does the above representation signify? The same neighbour who wants you to stay back and is sad if you leave, is also happy if you leave because he gets your property. Despite all negativism, somewhere the respondents 'knew' that for the constructed 'other'–the Muslims–both feelings were true; both the sadness and the happiness were genuine, brotherliness and greed actually existed side by side. Such is the strangeness, the contradiction in human character; such is the uncertainty and insecurity, the ambiguity and ambivalence. We all know it, have experienced it; indeed, it is present in everybody's life. Under peaceful conditions, most people can spend their lives under a relative disavowal of this stark truth. The partition victims, however, experienced it poignantly, as political unrest unmasked the darker side of human relationships.

Many of the migrants, children and adolescents, were thrown into the emotional conundrum without much preparation. Their process of development was disturbed. Thus their handling of their subsequent experiences was significantly influenced by their age, their prior preoccupations and their personality predisposition and temperament.[21] In some, the ambiguity gave rise to maturity; otherwise, it led to incomplete closure.

SILENCE AS A DEFENCE

The issue of silence has been addressed by students of human trauma. Research concerning survivors of the European Holocaust has demonstrated that encountering a violent shock numbs one, and if the wound is too raw even after passage of time, one wants to look forward and not back.[22] Yet the memory remains, binding one's emotions to the point of trauma, permeating the self with the impact of the violence. The various reactions to trauma, among which numbing is a major one, have been recorded as 'survivor syndrome'. Silence serves the purpose of avoidance of pain. When the event took place the person suffered severe pain, and subsequently it was unconsciously repressed or consciously suppressed to evade further reference to it.[23]

For my respondents also there was silence, but of a different nature. The silence was locus-specific, pertaining only to the period of migration, but not before and after. It is therefore unlikely that the silence was a mode of suppressing trauma. It was a distinct kind of silence, not confined at the expressed level, but imposed on one's memory. Even direct questioning and probing revealed very little. It was not that they remembered the events but did not wish to discuss these; indeed, it seemed that the memory was fashioned to exclude these. Probably in the chaos and confusion of migration, the registration of the affects and the processing of the shock were hampered; the script did not fall in place, the schema was built and broken, only to be rebuilt and destroyed once again. Maybe that is how their minds learnt to retain the events in memory: in piecemeal fashion, in the jump-cut technique. The period of migration, owing to the confusion and facelessness associated with it, was encapsulated in a kind of brisk objectivity, a sort of isolation from the rest of their affect-laden existence. The feelings of others were registered more or less intact, but at the expense of one's own. If we accept this interpretation, another oft-noted fact of Partition in Bengal can be explained. The observers have underscored their feelings of 'surprise' and 'disbelief' at Partition and migration. Typical statements are, 'Partition came about in 1947 with a jab of the pen.' Or, 'When it dawned upon us that Hindustan was a foreign land it was a shock.' Janak said, 'The consequences were unbelievable.' 'How could the twin cities of Dhaka and Calcutta be separated?' Namita exclaimed, 'You know, my girl, after we all settled here I sometimes begged my husband to take me to Dhaka. I could not believe that it was now a foreign land. The entire event was so unanticipated–we could not digest it.' The perceived suddenness persisted despite the fact that Partition had been discussed for months by the elders of the family who were already contemplating migration and arranging to move. 'We knew but never believed it; I cannot believe it till today. It is a bad dream,' said Manoj.

This dream-like quality of a life-experience may occur when the memory does not provide adequate cues to the continuity of thought and affect during the period when the event took place. It is like being informed about something when one is drowsy. The mind does not register the information properly, causing gaps in connectivity, and a discontinuity in identity. I reckon that the sufferers of soft violence become victims of this fragmentation of identity.

This feeling of suddenness and unexpectedness was prevalent in the politically sophisticated and the naïve alike. Some writers on partition memory have observed this unexpectedness and perceived suddenness. David Page recalls the words of Sir George Abel, Personal Secretary to the last two Viceroys of India. Page was a young man at that time. Abel expressed his astonishment at the sudden and fatal deterioration in Hindu-Muslim relations to such an extent that division of the country became imperative. 'I was in India for twenty years and I didn't manage to get at the bottom of it,' said Abel to Page. Page himself, in 1999, claims not to have understood it: it was truly sudden, he says.[24]

If it was sudden to the white rulers, it was more so to the natives, the victims. Indeed this cognition of suddenness by the people in general evinces once again the play of the primitive defence of denial under stark unpleasant reality. Partition remained a theoretical possibility, even a theoretical certainty, and migration the 'only option' for the Hindu community in East Bengal, but they never seriously visualized how life after Partition would be. Since Partition and migration would involve absolute disruption of the habitual life-pattern, the respondents probably erected a very strong cognitive defence against registering the message. Hence the entire experience of Partition and migration had this dream-like quality; by projecting it away from the immediate reality, the pain could also be projected out. Thus partition experience had probably a resemblance to psychotic thinking. Indeed, the word 'insanity' or '*paglami*' has been used too often in connection with Partition.[25] But that only temporarily. Soon stark reality was before them and they had to build their lives anew. The events of Partition and migration having been blocked out, it were as if the pre- and post-migration memories had been spliced, like a film with no continuity.[26]

It is possible that as a result of the dissociation, many refugees only gradually absorbed the traumatic message—that they had lost their homeland forever—fully realizing it only when the definite and concrete legal 'Act' of 'Enemy Property' was enforced. Hence, it was a slow trauma, a gradual recognition of the 'real' which hovered over their physical, psychical and social existence. Those who could not adjust to it through a mature mode of resolution, retained the pain as an omnipresent negative emotion in their thoughts and actions in their later lives.

THE IDEALIZED PAST

Now, once again, I pick up the thread of the exceptional attachment of my respondents to the homeland, seeing it as part of their coping with their loss of self-definition. In an effort to sustain some stability in identity, these persons remained fixated on the comfortable past. The past, however, is dug out from memory, which is naturally, and in the case of my respondents particularly, distorted. The identity that is born from this effort, anchored as it is in the reconstructed reality, also entails an illusory quality, a mis-recognition so to say.[27] Within the narrative space, the respondents thus reconstructed idyllic versions of their past: an effort that facilitated a closure for their ruptured souls.

The creation of this myth, I submit, took place to a great extent within the process of the narration itself. The myth had already been born in a nebulous form; but its solidification needed the narrative environment. Many of my respondents had narrated their experiences to other people, to their family, to their friends. It had been refreshed or revised each time it had been recounted, and this process of creation, or re-creation gave them pleasure.

Allow me to elaborate. While interviewing these senior persons, I detected a kind of joy in them as they dwelt in the idealized past. They smiled in indulgence, their eyes sparkled, their tone acquired a softness, a melody, their language became lyrical. Such happiness has been noted by earlier observers as well. Subhoranjan Dasgupta recounts how his friend Belal Chowdhury at Chittaranjan Park in Delhi felt that the migrant Bengalis like himself, though quite well established in the capital, were keen to reminisce on the minute details of their towns, villages and friends; they were 'happy prisoners of the past'.[28] This happiness, one can readily see, has a childlike component. The past is a shelter, a happy haven where one would like to rest without the intrusion of outer demands and disturbances. One would willingly be a prisoner of this refuge.

This kind of voluntary bondage to an imagined sanctuary is a common occurrence in psychoanalytical narration; the client seems to attribute her present status to certain significant experiences in the past and is unwilling to move away from it. Ernst Kris comments upon this kind of repetitive preoccupation with the past as 'imperceptible transition from reporting to remembering, from repetition to recall'. At times, it reduces to 'regressive evasion': a flight into the past, avoiding its relationship to later stages of matured identity and involvement with contemporary issues. Kris calls such efforts to perpetuate one specific segment of the past at the expense of others as the 'personal myth'.[29]

In some of my respondents, such clinging to the past and the larger-than-life projection of their 'desh' was remarkable. In Arun's statement 'Kumilla is extraordinary', the glory of the homeland spilt over to the entire locality, the history and the culture of the place. He elaborated, over three days, the social and political history of Kumilla district. He eulogized the reigning clan and Raja Virvikramdeva, and spoke enthusiastically of the pomp of the subdivision, the various 'tanks and banks' (lakes and banking offices were part and parcel of the town) it held, the places to visit, like Dharmasagar, Ujir dighi, Najir dighi, Rani dighi, Suja Musjid, Iswar Pathshala and Victoria College, even of the excavations and relics of an ancient civilization found at Mynamati. He took almost a personal pride in the talent of the eminent persons born to Kumilla: musicians Sachin Dev Barman, Allauddin Khan and Gyan Datta, dancers Manibardhan, Manishankar, Shantibardhan, authors and poets Bijay Bhattacharyya, Sanjay Bhattacharyya, and so on. Arun's face lit up and his entire attitude changed when I told him that my parents were also from Kumilla. At some point, he took me to task for being ignorant of the glory of Kumilla. For a few hours, Arun became the spirit of *his* Kumilla. One tentative explanation of identification with the past comes from researches on the European Holocaust. Displaced persons all over the world suffer challenges to their identity, and therefore develop stronger attachments to the time and place which saw the germination of their identity. This remembered past is the prop against which their faltering identity is balanced. For example, the Jewish insistence on remembering and ritualizing ancient practices has been interpreted as a manifestation of their urgent need to maintain their identity and solidarity.[30] This bonding to the past also implies a kind of immovability; a static element in the mentality, a resistance to change. In other words, this explanation again corroborates Kris's hypothesis.[31]

The fixation to the idealized past, however, serves another purpose: it puts the good and the evil in sharp contrast. 'Everything here is bad, everything there was good,' commented one respondent in her intense emotion. Scrutinizing such feelings, Dipesh Chakrabarty maintains that the description of the sanctity and beauty of the village made the violation and defilement an act of sacrilege.[32] Pradip Bose writes, 'The idyllic here is invoked to put in sharp relief the traumatic.'[33] I agree completely with the interpretation. However, I want to add that such contrast is not only a characteristic of refugees; it is embedded in the very nature of any narrative.

Essentially, a narrative has a dramatic character. A self-narrative, like any story, has a tendency towards compactness, consisting of an organized sequence of events, which stand in relief to each other. In a typical story, film or drama, the calm and carefree life is followed by an unexpected disaster, with the intention to impress upon the viewer the enormity of the violation. The poet or scriptwriter residing in every narrator does the same: modifying the memory to create dramatic effect. This dramatization in turn, strips the sequence of events from the irrationality and randomness inherent in any natural experience, and gives it a perspective, a closure. If some of the situations were originally characterized by contradictory emotions, during narration they are modified towards a consistent whole. If some events are inimical to the narrator, these are selectively silenced in the narrative. After repetitive telling and retelling of the stories, with gradual modification, the person starts believing one or the other version as the true course of events and affects. Thus, through narration, through the frame of words (or letters, to be Lacanian) the personal myth is perpetuated in emotion.[34]

I recall here a Bengali song composed by Salil Chowdhury and sung by Hemanta Mukhopadhyay in the late 1950s. Its opening line is 'Kono ek gayer badhur katha tomay shonai shono' (Listen while I tell you the story of a village wife). Those who have heard the song will remember how the nostalgic languor, created by the lyric and the tune of the first part, describing in very simple imagery the peace and security of the village woman, is torn apart in the second half that unfolds the horrors of war and famine. This second part is characterized by sudden change in both words and music, which contrasts the feeling of steadfast sweetness. The song ends with what seems to be an eternal lament. Many of the interviews reminded me of the song, in their juxtaposition of idealized beauty and subsequent horror.

I was reminded of this song for a second reason too. Whenever I have listened to it, I have felt that the song, concerned though it is with the plight of the village in Bengal, is addressed to urban listeners; those who have not intimately known village life. It is not the feeling and language of the village wife that it speaks of. The daily hassles of her life are unknown to the listeners; theirs is only an idealized version of the village. The words of the song, characterized by urban sophistication, create a distance between the listener and the sufferer. Indeed, the song ends by requesting the listener to think of the shattered dreams and hopes of the village wife whenever he happens to pass through such a village with abandoned, broken huts. The listener does not share the pain; he simply gets a glimpse of the pain from without. At times the narrations of my respondents generated a similar feeling of distance in me, as if they were giving me nothing but a story. Yes, occasionally I almost felt rejected, distanced by the stereotyped delivery of the narratives.[35] This made me try to probe deeper, through introspection.

The feeling of being rejected also came from the respondents' silence on some points. Their silence was not the silence of sufferers of brutal violence, many of whom refrain from communicating the horrors of their experiences even to their close ones. My subjects were quite articulate and spoke freely about their experiences. In many cases, their spouses and children were sitting with them, affirming their statements or even reminding them of some small event, indicating that they had discussed it quite often. Yet, there was this silence: a partial and selective silence about some issues, as if I were not permitted to enter these spaces of their memory. Their eagerness to speak was not always eagerness to tell *me* the story, but to tell it to themselves.

The story was only partial, at least, emotionally partial. It was a myth they unconsciously chose to retain. A silence it was, a silence called eloquence.

UPROOTING AND SEARCH FOR IDENTITY

The realization of the gap in emotional memory, the pervasive 'fear psychosis'[36] and the riddle of partial suppression of emotion on the part of the sufferers of soft violence generated a strong personal reaction in me. I wondered how the terror had been so strong as to cause such distortions on the cognitive and affective planes. It has crossed my mind that in the realpolitik of the period the threat might have been construed in such a manner that small events took gigantic proportions, as portents of catastrophe. The rumours, the whispers, may have been deliberately encouraged so as to affect the perceptions of the Hindus of East Bengal; a subtle psychology to create an atmosphere of insecurity leading to terror.[37] The Bengali community has never been reputed to be particularly violent. This stereotype might have led to the use of 'atmosphere' and 'rumour' to fuel fear.

In other words, the panic was 'real' and designed to be panic. To test this hypothesis we must explore the history of the time, and I am by no means a fit person to do this. Rather I am arguing the opposite way–from the emotional history of the individuals to a socio-political history. I suggest that the creation of panic might have been part of the political strategy.[38] Many of my respondents implied this. One fact that came up repeatedly was that influential and non-communal administrative personnel were systematically transferred out of Hindu localities, and external forces given entry (particularly in Noakhali, Barishal and Chandpur) so that the familiar social composition changed. Many felt that even during the riots the military forces were brought in a bit too late, before which the threatening hooligans and rumours were allowed free rein. There was, in name, an official structure; but under the circumstances, the public could put little trust in the representatives of that structure. Once the anxiety mounted, events took their own course and the purpose of the designers was served.

Psychologically this had another disastrous effect. To grasp its full impact, we have to look at the post-migration condition. The refugee Hindus came to their 'true home': where the land should belong to them. But here again they met with rejection, swindling, humiliation and blame for the ruptured economy. Therefore, it seemed they belonged nowhere. They had been tricked out of their homeland; indeed, if they had not been shown the illusion of a free abode in India, at least some of them would have erected a stronger resistance and only violence and bloodshed would have resolved the matter. It was the positive mirage of the 'own land' that encouraged migration. Disillusioned after moving to West Bengal, the migrants underwent a strong identity crisis, not merely because of the loss of their homeland and property, but because they were not welcome in their new home either, and thus belonged nowhere. Too many respondents said, 'We were cheated'.

The Bengali word *chinnamool* means uprooted, removed forcibly and absolutely. More specifically, the word evokes the image of an uprooted tree with roots dangling. These people were chinamool; detached forcibly from their identity that lay in the stability of reference points in their social environment. And the new land of India failed to compensate for the loss, politically, socially, personally.

Here once again a difference with gross physical violence needs to be highlighted, keeping the age of my respondents in mind.[39] Physical violence forcibly causes loss, while in soft violence of the sort reported here the loss is not of an external object of attachment, but of an internal object of identification. The child whose father has died can remember him as the loving and caring one, but the child who has seen the father turn gradually from a loving parent to a jumpy, preoccupied, helpless and disheartened person is more confused, though there is no cause for actual mourning. As the child watches the perplexity of his parents during decision-making, observing their fears and helplessness, the real parents live on, but the internal parents die. The process of silent mourning starts without any external reference and thus adds to his confusion.

Thus, the most poignant and long-lasting effect of Partition on the young migrants was, in my opinion, neither financial, nor related to career. The trauma of these refugees was the loss of meaning at a very significant phase of their life, the period from early adolescence to early adulthood, when identity crystallizes.[40] Their pain stemmed in this jeopardization of meaningful existence, the organization of the interpersonal world. For some of them, this is still their intra-psychic preoccupation; they are still groping for meaning and coherence, and perhaps would have to part from this world before they know why the green earth beckoned them.

Not everybody, though. There were children with greater strength who were not threatened by their parents' fear, but assumed a mature stance and tried to somehow master the situation. Some of them took over the role of the parents; they tried to be the protectors of their families. These are the positive products of migration, the determination and the ability to take responsibility for others. This is where the pre-migration personality assumes significance. The young person's self-perception and strength of personality determined, at least partially, his or her response to the trauma of Partition. In the following chapter, I shall give some examples of reactions to soft violence that had ontogenic origins in certain personalities.

Notes

1 Gyanendra Pandey. 1997. Community and violence: Recalling partition. *Economic and Political Weekly* 32 (9 August): 2037.

2 I am indebted to the following sources for my understanding of historical facts: Partha Chatterjee.1984. *Bengal 1920-1947: The land question* (Kolkata: K.P. Bagchi); Joya Chatterji. 2002. *Bengal divided: Hindu communalism and partition, 1932-1947* (Delhi: Cambridge University Press); Ikram Ali. 1993. *History of the Punjab (1799-1947)* (Delhi: Low Price); Ajit Bhattacharjea. 1998. *Countdown to partition: The final day.* (Delhi: Harper Collins); Mushirul Hasan, ed. 1993. *India's partition: Process, strategy and mobilization* (Delhi: Oxford University Press); Gyanendra Pandey. 1994. The prose of otherness. In David Arnold and David Hardiman, eds, *Subaltern Studies VIII: Essays in honour of Ranajit Guha* (Delhi: Oxford University Press); Gyanendra Pandey. 2001. *Remembering partition. Violence, nationalism and history in India* (Delhi: Cambridge University Press).

3 As early as in 1957, the difference between Bengal and Punjab partition was coming up in contemporary articles. See for example, Taya Zinkin. 1957. Focus on Bengali refugees. *The Economic Weekly Annual*, 89-90. But this is not to say that the riots of Bengal, though less in quantity were of less qualitative impact, not only in the context of Bengal, but also in the context of Hindu-Muslim divide in entire Inida. See Suranjan Das. 1993. *Communal riots in Bengal 1905-1947*. Oxford University South Asian Studies Series (Delhi: Oxford University Press).

4 Prafulla Chakrabarti has identified 'psychological pressurization' as the major cause of migration for the Bengali Hindus. See P. Chakrabarti. 1999. *The marginal men: The refugees and the left political syndrome in West Bengal* (Kolkata: Naya Udyog).

5 Sandip Bandyopadhyaya. 1996. The riddle of partition: Memories of the Bengali Hindus. In R. Samaddar, ed., *Reflections of the partition in the east* (Delhi: Vikas): 59-72.

6 Ibid., 64.

7 Freud defined 'overdetermination' as the multiple and overlaid causation of a psychic event. It is indeed one of the major tenets of psychoanalysis that almost all behaviours have multiple sources and interlinked associations. See S. Freud. 1900. The Interpretation of dreams. In J. Strachey, ed., and trans., *The standard edition of the complete psychological works of Sigmund Freud*, vol 5(London: Hogarth Press).

8 This aspect of fear rather than violence per se as the major motivator of migration in the east has been recognized explicitly in some of the recent historical treatise on the subject. That it was not the fear of *praan* (one's life), but of *dhan* (income) and *maan* (self-respect) that drove them out has been reported in many memoirs. Mushirul Hasan had suggested in his edited book entitled, *India partitioned: The other face of freedom*, 2 vols (New Delhi: Lotus, Roli Books, 1995) that ' Most were driven out of their homes and drifted from one place to another out of fear, panic and a sense of hopelessness. They were indeed hapless victims of a triangular game plan, worked out by the British, the Congress and the League without care or consideration for huge number of people who had no commitment to a Hindu homeland or fascination for an imaginary *dar ul-Islam*. They had no destination to reach, no mirage to follow' (vol 1, p. 33). Haimanti Roy, in her PhD dissertation had detailed this play of fear in migration in Bengal (see H. Roy, 2006. '*Citizenship and national identity in post-partition Bengal, 1947-65*', University of Cincinnati, Arts and Sciences: History, downloaded from http://etd.ohiolink.edu/view.cgi?acc_num=ucin1147886544).

9 E.V. Walter. 1969. *Terror and resistance: A study of political violence* (New York: Oxford University Press).

10 N. Chomsky. 1988. *The culture of terrorism* (Boston: South End Press).

11 Walter V. 1969. *Terror and resistance*: 8.

12 Ibid., 14.

[13] Bandyopadhyaya. 1996. The riddle of partition: 65.

[14] See for elaboration of the dissociative process, E. D. Parks and R. Balon. 1995. Autobiographical memory for childhood events: Patterns of recall in psychiatric patients with a history of alleged trauma. *Psychiatry: Journal for the Interpersonal and Biological Processes* 58, 199-208.

[15] Although I refrain from commenting on issues like how building of the identities as nation-states contributed to this ambiguity, I feel the urge to quote a potent comment by Gyanendra Pandey that incorporates the psychological complication of this period: 'It is in the unrecorded, or at least, unintegrated histories of other traditions and practices–that we shall find much of the specificity, and diversity, of our lives and times, of our nation-states, of our capitalist economies and our modern institutions? Perhaps it is precisely in the ambivalences that we shall find the particular violence of our histories'. Pandey. 2001. *Remembering partition* 13.

[16] Recent advancement in cognitive psychology has provided ample evidence as to how 'events' change the organization of the memory structure. One influential theory states that autobiographical knowledge is organized in 'packets' of general events that in turn contain a kind of index to highly detailed event-specific knowledge. See M.A. Conway and D.A. Bekerian. 1987. Organization in autobiographical memory. *Memory and Cognition* 15, 119-32. When we are browsing through our life-time experiences, as in the case of my narrators, the retrieval process would be guided by the salience and clarity of the general event, and from there, hierarchically to specific events. Salience of events in turn is determined by the intensity of the affect associated with the event at the time of experiencing. Since violence generates strong emotion, the associational bond during retrieval would automatically lead to the memory traces of such events. On the other hand, since autobiographical memory is retained mainly in terms of events, absence of events would impair the retrieval of affects.

There is a second point in it as well. This pertains to the change in earlier memory after a salient event takes place. Most experiments indicate that a new and significant experience does not obliterate or alter the pre-existing memory trace, but it influences the salience of the item during retrieval. That is, the violent event, once it has occurred, would supersede the earlier experiences during retrieval (hence the opening theme of violence for the sufferers); but once the other aspects are probed or cues provided, the earlier traces can be retrieved. For a detailed review, see S.M. Smith. 1989. Environmental context-dependent eye-witness recognition. *Applied Cognitive Psychology* 6, 125-39.

[17] Although Freud started investigating trauma in relation to sexuality in repression, he gradually came to recognize the self-related aspects of trauma too. See J. Breuer and S. Freud. 1893. On the psychical mechanism of hysterical phenomena. Preliminary communication. In Strachey, ed. and trans. *The standard edition of complete psychological works* vol 2, 3-17; S. Freud. 1927. Future of an illusion. In Strachey, *Standard edition of complete psychological works* vol. 21, 5-58; S. Freud. 1929. *Civilization and its Discontents*. In ibid., 59-148. For a review of the concept of trauma in psychoanalysis, see L.E. Kirshner. 1994. Trauma, the good object and the symbolic: A theoretical integration. *International Journal of Psychoanalysis* 75, 235-42.

[18] A. Haas. 1996. *The aftermath* (New York: Cambridge University Press).

[19] V. Das. 1990. Our work to cry: Your work to listen. In V. Das, ed., *Mirrors of violence: Communities, riots and survivors* (Delhi: Oxford University Press): 345-97.

[20] For the relation between general anxiety and panic in terms of cognitive and affective characteristics, see A.T. Beck and G. Emery. 1985. *Anxiety disorders and phobias. A cognitive perspective* (New York: Basic Books).

[21] The role of the quality and length of the pre-traumatic life on the subsequent adjustment to trauma has been discussed from an Eriksonian perspective by M. Kestenberg and J.S. Kestenberg. 1988. The sense of belonging and altruism in children who survived the Holocaust. *Psychoanalytical Review* 75, 533-72. See also, J.M. Vogel and E.M. Vernberg. 1993. Children's psychological responses to disasters. *Journal of Clinical Child Psychology* 22, 464-84.

[22] Here one may be reminded of Bion, a psychoanalyst, who himself participated in the war and claimed that he had actually died in the war. He postulated that one may or may not desire to confront and process knowledge and learn from such experiences. He called these two motives +K and –K. Bion forwarded the notion that love, hate and knowledge are the three factors of deriving meaning from life experiences. See W. R. Bion. 1965. *Transformations: Change from learning to growth* (London: Heinemann).

[23] As early as in 1964 Neiderland spoke of the 'survivor syndrome'. See

W.C. Neiderland. 1964. Psychiatric disorders among persecution victims: A contribution to the understanding of the concentration camp pathology and its after effects. *Journal of Nervous and Mental Diseases* 139, 458-74. The literature on post-traumatic stress disorder is replete with the description of similar reactions. See W. Yule and R.M. Williams. 1990. Post-traumatic stress reactions in children. *Journal of Traumatic Stress* 3, 279-95. In 1988, a special issue of *The Psychoanalytic Review* was devoted to the study of child survivors of the Holocaust. The authors observed various kinds of distortions, from simple denial of danger to narcissistic omnipotence that seems to protect from awareness by an implicit belief in one's own invulnerability. Besides, somatization of different expressions have been reported. Some have observed that children are fully aware of the distress of their parents whose torture or murder they have witnessed, and subsequently avoid any reference to it, succumbing to a strange silence. See for example, I. Brenner. 1988. Multisensory bridge in response to object loss during the Holocaust. *Psychoanalytical Review* 573-86. Other significant references are: S. Fredlander. 1979. *When memory comes*, trans. H. R. Lane (New York: Farrer, Straus, Giroux); S.W. Whittlesey, J.R. Allen, B.D. Bell, E.D., Lindsey, et al. 1999. Avoidance in trauma: conscious and unconscious defence, pathology and health. *Psychiatry: Journal for the Study of Interpersonal Processes* 62, 303-12. In the Indian context, some of the significant contributions are by V. Das and A. Nandy. 1986. Violence, victimhood and the language of silence. In Veena Das, ed., *The word and the world: Fantasy, symbol and record* (Delhi: Sage); A. Nandy. 1999. The Invisible holocaust and the journey as an exodus. *Postcolonial Studies* 2, 3; U. Butalia. 1998. *The other side of silence: Voices from the partition of India* (Delhi: Penguin).

24 D. Page.1999. *Prelude to partition* (Delhi: Oxford University Press): ix.

25 Nandy talks about the 'collapse of the moral universe': The partition psychosis, *Outlook*, Aug 13, 1997, http://www.outlookindia.com/article.aspx?204034. Also see Ashis Nandy. 2007. Telling the story of communal conflicts on South Asia, pp. 40-64, in *Time treks: The uncertain future of old and new despotisms* (New Delhi: Permanent Black): 40-64. There are anecdotes and stories of actual insanity being saner than normality of the time. One may be reminded of Sadat Hasan Manto's story of 'Toba Tek Singh'.

26 Semanti Ghosh edited a book in Bengali compiling write-ups by reputed

commentators on Partition from both West Bengal and Bangladesh, both Hindu and Muslim. In the preface, Ghosh writes that she expected to have writings which would fill in the untapped or empty spaces in understanding this significant event. But she was disappointed, as only a few of the articles ventured to proceed into the unknown. Is it possible that Partition is an event which defies too deep entry into its history, memory or even into its historicized memory? Indeed, going through this book I too felt more emotionally touched by the poems and photographs complied at the end, than by most of the writings. See S. Ghosh, ed. 2008 *Deshbhag: Smriti ar stobdhota* (Kolkata: Gangchil).

[27] This misrecognition is not without its utility though. From a Lacanian perspective, it is through a creative remodelling of the situation-self interaction that an individual learns; in this sense, all learning involves a reconstruction of the world. This reconstruction represents the attempt of the desiring child to reach a sense of completion, without ever being 'really' complete. Thus, there is a close relation between misrecognition and maturity.

[28] S. Dasgupta. 1996. Life–our only refuge. In R. Samaddar, ed., *Reflections of the partition in the east*: 162-75.

[29] For a discussion on ideas fixated to some locations of childhood, see E. Kris. 1956. The recovery of childhood memories in psychoanalysis. *Psychoanalytic Study of the Child* 11, 54-88. The concept of personal myth was developed in the same year; see E. Kris. 1956. The personal myth. *Journal of the American Psychological Association* 4, 651-81.

[30] See E. Erikson. 1964. Identity and uprootedness in our times. In E. Erikson, ed., *Insight and responsibilities: Lectures on the ethical implications of psychoanalytical insight* (London: Faber and Faber): 83-107.

[31] An interesting opposing theory is that the victimized group is more prone to change, maybe because of its wish to avoid the connection with the negative past. Indeed Hagen observed that the stronger the victimization, the greater the motive to change. Others suggest that subordination does not necessarily produce change in society; challenges that are either too great or too small thwart change. See E. Hagen. 1962. *On the theory of social change* (Homewood, IL: Dorsey Press). For a discussion on Hagen's theory and fixation to the past of the Jews, see D. Heller. 1982. Themes of culture and ancestry among children of concentration camp survivors. *Psychiatry: Journal for the Study of Interpersonal Processes* 45: 247-61.

[32] D. Chakrabarty. 1996. Remembered villages: Representation of Hindu Bengali memories in the aftermath of partition. *Economic and Political Weekly* 3, 2143-45.

[33] P. Bose. 1996. Partition: Memory begins where history ends. In R. Samaddar, ed., *Reflections on partition in the east*: 75.

[34] We find reference to a similar process in the gradually changing versions of myths and folklore. Among the various versions differing from culture to culture, ultimately one version becomes dominant. See for discussion, A. Lord. 1973. *The singer of tales* (New York: Atheneum). In the Indian context, Romila Thapar discusses the various versions of the story of Shakuntala, the versions changing their nature according to 'historical demands'. See R. Thapar. 2000. *Narratives and the making of history* (Delhi: Oxford University Press).

[35] I am indebted to Rik Mitra, a young investigator in the same project, for this piece of illumination. In one of our in-house discussions, this enthusiastic young man expressed his utter frustration at being offered the same stereotyped stories by all the partition victims he interviewed. 'Seems they all have the same story,' he said, exasperated. I recognized the same disappointment in me at times, and wanted to probe deeper, through introspection.

[36] The psychiatric diagnostic system does not recognize any such disorder as 'fear psychosis'. The term is a popular but inappropriate nomenclature to indicate intense acute or chronic anxiety. Many of my respondents used the term and I have preferred to use it that way in the context.

[37] Prafulla Chakrabarti clearly states that such was indeed the case. He also believes that the Hindus were driven out of East Bengal through sheer psychological pressure. See Chakrabarti. 1999. *Marginal men*.

[38] That the spontaneous class struggle has gradually been changed into planned communal strategy has been suggested by earlier commentators like Suranjan Das. 1993. *Communal riots in Bengal*.

[39] See for discussion on effect of age on perception of trauma, T. I. Cann. 1988. The diary of an adolescent girl in the ghetto: A study of age specific reactions to the holocaust. *Psychoanalytical Review* 75, 589-618, and M. Kestenberg and J. S. Kestenberg. 1988. Sense of belonging and altruism in children who survived the holocaust.

[40] E. Erikson. 1968. *Identity: Youth and crisis* (London: Faber and Faber).

4

The Person, the Personality and the Perception

LIFE IS, AFTER ALL, a habit. People fall into certain modes of thinking and behaviour that at some point of their personal development have assisted them in coping. Like all habits, such practices are neither completely rational, nor consistent. In the course of life people leave a number of unresolved conflicts, yet they carry on with their efforts to put the discrete pieces together, to bring into their lives as much harmony as they can muster. Such is the buoyancy of humankind. And such is its folly.

As I read the narratives I had recorded, I had the urge to try and construct, from the behaviour and the attitudes of each of my respondents, an image of the total person. The word 'total' is audacious, as within the purview of a few interview sessions one can hardly understand the 'total'. Let me simply claim that I ventured somewhat deeper than the obvious verbal content of the recollections and tried to paint an image of the person as it appeared to me. One may compare the attempt to that of reconstructing a whole dinosaur from a few bones of the jaw, where some accepted principles based on observed configurations are utilized to fill in the gaps in available data.

Most writings on the effects of Partition (or man-made or natural disasters) emphasize the commonness of reactions among people from diverse backgrounds. This is, of course, important. My contention in this chapter is, however, different. It is that the ultimate meaning of any experience is processed through the personality of the experiencing individual, and the pre-existing modes of personality are crucial in determining the impacts of such experience. Through scrutiny of selected personalities, I intend to demonstrate that violence may not have a singular effect on all; apparent similarity may garb opposite meanings, and apparent contradictions may mask identical perceptions. This understanding does not nullify the commonality of the reactions explored earlier, but supplements it.

Methodologically, a cross-sectional approach would not suffice for this venture. Even a cursory glimpse of the 'person' necessitates an understanding of the development of his cognitions and emotions. One difficulty I encountered here was that my data were obtained at a specific point of time; yet, I attempt a longitudinal interpretation. My aim is to appreciate how the accounts of Partition might have been affected by extra-partition factors: the respondents' personality predispositions, their childhood experiences, their role models and their experiences of love and frustration in other spheres of life. The focus here is not on the experience of Partition, but on the experiencing person, and on the defensive configuration of the person.[1] This configuration was born in the respondents not out of their partition experience; by 1947, the major personality characteristics of these youngsters had already taken nebulous (or, occasionally, for the older ones, relatively defined) shapes. This pre-existing personality influenced their cognition of the event of Partition. Clearly, the same reflection of character pattern was discernible in other aspects of their lives, in their comprehension of the world at large, in their modes of handling myriad experiences. Cues to such defensive modes can be detected through analysis of the content and form of the narrations, of events related or unrelated to the partition issue. In earlier chapters, I have used a similar approach to study discrete events, as in the cases of Girish and Sudhanya. Here, the same technique is used to scan the entire narrative and, therefore, the entire reconstructed life-history. So I have shifted from the phenomenological end to the interpretative end of methodology.

These interpretations are my personal and professional understanding of the dynamic interrelationship between the core and the context[2] of the social perceptions of the respondents, and entail a commentary on the process of production of their memoirs. Let me hasten to state at this point that I elaborate at this length on the personal history and dynamics of selected individuals, because I believe these are not isolated instances. These represent specific types of perception of the trauma of displacement and thus provide clues to certain response modes. At the same time, the divisions are not comprehensive; I definitely do not claim to have covered 'all possible' prototypes.

I have presented rather detailed life-stories of three pairs of men. The first pair we have already met; they are Dipendu and Manish from Barishal. They represent the most typical victims of soft violence; those whose families were driven out of East Bengal by sheer terror, and their narrations evinced emotional perplexity. Dipendu and Manish apparently demonstrated substantially opposite personal and communal attitudes. My intention is to demonstrate how owing to their disparate childhood experiences and predetermined personalities the defensive configuration resulted in two dissimilar facades covering a similar uncertainty beneath. Shashanko and Barun, of the second pair, were declared supporters of fundamental Hindu politics. They differed from the earlier pair as they had witnessed violence perpetrated on others as well as faced serious threat themselves. Both were involved in the Hindu nationalist political stream of India. In the exposition of the life-experiences of these two men, I intend to imply that the meaning of Hindu political affiliation, though apparently having a common core of resentment against the Muslims, was intrinsically different for each of them. Their experiences, coupled with their pre-existing temperamental and personality dispositions, resulted in different motivations for the apparently similar political affiliation. The third pair consisted of Achintya and Tarapada. These two persons had dissimilar experiences, they came from widely disparate social strata, they harboured opposite political beliefs. Yet, they shared at the core a trusting and flexible nature, which enabled both of them to exercise relatively unbiased judgement on communal issues and on life in general.

In describing these persons, I not only changed names, but in certain instances other personal and familial details also (which I considered irrelevant for the concepts emerging in the discussion, but may provide clues for identification). It was a compromise between my attempt to guard the identity of the persons, and a commitment to holistic approach to understanding a human being. I have been unable to solve this dilemma between ethics and truthfulness to my satisfaction. On the whole, I would ask the reader to look at these narrations as fictions based on real life representations.

LAMENTATION: DIPENDU AND MANISH

Psychologists have frequently categorized human beings in terms of their quality and quantity of social responsiveness. Some individuals interact more with other people and thrive on interpersonal warmth; some shy away from personal contacts and feel safer surrounded by neutral objects. Some weave their lives with the smooth threads of expressed relationships; some take refuge in the inanimate, perhaps in nature, books or music. As the event of Partition and consequent uprooting was thrust upon these two categories of people, they probably reacted with their own habitual defensive manoeuvres: the former category overusing interpersonal relationships to diffuse intergroup differences; the latter resorting to further withdrawal, sometimes accentuating ingroup-outgroup distinctions and even rejection of the outgroup to some extent. The pain of separation and being forced to experience animosity were the same for both, but the long term effects differed as they looked at Partition from two distinct angles.

Dipendu's Story

Dipendu was born in Barishal town. When he left his hometown with his family around 1950, he was not yet in his teens. Now retired, he resides in Kolkata with his wife and two unmarried sons. His colleagues testify to his being a gentle, polite and helpful person, with a perfectionist streak and a strong sense of morality. Those close to him add that he can be very stubborn too, though rarely directly aggressive. He is an emotionally and aesthetically sensitive person with a creative spark in art and painting. He also possessed in his youth a flair for athletics. However, he never seriously pursued any of these talents beyond organizing local sports and cultural programmes. He is one of those who 'could have done much', but never did.

I was personally acquainted with Dipendu even before this study. Knowing him to be from 'East Bengal', I requested interviews with him. He acquiesced and invited me to his residence. Though a bit hesitant prior to the appointment, he became animated during the very first interview session. Dipendu's father was a well-known lawyer in Barishal town. His mother was a housewife. They lived in a predominantly Hindu locality. Theirs was a well-to-do family, respected by Hindus and Muslims alike. Dipendu, the youngest one of five siblings, was well cared for, if not downright pampered and overprotected. He studied at a local school where he had both Hindu and Muslim friends. He could not recall any tension between the communities before 1949-50. The children played together, they participated in each other's daily activities as well as in the respective festivals.

Dipendu was growing up in this congenial and protected social environment, a sensitive boy with a natural inclination towards art, and a budding talent for sports. The past was happy, the present was easy flowing, and the future seemed to be sufficiently secured, when Partition came about.

The 14th of August in 1947 did not have any memorable impact on Dipendu. He was, of course, aware that officially their home was now Pakistan. That signified nothing, he said. Yet, he remembered the 30th of January 1948, the day Gandhi was shot. The mourning was spontaneous and *arandhan* (no cooking) was observed at every home, Hindu or Muslim.

Dipendu recalled that the scenario changed for the worse in

1949. I have already described in Chapter 2 how the increasing terror and the course of events finally culminated in his family's decision to migrate. We may recall the gracious Muslim friends who tried to lend them a hand, the increasing mood of depression all around, the apprehension of attack on their family at a time when the father was absent, the father's return and the immediate preparation to leave. Dipendu, his mother, sisters and brothers travelled with a neighbouring family by steamer to Khulna where they had to take shelter with an influential Muslim friend of his father. This 'chacha' arranged to guard them carefully and got them onto a tightly packed train heading for Sealdah. After a long, tiresome and oft-interrupted journey, they reached their destination.

At Sealdah they were at a loss. The family which had accompanied them this far now disappeared. They were greeted only by volunteers who offered them unpalatable food and temporary shelter. It was a moment of disillusion, disgrace and the beginning of prolonged insecurity. Initially they took refuge with various relatives, some members of the family staying at one place and some at another. Meanwhile, Dipendu's father joined them and they managed to shift together in a house in central Kolkata that had been abandoned by a Muslim family after the Calcutta riots. It took them many years to settle. However, since Dipendu's father was a professional with some contacts in Kolkata, they ultimately managed to become financially stable. Of course, the prosperity of their Barishal life was never regained. Lost was Dipendu's ambition of becoming an artist or a sportsperson. He managed to carry on his academic pursuits, but his elder brother had to discontinue his studies and take up a job.

Dipendu considers himself a socialist and a supporter of leftist politics in West Bengal. His political leanings, he said, were a result of family influence as all his relatives were oriented towards Communism. He added that during their difficult years, the Communist leaders and workers were their only friends, regularly keeping in touch and enquiring after their welfare. Considering the indifferent attitude of other political parties, particularly the

Congress, supporting the Communist Party was an obvious choice for the refugees.

Regarding intercommunity relations, Dipendu was strongly positive. He recalled excellent relationships in pre-partition Bengal. There was considerable logical consistency in what he said, and he emitted a secular humanistic attitude. His account was full of benevolent Muslims, and he spoke rather cursorily of the communal ones. He further added that his parents maintained regular contact with their old Muslim friends. After their deaths, the contact was lost, but Dipendu maintains his high regard for Muslims.

In general, Dipendu always speaks slowly, impressing every word on the listener and occasionally using a dramatic pause. The same manner persisted throughout the narration. It seemed to me, from his non-verbal expression, that he was sincerely trying to convey the feelings of his childhood days. But somehow he did not seem quite satisfied with what he was able to communicate. Indeed, he wanted to qualify his statements even after the interview was concluded.

Manish's Story

Born in a village of Barishal, Manish too migrated with his family to Kolkata in 1950. He was a college student at that time. Presently he lives in Kolkata with his wife. He has a daughter who is married. Manish is reputed to be a strict, sincere person and a perfectionist. Occasionally he can be anxious, irritable and vulnerable. Particular about maintaining ethical standards, he feels a general dissatisfaction with the state of world affairs. He is a prolific reader and enjoys scholarly critical discussion.

Manish's daughter happens to be my friend. Learning about my interest in Partition, she asked me to meet her father. I went by appointment to their place, where his wife and daughter received me. A bit later, Manish, dressed in neatly ironed white pyjama and kurta, entered with a newspaper in hand and lowered himself on a sofa adjoining mine. While I explained the purpose of my visit, he was apparently reading the paper, holding it in such a way as to cover half his face. He was, however, attentive to me, as he asked about the details of my work and what I intended to do with the information I gathered, all the time holding the newspaper up. Then suddenly he sat up straight and put the paper down, as if mentally ready to face the situation.

Manish's original home was a small village in Barishal, out of reach of so-called civilization. There was no school, college, doctor or health service and no electric connection. The nearest town was three miles away. Manish himself was born in a *dhenkighar* (a room usually used to husk and store rice, but also used for delivery of children).

Manish's father had expired when Manish was a mere infant. Therefore, Manish and his widowed mother stayed with his uncle's family in the village. They were financially dependent on the uncle, and so his mother was occasionally subjected to derisive comments by her in-laws.

Manish's account of the pleasures of childhood was replete with the beauties of the rural landscape, the river, the paddy fields, the flowers, the festivals, the *bratas* observed by the women, the slow and smooth life.

Manish was always good at studies. He started at the village pathshala and then came to Barishal town with his mother and an elder brother to study. He passed the school-leaving examination with flying colours and took admission to the famous BM College. Till then, Manish recalled, despite communal discrimination, hostility per se was not palpable. Of course, there was social separation between Hindus and Muslims. For example, Muslims were never allowed inside Hindu homes, and they observed their festivals separately. However, there was no animosity.

From 1949, gradually, tension mounted, and occasional riots broke out. In Barishal town, word spread that on the Hindu auspicious day of Shivaratri there would be a pre-planned attack on them by the Muslims. All the Hindus took refuge in the 'Deputy House'. It was a battle-like situation. The Hindus arranged several lines of defence. From the afternoon onwards, they heard war cries and some nearby houses were set on fire. They could see the flames all around. The call 'Allah Ho Akbar' still haunts Manish. He recalled how the youngsters were forced to drink milk and salute their elders as if it was the last day of their lives. However, for some unknown reason, the 'Deputy House' was spared. They learnt later that the local Muslim commanding officer took preventive measures to deter the attack. However, after this event, rumours spread and so did fear and insecurity. Finally, in 1950, the family decided to migrate. Manish and his brothers and sisters left Barishal accompanied by an old aunt; his mother stayed behind for some reason. After a protracted journey, they reached Sealdah, but had no place where they could stay. They stayed for days in the temporary hut erected inside the station, surviving on the meagre food provided by volunteers. They had a relative in Kolkata, but he did not offer them shelter. The same relative, however, found an abandoned house in south Kolkata for the refugee family. In the meantime, their mother arrived and the family was reunited.

Manish was keen on continuing his studies, but felt morally obliged to earn for the family. His elder brother had already taken up part of the responsibility. Finally, Manish managed to get a job by day and study at night. He described how he was mistreated by some educationists and denied admission in some colleges, because he was a refugee and did not have his papers in order. Gradually they settled in Kolkata and Manish took up higher studies as a challenge. He narrated how he had been repeatedly thwarted in his attempts and how some of his colleagues mistreated him. Ultimately he managed to finish studies and acquired a moderately satisfying job.

Recently Manish visited his old village in Bangladesh where he found the same backwardness that prevailed in his childhood. The gloom, the poverty, the darkness of superstition and unhygienic practices were all unchanged. The villagers were, if anything, even poorer. He met Maqbur, the person who used to work for them and who burnt down their house after they abandoned it. Maqbur's present financial condition was miserable. Manish attributed the predicament of his former homeland to the inefficiency of the Bangladesh government. However, this visit to his village was like a pilgrimage for him.

Manish has never been a zealous supporter of any political party. He appreciates Gandhian philosophy, though he is not happy with its application in India. He bears particular dislike for the Communists of West Bengal, and he also believes that Muslims are not trustworthy.

Manish initially struck me as hesitant and guarded, becoming relatively relaxed by the end of the first day's session, and positively eager to talk from the second day onwards. He wanted his daughter and his wife to listen to all he said, and to insert their comments so that no noteworthy fact was missed. He spoke in well-chosen words. He also frequently referred to the theoretical models of the South Asian economy and discussed the relevance of views forwarded by Amartya Sen and other scholars. With time, he became more at ease and occasionally reverted to the Bangal dialect, and even sang out a few lines. The tendency of theorizing, however, remained until the end when he forwarded his own theory of Partition. In addition, he spoke elaborately about his academic career and of his later achievements. Apparently, he felt most comfortable in theoretical discussion.

Manish explicitly retains a pessimistic attitude towards life. I have discussed my conceptualization of the dynamics of his mistrust of the Muslims and the ensuing conflict thereof in an earlier section. I have shown how the negativism has invaded more than one area of his social perceptions. He felt persecuted first by the Muslims in East Bengal and then by his colleagues. He remains not too happy with his lot and the course his life took.

Experiences and Personalities

Dipendu and Manish apparently shared many aspects of their personalities. Both were remarkably polite, morally sensitive and perfectionist, occasionally to the point of being rigid. Their experiences were similar as well. Both were adolescents at the time of migration. Both were kayastha Hindus from Barishal and migrated around 1950 under comparable circumstances.

The post-partition experiences of Dipendu and Manish also corresponded on many points. They landed alike at Sealdah and spent a few days among the thronging refugees. The experience was far from what one would expect when alighting in their 'own' country. Volunteers from various social service organizations catered for them, but they were made to feel like beggars, and even insulted. Dipendu recalled his sense of humiliation when a man offered him some food in a dirty bowl. 'I could never accept food that way,' Dipendu exclaimed. 'After the love and care with which my mother served food, how could I accept this disgrace?' Sensing his refusal, the man laughed sarcastically and said, 'Who cares if you eat or not?' Dipendu was furious. Similar 'culture shock' took place in other spheres of his life too. The natives of West Bengal looked upon the refugees as a burden. Acerbic comments were common. Shielded within a refined family milieu, Dipendu never used abusive language. Now his local peers freely uttered all sorts of vulgarities. He laughingly commented about his shock the day some mate called him *shala*. He had to learn to live with the 'facts of life'. Manish also recalled the uncertainties and bitterness when they had to spend a few days in the temporary huts erected at the station. They had some distant relatives in Kolkata, but they did not offer them shelter. Like Dipendu's, Manish's family also finally settled in one of the numerous houses abandoned by Muslims who had left Kolkata.

Dipendu and Manish completed their higher education. The world was unkind to them and they had to struggle hard. They narrated how vulnerable they had felt. It was impossible, almost obscene, to demand any privilege, or to express a desire to fulfil any personal ambition. Both considered themselves fortunate that their studies had not been interrupted.

Both felt that in pre-war Bengal, despite some discord and discrimination between the two communities, an overall harmony and mutual acceptance had prevailed. Dipendu acknowledged that communal riots were part and parcel of life in East Bengal.

Yet, he stressed the positive aspect of the intercommunity relationship, recalling the close relationships his family had shared with their Muslim friends. Manish on the other hand emphasized the social distance between the two communities. According to him, Hindus used to mix with Hindus and Muslims with Muslims; the Muslims were mainly uneducated and of lower financial status; they were in a socially subordinate position too, and not allowed inside Hindu houses. However, this was not hate, Manish claimed. Mutual love, compassion and understanding prevailed between the two communities, he asserted, at least before 1946.

Dipendu and Manish fathomed the impact of Partition in a similar manner. Partition per se, had no significance for either of them at that time; the event was not felt as an augury of disaster by these youngsters. The difficulties were discerned about one and half years later. Their real trauma resided in the realization of the inevitability of uprooting and forced migration to an unknown land. Dipendu expressed it with passion and Manish in a factual fashion; nonetheless it is clear that the wound still bleeds.

Dipendu and Manish alike reported the mounting communal tension after 1947. Both were living in Barishal town in February 1950. Both had heard rumours of violence at various pockets of the country, of trains carrying corpses, of brutalities, but neither had witnessed actual physical carnage. Both saw fires on the outskirts of the town. Two similar events of threat of attack and violence by Muslims precipitated the migration of both their families. Although the attacks never came in reality, the anxiety was insufferable.

Neither had encountered brutal violence in the course of their journey. Both, however, nurtured a similar notion of violence, comprising not only torture and massacre, but the realization that one no more had any right over one's land, property, dignity, even one's body. Both narrated specific incidents that marked such violence. Dipendu spoke of a lady whom he called kakima (aunt). She was from the neighbouring aristocrat family. When they boarded the steamer together, they had to undergo a 'search' by the Pathan army. The soldiers seized everything from everyone.

'Our kakima was strikingly beautiful,' recalled Dipendu. 'We adored her. She was something sacred, unattainable for us; she was so stunningly gorgeous! These fellows touched her body in the name of searching and took off all the ornaments she had. It happened in front of everyone. Nobody had ever manhandled her like that. It was a violation of sanctity.' This was 'sheer violence' to the young boy. When Manish was migrating, he was accompanied by an old aunt. She also had a few ornaments and some money with her. Near the border, some army men accosted them and simply claimed everything she had. '"Hey old hag, submit whatever you possess", they ordered. There was so much contempt and demonstration of brute force in their approach that I felt extremely vulnerable', Manish recalled. For Manish, too, violence lay in the violation of human rights.

The duo also shared a feeling of guilt about being the relatively fortunate ones in post-partition India. Despite difficulties, both of them had thrived, at least in comparison to a large number of refugees whose lives had been shattered forever. Both attributed their success to an 'external locus of control', considered it their good fortune, and felt sympathetic for the relatively unlucky ones. The apparent similarities were, however, punctuated by a number of dissimilarities. Some differences were demographic in nature. Dipendu was a town boy; Manish was from a remote village. Both were minors, but Dipendu was younger than Manish and came from a financially well-off family, had both parents living and protecting him during his childhood. Manish's pecuniary condition was unstable since his father had died at a very early age. After migration, Dipendu's father and brother earned for the family; Manish had to help to support his family.

These were but background differences that contained other psychological dissimilarities in terms of the interpretation of life-events and the resultant affective tone. The mode of presentation of the two narratives was strikingly different, implying different emotional responses to life and experiences. I wish to underscore two such differences. One was in recounting the childhood days in Barishal, in their spontaneous recall of the lost pleasures. Dipendu's early account was full of loving and caring persons surrounding him. He talked happily about his mother who was, 'an exceptional lady'. It was remarkable, he thought, that she used to read books regularly–novels as well as religious ones. She worshipped God, yet remained uncontaminated by any superstition or sectarian prejudice. Dipendu described elaborately his friends, neighbours, teachers and his father's friends too, all portrayed as warm and protective. The contentment for Dipendu came from the association with people. When in later life he developed a political opinion, this too was derived less from ideological analysis and more from interpersonal influences.

Contrarily, Manish's account of happy memories constituted mostly of the natural beauty of his village and the uneventful, relaxed way of life. He too spoke fondly of his mother, particularly about her struggle as a widow raising her family. Nevertheless, his delineation had a tone of idealized fantasy, almost like a poem. He remembered his 'eternally suffering mother standing alone under a nut tree' when he left for his grandfather's house. Manish dwelt more on the vast paddy fields, the river, and his daily infinitesimal interactions with nature. He recalled how they used to tell the time by the position of the sun and the moon and the blossoming of flowers, how they used *jaan*, a method of driving fish through a narrow canal so it was easy to catch them, and how in the evening the cows would be driven towards the cowshed. He relived the smell of boiling rice and of jute left in the water to rot. He described the various village rituals observed mostly by the women, such as Maghamandal *brata* and Punnipukur *brata*. He recalled a few adages of the time, and even joyously sang aloud a few lines of village song. For Manish bliss emerged from the proximity to nature.

The only component of the natural environment Dipendu described was the Pareshsagar Dighi, which had seemed unusually vast to him as a child. He wondered whether it would still look so expansive. Contrarily, the only people apart from his mother whom Manish recalled with loving words were his teachers, Jatindra Nath Datta and Anil Kumar De at the BM College. He named his childhood mates only when asked. He also recalled a village lady with respect, because she was the midwife when he was born: 'She is the *dhatri* or *dharani*,' he said, 'since it was because of her that I saw the light of this earth.' Once again, the relationship was not of close attachment, but of secondarily developed idealization. When Manish spoke of his political ideology, he related it to his rational appreciation of the Gandhian doctrine; interpersonal influences, if any, were never mentioned. This was in stark contrast to Dipendu who related his political affiliation to his benefactors' ideology.

This difference in recall, in the process of memory, reflects the distinctive ways in which these two persons cope with traumatic experience. Under duress, an individual seeks refuge spontaneously in the happy sensations and memories of early days. Dipendu, in this effort, seemed to cling to the memory of good people, even at the cost of the physical-natural environment; Manish probably felt more at ease within the embrace of Mother Nature.

A second difference centred on the attitude towards the Muslim community. Throughout his narrative, Dipendu emphatically presented a pro-Muslim and eloquently secular attitude. He spontaneously spoke of the fraternal bond between the communities despite the fact that theirs was a Hindu locality. He recognized the conflict between Hindus and Muslims, but this was at the level of the general political environment. At the individual level, he recalled only mutual affection. During the narration, he tried to justify this contradiction. At times, he posited that theirs was an extraordinary family; at others, he declared that Barishal was an enlightened and exceptional district. On still other occasions, he claimed that the fraternal feeling was the general and natural heritage of undivided Bengal, to be ruptured only by the unprecedented political conspiracy. Apparently, he had not been able to solve the riddle. In contradiction, Manish revealed definite sentiments against Muslims. He was initially hesitant to express his resentment explicitly, but ultimately declared Muslims to be 'naturally ferocious and racial' and 'not trustworthy'. If his initial reticence stemmed from his politeness, his mistrust for the community came out forcefully as he embarked on the topic. However, his discomfort in this negativism was evinced in his contradictory statements as he was unsure whether his attitude might be labelled hate.

Dipendu and Manish further differed in their acceptance and communication of the trauma of Partition and migration. Dipendu attributed the change in the entire course of his life to the event of Partition. 'My aims were shattered. Had I stayed in Barishal, I would have been a player, I had athletic talent; I could have even become an artist. But here, in Kolkata, I could not dream of pursuing these ambitions.' he said. He felt that people would have laughed at a refugee wanting to learn oil painting, when his family was struggling for daily rice. Yet, he recognized one good effect Partition had on him. 'Over there I was sheltered; I was overprotected. I even had a governess to look after me who took care of my every need. Here I was left to the street. I learnt to face life.'

Manish expressed downright condemnation. At the same time, he tried to present a generalized and theoretical stand. Referring to the effect of Partition on his personal life, he exclaimed, 'Disastrous!' Then he pondered for a moment and added, 'We were never well off. But I was brilliant in studies. I could have pursued a fine career much more smoothly [pause]. I cannot think of the effect of Partition in terms of my personal life only. I have to think in terms of the community. The effect of Partition was disastrous for all three segments of the land. None of the nation-states has prospered from it.'[3] Then Manish went on theorizing over why Partition brought about nothing but misery. He contended that every action contains a combination of the *trigunas*; any effort to succeed must have some component of *sattva* and *rajas* and less of *tamas*. The act of Partition only combined *rajas* and *tamas* as it was motivated by selfish vested interests; the result was therefore chaotic violence. 'Born in *tamasikata* it has resulted in pervasive *tamas*: darkness,' he concluded. Here again, at least apparently, Manish was much more pessimistic than Dipendu.

So what does this difference in reconstruction signify? We have already assumed that whatever was recalled was not an exact reproduction of what happened, but the best compromise between the actual event and the event one desired to remember.[4] Which determinants operated to select what was to be remembered and what not to be? I consider personality, shaped out of early childhood experiences, a significant factor in this regard. More explicitly, my proposal is that depending upon the personality disposition of Dipendu and Manish, some components of their memories were lost, some surfaced intact and some were underscored. In other words, different defensive configurations were more easily available to each.[5]

To understand the personality-event interface in their lives we must once again review the overt and covert personality features of these two men. Psychologically speaking, the reputation of their being moralists and perfectionists, may be related to their need to systematize the uncertainty of life-events into a 'model', to draw an ordered existence out of the chaos. At a deeper level, it implies a specific style of aggression management and a subsequent effort to keep the resultant intra-psychic anxiety defined, focused and well within bounds.[6] Probably for both Dipendu and Manish, the experiences of their early years inhibited free expression of retaliatory aggression, leaving a trace of dissatisfaction and incompleteness. They shared this basic anxiety of unprocessed anger. In adulthood, they adopted traits of orderliness as a defensive mode.[7]

Yet, their self-presentations differed. Dipendu was outwardly expressive and affectionate. Manish was relatively less comfortable in expressing interpersonal sentiments. Dipendu was inhibited in expressing aggression; Manish spoke out his dislike more freely, but was never completely satisfied with it. Dipendu apparently tried to make a positive interpretation of the course of events; Manish was rather bitter and negative about his life-experiences. In other words, Dipendu had difficulty in expressing anger; Manish was uncomfortable with expressing emotional proximity.

It may be hypothesized that for these two persons, the trauma of forced uprooting, the inevitable anger at the disruption and subsequent anxiety, immediately mobilized the 'defensive' patterns that had developed in the course of their earlier life. To understand the dynamics in detail, we have to scrutinize the 'meaning' of their childhood experiences over which the trauma of uprooting was superimposed. Dipendu's childhood, as described by himself, was 'overprotected'. He was the passive recipient of care, not the active designer of his life. One possible consequence of this kind of childhood experience is that 'trust' in life is generated as a blind belief in 'goodness', and is shattered easily as the evil side of existence is exposed.[8]

An episode Dipendu recalled from his childhood may be thought to symbolize his approach to life. There was a fakir who would come to their house in Barishal every morning and utter blessings on the children. He would stroke their small heads, murmuring meaningless 'mantras' that sounded like 'hooommm-hmmm'. So the children called him 'Hoomwala'. Dipendu was fond of this serene and benevolent figure and waited for him to come each morning. One day Dipendu was passing through the marketplace when he suddenly saw 'Hoomwala', clad in the same black robe, but his tranquil facade gone. He was quarrelling with some people and uttering filthy abuse. Dipendu was so shocked that his world, his belief in humanity, seemed to fall apart. He was deeply pained. 'I wished I had not seen him that way. I wished I had not gone to the marketplace.'

Probably a similar reaction was generated in this sensitive boy when the insecurity of Partition descended on his family and they decided to leave Barishal for fear of Muslim attacks. The friendly Muslim community now suddenly appeared as enemies. The indignation he felt at this turn of events could not be expressed freely; he wished he had not seen this vile side of human nature, just as he had not wished to see 'Hoomwala' in his angry avatar. As the ambiguity of reality was thrust upon him, he had to choose between disillusionment and fantasy. He opted for the same mechanism as he had for 'Hoomwala'. Since he had been accustomed to being cared for by others, to being passive, he was not able to rise actively to the feeling of disaster. He grudgingly thrust himself into the commotion of the situation, allowed himself to be swayed away by it, but did not want to confront complete disenchantment. He coped by developing a partially realistic cognitive frame and suppressing parts of his memory; he recalled only the goodness and survived on it. Yet, as he built up this inner sense of munificence of humankind, he did this painstakingly, distorting reality, suppressing the malevolence. In the process, some other components of his surroundings were simultaneously forgotten. In Dipendu's case, in his fervour to establish the 'good universe', it was the physical-natural environment that lost its impact.

On this track of transforming unpleasantness into pleasant memories, whatever indignation Dipendu felt, whatever wrath he had for his misfortune, was projected onto some unknown agency. He was not allowed, intrapsychically, the vindictive pleasure of pinpointing a specific person or community, because that would immediately puncture the ideal goodness he had erected with such effort. His aggression was, thereby, left unresolved as he was unable to direct it towards any focused 'enemy'. According to the natural psychological mechanism in such cases of conflict over aggression, some of the anger was directed inwards, disabling him in pursuit of his talents.[9] He could have taken the thwarting of his ambition to practise his talents as a challenge to his tenacity. Instead he gave in and wasted his talents, as if he wanted to tell his fate, 'I will not prosper, not receive your grace, since you have forced me to see evil.' His obliging and readily altruistic mode of social interaction befitting his passive approach to the world kept his resentment under cover, and provided him with a passive aggressive mode of coping that occasionally breaks out in the form of 'stubbornness', familiar only to the people close to him.[10]

For Manish, the backdrop was different. With his father's untimely death, he started his life in loss, harnessed to monetary constraint and left with a feeling of helplessness. He opened his narrative with the description of the poverty and dilapidation of the village as well as of their family. He ended his narration in frustration. Unlike Dipendu, he had learnt to be angry and to express his indignation; he was able to fight his way out. From his childhood account, one gets an impression that he had had a single aim in life, to obtain a respectable career. But this was not the entire story. There is a second characteristic of his style. Undoubtedly, he fought out his course to success, but at times under stress, he shrank back; he withdrew. The fatherless boy, helpless though furious with the persecution of the adult world, occasionally peeps through the mask of the learned man. Manish seemed rarely comfortable with his aggression, he was afraid of retaliation and punishment. For him too, a simple childhood story told out of context, but emerging as an unrelated association during the narration, provides a clue to his attitude. This was about a man who apparently worked for their family, whom he called Uddhab-dada. This man was strong and had some authority over the youngsters. Manish narrated how one day he defied the order of Uddhab and went out to play, then came back home clad in dirt and mud. Seeing Uddhab-dada around, he was so terrified that he just hid in his room lying face down, pretending he had never gone out. In this ostrich mode of coping, he had forgotten that the mud and dirt on his body would betray him. He could not express his indignation against powerful authority directly.

Throughout the sessions, Manish's narration was characterized by his insecurity and relative discomfort with people around him. The absence of human faces in his childhood account, his focus on the natural environment, his complaint against his uncooperative acquaintances in later life, his theorization of the fallout of Partition, highlighted his discomfiture in accommodating the ambivalent human relationships in his life. This does not mean that he is emotionally stiff and completely unable to relax; indeed his eyes sparkled with mirth as he painted pictures of the opalescent rural life in Barishal. His natural affection and concern for others including myself also showed in small gestures. Nevertheless, now and again he was obliged to seek sanctuary under his over-rational armour.

It may be hypothesized that the poverty, the humiliation of his mother by his relatives, the fear of losing what little his family possessed, had formed the basis of his cautious and probably justified mistrust. Had he been allowed to stay in Barishal, the flowing river, the aroma of paddy and jute, the fishing adventures, coupled with the admiration and honour he got as a brilliant boy and the inevitable gradual recognition in a profession would have calmed him down, replenished the love he had been deprived of, soothed his simmering soul. But that he was driven out of this developing security by 'them' had been 'disastrous' for him; not so much for his career as he thinks, but in destroying his ability to take life with easy trust and to express emotions freely. In due course, he attained a respectable position in his career, prospered in a material and social sense, but was still not able to obtain a security born out of a true sense of belonging. Just as he had not been able to look Uddhab-dada directly at the face, he could not look at the human world with confidence.

In the course of his experiences, his dislike of Muslims was born. Habituated to focusing on a specified adversary, he adopted a mode of defining the 'other' as undeserving of trust. Rationally he knew that the common Muslim people could not be responsible for his personal disaster. He admitted it frankly. Yet, he had to fix a target for the blame, so he developed a negative image of the generalized enemy called the 'Muslim community'. Any positive experience with individual Muslims was never highlighted; these were probably suppressed just as Dipendu had suppressed the negative interactions. Manish, despite his rational understanding to the contrary, fears the Muslims, mistrusts them, and avoids them because this helps him to keep his inner equilibrium.

Whenever there is anticipated social disruption and prevailing uncertainty, one's judgement may take two illusory patterns. One is known as a 'Positive Illusion Strategy', where alarms are minimized to give a semblance of security; in other words, in such cases, people under-report personal victimization and negative experience. A second strategy is known as 'Zero Miss Strategy', where one becomes oversensitive, constantly on guard, defensive to the extent of seeing red even when the situation is neutral.[11] Our two cases represent these oft-used strategies. Neither of them presented in their narrations the inevitable ambiguity of the emergent social circumstances of Partition; they failed to acknowledge the shades of grey that characterize any given moment during such political tumult. Without enough scope to mend their pre-existing vulnerabilities, they were, under socio-political constraints, desperately protecting their ego-integrity. This is probably why in their accounts there was a partial suppression of one or the other aspect of the environment: a 'lack'; an internal hushing up; a void. Dipendu and Manish spoke of their pain through their silence.

CREATION OF THE ENEMY: SHASHANKO AND BARUN

Among my respondents were some who not only attributed negative traits to Muslims, but went on to confirm this in their political involvement. We scrutinize here the narratives of two active supporters of 'Hindutva', and judge the similarities and discrepancies in their psychological structure.

Shashanko's Story

Shashanko is an executive manager in a private company. He lives with his wife and an unmarried brother in a house at Maniktala, an old neighbourhood of central Kolkata. This particular neighbourhood had been the witness to much violence. His son and daughter have settled abroad, and occasionally come to visit their parents.

Shashanko's ancestral home was in a remote village near the border of Noakhali district. Shashanko is proud of the fact that he comes from a royal Hindu lineage. The family lived in Noakhali town and used to visit the village home during the vacations. Around 1944 they started living in their village home rather permanently. In 1946, when Shashanko was not yet in his teens, trouble broke out all around. They could see fires in neighbouring areas, and heard of rioting and forced conversions at Noakhali. Then problems cropped up in their locality too. As a measure of caution, the young girls were removed to the town. Shashanko's father and uncle did not want to displace the rest of the family without resistance. They would fight back, they decided. They started equipping themselves for a direct confrontation. Shashanko described this preparation with enthusiasm.

'The Mussalmans who worked for us supported us. The outsiders disturbed the situation. We called the blacksmith in the wee hours of the night and he manufactured weapons like spears, bows and arrows for us. All preparations were made with the utmost secrecy. Because of the huge trees in the garden and the canal, the inside of our house was shielded from the outsider's view. A carpenter was called in to help make guns. We children were assigned the task of looking after the weapons. We polished the guns with charcoal and oil. We already had swords and sacrificial knives because during Durga Puja we used to sacrifice goats. Our elder brothers practised shooting the arrows at targets on moonlit nights. That year we did not observe Lakshmi Puja. Two friendly Mussalmans—Rahamat and Keramat—had informed us about the preparations at the other end ... We heard that the Mussalmans would attack us that night. Only one room and the courtyard were kept for use, all others were fenced with thorny plants. All inflammable objects were dropped in the water. We also hoarded rice, pulses and other food. We ate khichuri together. What a grand feeling! Everybody greeted one another. Nobody wept, not even the mothers. That day we understood what it meant to be the true descendants of a kshatriya king. Everyone was given small daggers, even the younger ones, and a handful of poisonous dhutro seeds. Somehow, I do not remember whether we, the youngest, were also entrusted with the poison. Anyway, we were told to attack first, and then to die if necessary. Our elder brothers took the spears; the older ones took swords and guns. I recall my father taking a gun himself.

'It was late afternoon. There were frightening noises all around. The Mussalmans were shouting "Naraye Taqdir" and "Allah Ho Akbar". A few thousand [Mussalmans] entered our house. Some elderly men of the village headed the procession. They told us, "You have to surrender to us and convert to Islam." My Jetha [uncle] responded, "If you are our friends, go back; if enemy, come in." The intruders shouted back, persistent in their demand. Suddenly all of us rushed forward. We charged them head on. Uncle hurt two of them with swords. Father started firing. The assailants were taken aback. They had not foreseen that we would be so prepared. They fled.

'After they retreated, we laid *chowkis* [light string cots with wood or bamboo frames and legs] on the courtyard and started planning for the next day. We knew the Mussalmans would attack us with renewed strength. Around 8 or 8.30 at night three Mussalman men of the village, Rahamat, Keramat and Habib, came in. Their mother was indebted to us and had ordered them to save us at any cost. They implored us to leave the house; they would get us to safety. My Jetha initially resisted. "We will die, all of us, together," he said. Ma and Jethima fell at his feet and pleaded, "Please listen to them, save our children." Finally Jetha said, "I will shut myself in the puja room and ask permission from my God [Thakur]." He came back after half an hour and reported that "Thakur" had consented to an effort to save the children. It was just after the rainy season and there was water all around. The jute-carrying boats were brought in. We children were sleeping on the chowkis. They woke us up and bundled us into the boats. We were still in our underpants and vests. They covered us with jute and these three Mussalmans and a fourth boatman took us to the Thana, six or seven miles away from the village. Twice or thrice Mussalman thugs stopped the boat and cross-examined our escorts who lied about our existence each time. The Mussalmans were keeping surveillance to prevent the Hindus from escaping. At one point, a little girl, one of our cousins, cried out aloud. She was told that if she cried again, she would be thrown out of the boat.

'Around four in the morning, we reached the town. My elder brothers were working in Kolkata. We did not know where my elder sisters were. We were sheltered in a local man's house for a few days. We had to eat the dirty putrid-smelling khichuri of the langarkhana. Believe it or not, till today I cannot take khichuri. I still remember the stink.'

Shashanko later learnt that nobody had detected their flight. Next day a more determined group had attacked their house. The family resisted, but ultimately everything was looted. Even the valuables which had been hidden under the water in the tank were found and taken. Fortunately, nobody was killed. The next day the military arrived. The family was shifted to the town under army protection. A number of Hindus had assembled there on the bank of the river. Shashanko and his cousins were united with their family.

'I can still go back those fifty years and see myself, a small bare-footed boy in a netted vest and torn pants held up by a string. If the military had not intervened, there was no way our family would have survived the next assault,' Shashanko said.

Independence came amidst this confusion. Shashanko dimly recalled his participation in processions and slogans in favour of Pakistan. In the course of time, the family decided to come to Kolkata. Shashanko's father had resisted the move since as a freedom fighter. For his part, he considered it below his dignity to be labelled a 'refugee'. Shashanko wanted to build a successful career and he succeeded. He was interested in politics too, and he identified with the anti-Congress and anti-Muslim groups. He was also a staunch anti-Communist. He feels persecuted by the CPI(M), the then political power in the Government of West Bengal. He reported being harassed by its cadres in his neighbourhood, and as a result has restricted his political involvement.

Shashanko did not spontaneously speak about his family, but when I asked him, he spoke with feeling. 'My parents—they were really ideal parents. I adored them, you know.' He described his father as a man of principles, an 'exceptionally honest man'. He was involved in the freedom movement and supported the Congress. Shashanko spoke of his father's educational excellence. Then he spoke tenderly about his mother, described her generous nature and mourned her death. His emotion and respect for his parents were palpable.

Shashanko had well-framed political opinions. He explained why Hinduism was the only way out for our country. 'Hinduism is a great religion and India's past was glorious because of the practice of Hinduism,' he declared. He believes that the Muslims are the source of all disasters in India. He spoke at length on how he had seen in the course of his personal and professional life the undue advantages enjoyed by the Muslims of India. He spoke laughingly about one highly placed Muslim man who has 'a clear brain, clear because it is completely devoid of grey matter'. He blamed the short-sighted negative politics of the Congress and Communists for this situation. 'The Mussalmans do not even bother about getting their house plans sanctioned by the municipality.'

He feels offended by the attitude of the rich Muslims who are eager to keep their identity separate from their fellow Muslims belonging to lower social strata. He expressed the opinion that highly placed Indian Muslims do not want their own community to flourish. 'Those who have studied at madrasas cannot get a job anywhere. Yet they will not be allowed to join the mainstream education system.'

The mode of exposition of his attitude, however, was rather ambiguous, and he constantly qualified his statements by reiterating that he had been saved by Muslims. 'This is not to say that I hate the Mussalmans. There are of course many good Mussalmans.' He has many Muslim friends. They often come and stay with his family. 'Yet,' he continued, 'I am top to bottom a conservative Hindu. Look how we have been sacrificing our own benefit for them. For example, we have renounced Sanskrit, but retained Arabic and Urdu. The government is providing subsidy for Haj-goers, but not for the pilgrims to Sagar.[12] He described the plight of the Muslim residents and their callousness in hygienic matters in certain pockets of the city. 'Look at the nasty way they live. Go to Park Circus [a predominantly Muslim area of Kolkata]. See for yourself the misery and poverty of the residents there. No civilized man can stay in those pitiable conditions.'

Then he commented on the state of affairs in Bangladesh. 'Look at the plight of the Muslims there. I agree that earlier at our country houses they were given separate utensils to eat from. They were discriminated against by the Hindus. Now that they are being given equal status, what are they doing?' He elaborated on the political genesis of communalism in India and drew a comparison with England. 'In general a Muslim, or for that matter anybody, is not communal. It is something politically injected into a man,' he said. 'Such things happen everywhere. When a political party supports a minority, it is usually to increase its vote bank. For example, in UK, most people of Indian origin support the Labour Party, because it is pro-Asian. Recently, however, they have become more politically sophisticated and many of them now support the Conservative Party.

Through his interaction with his Muslim acquaintances, as mentioned earlier, he had reasons to believe that the rich and educated Muslims themselves discriminate against the poorer ones. He felt that if the educational level of the Muslims could be brought at par with that of Hindus, the communal feelings could be fought against. It is a conspiracy of the Muslims themselves to keep the poor section of their community barred from proper education, he observed. And despite their own lack of merit and credentials a few from the same community are usurping top positions by virtue of their religion alone.

I considered the above narration an expression of Shashanko's ambivalent feelings about the Muslims. From his juxtaposition of positive and negative, it appeared that he was oscillating between condemnation of the Muslims and sympathy for their plight. I asked him kindly to clarify his political ideology.

Shashanko readily obliged. He declared that the very existence of Hindus in India is endangered by the Muslims. Shashanko was worried that the 'scientific faith of Hinduism' is being overpowered by Muslim dogma. He stated that nothing but Hinduism could keep a vast country like India united, as its spirituality and philosophy are part and parcel of the country. There is political, historical and geographical harmony in Hindu concepts. For example, he said, the rivers constitute one major bond of union in this country, which is why they have always been deemed sacred. He considered the folktales and myths of India too as intrinsically meaningful. For example, the tale that Sati's body was scattered all over India reminds one that these distant places are bound by a common creed. 'There is no hope for India unless Hinduism is restored to its rightful place,' he declared.

Shashanko further lamented the fact that our history books give detailed information on the lineage of Muslim and Christian sovereigns, while the history of the Hindu people, the true history of the nation, is glossed over. He pointed out that the lane where his house stands is named after a Muslim. He recalled that someone had proposed that the lane be renamed after a famous artist who had lived and died there. The committee set up to decide this included a Communist member who said that the change would hurt Muslim sentiments. Therefore, the original name was retained.

Shashanko's antagonism came out strongly in connection with his own political affiliations: 'I have always been politically against the Mussalmans. The reason perhaps is my childhood experience of riots. It has played its role in my subconscious. Not that I will kill a Mussalman if I see one, but I dislike them. The Mussalmans are a real menace to the peace of India. They are responsible for a major portion of all our troubles: the social restlessness, murder, robbery and other anti-social activities. Most of them are anti-Hindu and anti-India. And our own political parties pamper them. The Congress and the Communists are equally responsible for the state of affairs.' He equated the Muslims and the Communists in their dogmatic approach. 'The Communists think that you kill the Bourgeois and you achieve all; the Mussalmans think you kill the Kafir and you get everything. The Christians are different. They understand business.'

He ended the session on a pessimistic note. 'If the Hindus and Mussalmans are not politically aware of the danger, I do not see any hope.' He referred to a politically influential Muslim leader of West Bengal whose dishonesty and immoral transactions were being discussed in the newspapers and said that such persons are the core problem of the country. He concluded with the repudiation of the leftist secularism. 'And what to say about the Communists? The very word "secular" is pointless. It is a myth.'

Shashanko's way of speaking interested me. The flow of his speech was not consistent throughout the narration. When he was discussing the crisis at his village home and particularly the attack, resistance and flight, he spoke in a smooth and assured manner. But whenever it came to expressing his attitude to Muslims, his tone fluctuated, sometimes talking about the harm done by the Muslims with easy conviction, at other times less sure, using words like 'maybe', 'perhaps' or 'it could be', belying his hesitation. He seemed rather astonished when I asked him to talk about his family. I had the impression that he had a predetermined mindset as to what a person studying Partition would want to know. He had a story to tell and he was prepared to deliver it to me. As I persisted in my quest for the total person, he grew less sure and his responses were characterized by the usual pauses of an unprepared conversation.

Barun's Story

Barun's case was singularly impressive because in him there was absolute rejection of Muslims in general; the dislike was unequivocal. Yet, unlike Shashanko, Barun did not suffer any personal harm from the Muslims. His resentment against the Muslims grew out of what he witnessed. When I rang up Barun for an appointment, he immediately told me that I might find his association unpalatable, as he is an admirer of Nathuram Godse. 'I thought I must let you know this at the very outset.'

Barun lives in a modest house in Kolkata with his wife and daughter. I went to his house on the scheduled day and found him waiting eagerly for me. 'I am a straight person and have one single purpose in my life. I will tell you all I know. I have nothing to hide,' he commenced. Then he asked me if I was a secularist. He asserted that he was not one and he definitely thought that India should be a Hindu country. His single mission in life was to collect evidence of the cruelty and torture perpetrated by the Muslims. Whenever he spoke generously of any individual Muslim, he simultaneously mentioned that this must not be taken to suggest any kind of indulgence towards them. 'The Muslims have no right to live in India,' he declared.

Barun's home was in a village of Noakhali but he lived in Dhaka with his uncle's family. Thus, he witnessed the riots and violence at both places. He started his narrative recalling his association with political persons in Dhaka, particularly with Lila Nag and Anil Roy of *Jayasree Patrika*, and Hem Ghosh. He had been a devoted social worker from his young days, associated with the Forward Bloc. He described how, around 1945, most young people got involved with the struggle for freedom. There were frequent meetings and processions. But, he told me, the Muslims participated in such movements only when some Muslim leader was being held for trial, while the Hindus joined irrespective of the religious colour of the issue. He remembered being beaten by the police during one such procession. He narrated how he had been blessed by Hem Ghosh, who himself had received the blessings of Swami Vivekananda. 'I felt as if an electric charge had passed through my body.'

Then he described the riots in Dhaka in 1946. He was about fifteen at the time. Here took place the key incident that shadowed his entire life. I shall present a long portion of his narration, though of course, in a slightly modified form, especially where names have been used.

> 'The 16th day of August was Direct Action Day. The riots in Dhaka started immediately after. When the rioting broke out, we were on the streets. Somehow, we managed to run home. There was fire all around. The Mussalmans were shouting day and night "Allah Ho Akbar" and "Naraye Taqdir". Many women and children defecated in their pants when they heard the sound. On those days, almost nobody could eat, no, not because of dearth of food, but simply out of fear. We depended on the Singhs who owned a glass factory there. They had guns with them. After three or four days, the situation stabilized a bit. Then we heard that trucks full of corpses of Hindu men and women had been brought near the rail tracks. We used to serve as volunteers in many situations; we also helped to cremate bodies. So we went to see what had happened. There were these

trucks escorted by a battalion of Mussalman police. They [the police] were simply standing there inert. They told us that they would not arrange to cremate the bodies. We would have to do the horrible job. We decided to unload the truck and carry the dead bodies to the local cremation ground. We took off our chappals and climbed onto the truck.

'There were heaps of bodies—corpses—all stark naked. Some were rotting, some fresh. The putrid smell—it was ghastly! We stretched a plastic sheet on the ground and covered our mouth and nostrils with our own shirts. Then we started unloading the bodies. Here I saw a terrible scene. Firstly, there were two small bodies, those of children, but their heads had been chopped off. And then there was the naked body of a woman. Look at me, please [pause]. The naked body of a woman! She had vermillion on her hair. Her entire body was mutilated. She had been tortured and portions of her body were gone [pause]. Look at these places [moved his hands briskly to indicate the breasts and the genitals] here—and the lower abdomen—do you understand? Flesh had been torn off, bitten off from her body. I do not know what happened to me. I thought, we should keep documents. In those times, cameras were not to be procured so easily. Only one of our friends had a camera. I told him to get it. He ran home and brought it. I still remember it was a Rolliflex—or may be a Rollicod. My friend told that he would not be able to take a picture as his head was reeling. I had never pressed the shutter of any camera before. Yet I took the snaps. The naked bodies of the men, the mutilated body of the woman, torn apart at places! I still have the photographs. Wait, I will show you.'

Barun went and brought a large envelope from the steel almirah that was in the same room. While he was taking out the envelope, some papers and other things fell from the rack. I told him that he need not hurry; I might look at the photographs the next day as well. Nevertheless, he insisted on my seeing the pictures immediately. 'I must show them to you,' he insisted. 'Then you will know that I am not lying. I will tell you the truth and the whole truth and nothing but the whole truth. I have got these pictures published, you know.' Then he showed me the picture of a number of dead bodies lying side by side. The other photographs were elsewhere, he said.

> 'The truck was standing near the rail track. A train stopped at the signal. Many people got down from the train to enquire into the matter. One man fell unconscious seeing the body of the woman. Only six post-mortems were done. The rest were simply burnt. There was paucity of wood. Dhunuram and Brajalal Singh gave the wood . . .'

I asked Barun where these people had been killed and why the bodies had been brought to Dhaka. He replied that he did not know where they came from, probably from the outskirts of the town. Some young leaders of the Muslim League happened to be his friends. He had asked them why these bodies were not sent to the local cremation ground. They laughed and said, 'To threaten you people, so that you Hindus leave this land.' And they were successful, Barun asserted. Famous Hindus who taught at Dhaka University, for example, Professor Junargarh, left the country after the riots. The Muslim rioters used to boast of the violence they had committed, proudly recounting details of the brutalities. Three Nepalese policemen had been assigned at a nearby Muslim locality. They were 'Kafir', so the Muslims lay in ambush for them. Two of them escaped, but one was caught. Barun described the torture inflicted on this young Nepalese. 'Do you know what is at the back of all the violence committed by the Mussalmans? They would inflict all sorts of brutalities on those who do not follow Islam,' Barun commented.

> 'They banged on the Nepalese cop's chest and observed that it was strong and solid. So they placed a chopper used for cutting goats on his chest and banged it in with a wooden hammer. Thus, they slit his chest to send him to hell. *Dojkh*–they call it. This was the story they told us. I asked them why they were describing these horrors to us. They said, "Go back and tell your people that if by the grace of Allah we have Pakistan, this will be done to all of you." '

By the end of September, the situation was under control. Barun rushed to Noakhali to his parents. Near Luxam, he saw thousands of Muslims shouting 'Pakistan Jindabad'. He also saw sprayers and tins of inflammables–kerosene, petrol and other things–being sent to various places, especially to the Muslim League offices. He told his father that they should be cautious, as there had been brutal riots at Dhaka. His father, however, believed that nothing would happen in their neighbourhood since the Muslims were their friends. Actually, nothing happened there.

When riots began in Kolkata all communications were cut off; telegraph and all conveyance through roads and rivers were stopped. The Hindus in East Bengal were butchered. The outer world came to know of it only about two weeks later. Gandhi reached Noakhali on 27 November 1946. Barun's maternal uncles were Congress members. They accompanied Gandhi to various camps. So did young Barun. Gandhi, according to Barun, went to relatively safe places whereas the volunteers went to the remote villages. There had been mass conversion. Cows had been slaughtered and the blood poured over Shivalingas. Many people had been forcibly converted and were confused about their own religious identity; they did not know whether they could return to their own religion. During this religious crisis, the Ramkrishna Mission published a small booklet where they declared that abducted women and forcibly converted persons would be acceptable in Hindu society without any *prayaschitta* (Hindu ritual absolution for known and unknown sins). At this point, he got up, showed me a copy of the booklet, saying, 'This is the only copy of this book. It provides substantial proof of the occurrence of abductions and conversions.'

At Noakhali, the young man saw a second incident that infuriated him. 'The barbarians had imprisoned a Hindu lady in a room with walls of 'muli' bamboos and were watching her through the gaps. Her house had been burnt down, husband and children killed. The woman was out of her mind. She was crying and beating her head on the wall. Her sari was half torn; her mouth was foaming. The Mussalman men sat around laughing and jeering at the victim. They were enjoying the comic show enacted by the "wife of the malaun". One Mussalman man had decided to have her forcibly married after the fun was over. We could not rescue her.'

A third incident that Barun reported concerned a family who had come from Noakhali. The woman of the family had been abducted. She had one son and two daughters. The surviving family members told people that the mother of the three children had died. A mock *shraddh* (Hindu ritual performed after death) was arranged for the 'dead' woman. While the son was undergoing *mundan* (shaving of the head) he suddenly cried out, 'My mother is not dead!' The elders of the family silenced him and forcibly made him continue with the rituals. The boy performed shraddh for his living mother.

Barun thinks that all these incidents ignited his passion to record every bit of information he could gather about Muslim brutality against Hindus. He pursued his aim zealously. In the meantime, Partition took place. On 15 August 1947, he was sitting sadly at the doorstep of his house. A few Muslim men came on bicycles and called him names: 'Hey, you son of the "malaun", why haven't you hoisted Pakistani flags?' He told them that there were no flags available at the market; all were sold out. Then he remembered that these fellows had boasted earlier that if Pakistan was created, the college building would be wrapped in flags. He recalled their proud statement in the typical local Muslim dialect—'*Insallah, jadi Khodar hafeje Pakistan kayem hoy, college barhi pataka diya dhaikya dimu.*' He decided to go and see if the college building had really been draped in flags. He found only one small flag there. Flags were in short supply.

'It was but the beginning of scarcity—the immediate effect of Pakistan. Rice, wheat, biscuits—nothing was available at the ration shop. We did not get pen or paper, even.' Barun went on describing how the Hindus were singled out for oppression, how their houses were requisitioned by the government, and how the Dhaka Collegiate School was taken over by the Muslims and all Hindu boys were given transfer certificates. The headmaster of another school kindly admitted these boys to his school so they could sit for the final examination.

Barun soon became an ardent seeker of information. He used to assist the Swamiji of the Ramkrishna Mission by reading out hundreds of letters that poured in from remote areas as well as from towns and cities. From the letters he learnt about the persecution and torture that had taken place. In rural areas, fish, rice and coconuts of the Hindus were being looted and the owners were threatened if they tried to protest.

Barun recalled a significant political stance taken by those known as 'untouchables' at that time, now called Scheduled Castes (SC). He narrated the hypocritical role played by a SC leader who in the Sylhet election supported the Muslim League. After the election however, the Scheduled Castes became one of the most tortured communities of East Pakistan. Barun learnt that the torture was not limited to seizing their property forcibly. The women were the main targets. For example, Barun recalled one peasant complaining to the MLA that the local Muslim men had come to his son and bade him to sleep elsewhere since they themselves would sleep with his wife on that night. Another man said that his son was arrested for being a 'Connist' (this poor illiterate fellow could not even pronounce the word 'Communist'). This peasant also reported that the local Muslims were sleeping by turn with his daughter-in-law. The Muslims were, Barun explained, against the Communists because they did not believe in God. One Sunday a truck of local hooligans came to the party office and beat up the 'comrades'.

Barun recalled how after Partition, when many Hindus had already left the country, the Muslims wanted to mix with the remaining Hindus to learn the ways of a finer culture, though they hated the Hindus. They wanted to learn the recipes for sweets: 'pitha', 'patisapta' and 'puli'. However, Barun recalled with a smile, they could not achieve the same flavour and taste because 'all of their utensils smelt of *gost* [meat] and they cooked the sweets in the same pot where beef was cooked.'

Riots started in Dhaka on 10 February 1950. Dhaka Radio was broadcasting communal statements, while the foreign secretaries of India and Pakistan were sitting in a meeting for peace. The killings started virtually while the leaders were talking peace. Barun knew a number of highly placed persons of both religions. He was acquainted with a few Pakistan government officers and through them came in contact with a number of ministers. In 1950, one of his relatively influential acquaintances requested the foreign minister of Pakistan to look after his family. Thereafter, the Dhaka police used to enquire after their welfare once a week. At this time, there was an Ispahani plane shuttling between Dhaka and Kolkata, taking Hindus to West Bengal and carrying Muslims back. It was hard to get tickets. Barun happened to know the manager of Oriental Airways who helped him to arrange accommodation for those persons who were in real need, particularly children and women. 'And here I saw the selfishness among the Hindus. Since there were limited seats available in the plane, the families had to choose among the members. I have seen people sending their 40-year-old daughter to safety, keeping the 18-year-old daughter-in-law amidst the danger of violation.'

Barun recalled that women suffered the most during this migration. Young Muslim men took charge of 'searching' women at the airport, and under the official guise, they harassed and assaulted young women. Barun could find no way to prevent it; at the most, he could warn the families. 'At this time, I saw a horrible scene. A lady was staggering across the road with an eight- or ten-year-old boy. Her sari was wet with blood. Her face was pale. Her family said she had been tortured. At that time, I did not know the meaning of rape. Her husband had been away from home and a group of Mussalman men had forced their way in and raped her. She had touched their feet and called them her brothers, but they were merciless.' Barun rang up one of his influential acquaintances for assistance. It was apparent that the woman needed immediate medical attention, but the doctor was not available. Barun has no idea whether she survived or not.

He described another incident of a Hindu locality being attacked by Muslim hooligans. People came running to those parts of the town that were relatively safe for Hindus. Here Barun saw a woman crying piteously as she had left her infant son behind. The Muslims were looting their house. Her mother was consoling her, insisting she should forget that she ever had a baby. 'Consider him stillborn,' the older woman was entreating her daughter. But the mother was inconsolable. This pathetic scene kindled strong emotion in Barun. It was as if an inner voice ordered him, 'Sacrifice your life for the benefit of others.' He assured the lady that he would find her son. He wrapped a *gamchha* around his face and rushed in the guise of a Muslim to the mahalla where the Muslims were ransacking houses. He found the specific house and the child was still lying there unharmed. Other Muslim men were rummaging through the house. Barun shouted, '*Inshallah*, I'll take this son of the malaun, circumcise him and make him a Mussalman.' Nobody thought it unusual. He carried the child safely in his arms to its mother. 'The lady fell at my feet. I remembered Swamiji–it is by his grace that I have been able to help others.' Barun recalled.

Then he narrated an incident with a different tone. 'It was the 18th of February and I was standing in front of my gate. An elderly Mussalman man approached me and asked me if there was any vacant house in the locality. He was speaking in Hindi. He had fled from India with his family. I found an unoccupied house for him. Within a few days, I became very close to his family. He loved me like his own son. After a few days, the Mussalmans attacked our neighbourhood. I took shelter in his house. This man was very handsome. I could not pass for his relative. He advised me to claim that I was his servant, if the Mussalmans enquired about me. It was because of him that I was saved.

'You see, I do not hate all Mussalmans. I have high regard for this man. I still pray for him on the day of Mahalaya and observe the "Kabar chiyarat" for him.' Then he added: 'But don't think that by this I mean I look upon the Mussalmans as pardonable. Some people are exceptional everywhere.'

Barun remembered the death of Gandhi. Initially, like most people, he adored the Mahatma. Afterwards, Barun reconsidered the rational behind Godse's trial, started admiring Godse and abandoned his respect for Gandhi. 'Gandhi did a lot of things for the awareness of our countrymen, but I do not like him for his duplicity,' he finally commented.

Soon after, Barun came to Kolkata aboard a plane with a group of migrants. He had intended to go back, and only had the set of clothes he was wearing and a paltry sum of money. But immediately after this, the India-Pakistan air service was disrupted and his uncles who lived in Kolkata did not allow him to return. His parents were still at Noakhali.

Here too he pursued his documentation of injustice. 'I used to go to Sealdah Station every day. Such a nasty and putrid situation! You could smell the faeces from Rajabazar.' He described how the wretched refugees were carried in trucks to different camps. Often families were split up. Barun would warn the families to try and stay together, and he would request the truck drivers to wait for the whole family to get on the same truck. One family had come from a remote village of Khulna. The Muslims had tortured them in various ways, pulling off their clothes in the name of searching them. After walking for 8-10 miles, the husband, wife, three daughters and a son took shelter in a Muslim house. It was a moonlit night. Suddenly the father noticed that the girls were missing. Panic-stricken, he asked where his daughters were, and was told that they had been 'escorted' out by the local goons for some 'fun' in the moonlight. They might be returned in the morning once the amusement was over. The parents cried and begged for daughters' return, but to no avail. Threatened, they had to run for their life, leaving the three girls behind. Every day they came to Sealdah in the hope of finding them, but in vain. The mother went insane and one moonlit night silently walked out of her home.

One day Barun was sitting at Madhyamgram Station when he saw a woman refugee with an infant. The baby had been delivered on the way and was in a critical condition, suffering from severe dehydration and starvation. Barun bought some milk from a teashop and gave it to the mother. She dipped the corner of a dirty cloth in the milk and tried to feed the child, but it was too late. The baby died before their eyes. Barun could not beat the wailing of the mother. He left the place.

Barun believed that it was his duty to fight against the evil in his own way—'I must resist those who drove me out of my motherland,' he declared. He was also strongly against the 'hypocrisy of the political persons in general'; the Congress and the Communists. He named one leftist leader of West Bengal whose father had been forced to dig his own grave at Noakhali. 'And now he is a secularist! Sometimes I feel like beating up these secular persons,' he exclaimed.

Even today Barun spends all his time and energy collecting information from various sources on injustices perpetrated by Muslims. He spoke of an incident he had heard about. Muslims had attacked the RSP office in Dhaka. They reportedly cut one man to pieces and threw his flesh from the first floor so that the dogs and crows could consume it. 'Of course, I must admit that I have not seen it, but I have heard about it,' said Barun.

'I have excellent contacts in Bangladesh,' he exclaimed. He gets reports on the recent political chaos, how the Muslims are systematically wiping out the Hindus by forcing Hindu girls to marry Muslims, and converting Hindus on various pleas. The main victims of torture and coercion are, of course, women. He cited the case of a Muslim lady in Kolkata who confided to him that she was a Hindu girl who had been forced into marriage by a Muslim to bring 'refined culture and education' into the family.

Barun laughingly stated that though he is anti-Muslim, he has saved Muslim lives as well. He gave details of some such incidents during and even long after Partition. He said with pride that many sick people from Bangladesh come to him and he arranges for their treatment. He is also the local guardian of some of their children. When I asked him why he saves Muslims, he replied, 'It is my dharma to save anybody in distress. In such cases, religion is unimportant and humanity is what counts. Look, I am not a secular person, but I do not discriminate when somebody is in trouble.'

Barun, being totally committed to his cause, has an air of satisfaction and self-esteem. He talks confidently and challenges any opposition that might question his conviction. He takes pride in following his ideology, and often smiled with deep satisfaction while talking about his mission. He was certain of what he wanted to convey, and led me to his topics in his own way, not distracted much by my interruptions. His obvious enjoyment in talking about his experiences probably came from his emotional fervour.

At one point, Barun asked if his narration was of any use to me. As I remarked that I was intrigued by his accounts, and appreciated how much he had seen in his life, he said, 'Yes, I have seen so much. I have been seeing things since my early days. I am like a vulture who watches everything from the top.' To impress his points on me he was occasionally repetitive. He was particularly keen to have me visualize the violent scenes he had witnessed; he described some of them in detail a good number of times.

Throughout our meeting, I felt Barun to be an authoritarian yet affectionate person, with his own pattern of values and ideas. I observed he was soft and caring with his family. His care also extended to me. The first interview session continued till quite late at night. He was concerned about how I would go home, and although I assured him it was not a problem, he rang me up an hour later to ensure that I had returned safe.

Inner Perceptions

Both Shashanko and Barun were supporters of Hindutva politics and repudiated Congress and Communists alike. Both were self-declared anti-Muslim individuals. Their antagonism persisted despite having personal Muslim friends whom they loved dearly, and despite having had their lives saved by Muslims whom they recalled with gratitude. Yet, the psychological backdrop of the communal attitude of each of these two individuals had subtle discrepancies arising out of their personality and cognitive disposition. The anti-Muslim attitude of these two men was apparently the same, but in their inner perceptions they were poles apart. Let us scrutinize the nature of animosity towards the Muslims exhibited by each of them.

Shashanko had personal negative experiences: though his family was spared direct bloodshed, the material loss was substantial. Furthermore, the preparation for a possible attack by Muslims and the tension within the house were probably enough to traumatize the young child not yet in his teens. The natural antipathy thus developed was however punctuated by the sacrifice and assistance extended by Muslims during the crisis: the three men who endangered their own lives to save the children of the other community. Therefore, a seed of contradiction was sown at this early juncture. He was the victim of aggression as well as the recipient of grace from his Muslim neighbours.

Here I emphasize Shashanko's style of delivery, which had an element of drama. The storybook sequence of the reported events, the memory of the valour of every person, the uncle conferring with his 'Thakur' before sending the children to safety, and the mention of the royal Hindu heritage were less like a real-life description of a severe crisis and more like a secondary elaboration[13] developed over years by the family; a sequence of events told and retold and shaped in coherent images by the family members as a common family myth. As a pre-adolescent, it is likely that Shashanko was confused by the situation; nevertheless, the chaos and erupting emotions in the family under the circumstances were curiously missing from his narration, which had a mythical quality.

This is certainly not to say that the events recalled by Shashanko did not happen. What I mean is that the details of chaos and uncertainty might have been glossed over in his narration in favour of a well-organized description of adventure and courage. Yet, the same speaker revealed more spontaneous and mundane emotions when, after my query, he talked about his parents. Initially the same type of idealization was revealed in his general eulogy of his parents. Then little bits of memory born out of day-to-day interaction emerged gradually, such as his mother being fond of molasses or his father's resistance to being labelled a 'refugee'.

The oscillation between the idealized and the felt was most prominent in Shashanko's exposition of the attitude towards Muslims. He was expressing his ideological belief with reference to historical and political events. Here he was clearly following the Hindutva doctrine. Between the lines, however, he was extrapolating another theme. On the one hand was his experience of being politically and socially subjugated, and on the other was a kind of undoing; a reparation for his aggression, as he declared repeatedly that he did not really hate Muslims.

Did he or did he not? It is really difficult to tell. It is possible that his assertion of not hating Muslims was more an expression of surface decency rather than a genuine sentiment; or, it could be a streak of guilt. Dissatisfaction with life, particularly with reference to the socio-political situation in India and West Bengal, was his general mood.

Whence this dissatisfaction? Partly, of course, it came from personal difficulties in the political and social domains of his life. To look at it from a developmental angle, however, the roots of this dissatisfaction might be found in his cognitive schema from his young days. His glossing over the smaller nuances during a period of chaos, the dramatic and mythical style of his narration, and his emphatic and generalized statements about political ideologies combined to indicate an inner preference for the stereotyped and the idealized. I would call it a preference for forced organization,[14] a tendency to cut off the distracters and the loose ends, but with the qualification that this organization seemed to arise less out of an inner calm than from an unconscious concern for presenting a rational public persona.

Shashanko was neither introspective nor emotionally exploring in his narration. Unlike Dipendu and Manish, his inner life, what he loved, his anxiety were but sparingly revealed in his story. One might say that the face he wanted to present to me was one of a political spokesperson, to put across the point of view of the ideological cause that he thought he believed in. However, his ideological statements were laced with his personal resentment and bitterness.

Shashanko was apparently successful in his career, but somewhere he bore a grudge against certain categories of people. One category was, of course, the Muslims who had suddenly become powerful and disrupted his familial stability in Chandpur. He was against the Congress in India during the Emergency. Then he was against the Communists who, according to him, 'are complete tyrants and torture you cruelly if you go against them'. He reported having been threatened by the local CPI(M) leaders when he opted to stand for election as an opposition candidate. Why did he repeatedly thrust blame upon specific groups, and what was there in the doctrine of Hindutva that appealed to him?

Before trying to answer these questions from my data, I want to draw attention to two characteristics of Shashanko's personality as revealed in his narration. One was the appeal that success in life held for him. From the very start, he had aimed for a high position. Curiously, his ambition was fired by the life of none other than Muhammad Ali Jinnah, after he read his biography *Dialogue with a Giant* by Beverly Nichols. For Shashanko, this Jinnah was the ideal, the successful Jinnah, not the Muslim Jinnah. Like Jinnah, Shashanko spent a few years in England for higher studies before returning to build a successful career. At the same time, his resentment was directed most strongly towards those Indian Muslims who in his opinion undeservedly enjoyed superior status.

The second feature is Shashanko's emotional response to Partition. While he lamented his uprooting, his major feelings were those of confusion and the meaninglessness of life. He recalled an incident he witnessed in East Bengal where an insane man called Ramesh was exploited for the selfish purpose of demonstrating communal cleavage. Ramesh had always been jeered at by Hindus and Muslims alike. But during the political upheaval he was converted to Islam. A big procession was organized by the Muslims in the town with Ramesh at the front; they claimed that he had lost his mind because the Hindus had neglected him, and now it was the Muslims who accepted him.

As Ramesh was converted to Islam, he must have been declared to be of sound mind, temporarily at least! He was bestowed with some fancy Muslim name too. After the procession was over, of course, Ramesh reverted to his original position of being persecuted by Hindus and Muslims alike.

Shashanko interjected this event during his narration; probably because he felt that this incident symbolized what Partition did to its victims. Partition gave a different tinge to the interpretation of everything, including madness. One lost one's innocence: the right to think independently. 'I would have led the life of my choice if we had remained in our own place. It may or may not have been different from what it is now,' he said. 'But that would have been determined by my own desire.' Partition robbed him of his free will and control over his own life.

I think these characteristics, the feeling of being unjustifiably deprived of control, and the wish to attain exemplary success, were decisive factors in Shashanko's life. The chaos and insecurity of undefined identity were agonizing to him. He preferred to overlook the uncertainties of the time and to emphasize the idealized courage demonstrated by his family because that would defend him against the loss of control he and his family had suffered in the face of the attack. Even in later life, a residue of this insecurity lingered; he had to find some ideological and moral opposites to blame, he had to create this 'bad other'.

It is here, I suppose, that the ideal of a Hindu nation–particularly with its links to the glorified past of India–appealed to him. Through identification with this Hindu past, he could develop an identity that was meaningful to him as it could not be obliterated; it was inherited by birth and therefore indelible (in fact, I think what pained him in the case of Ramesh was the obliteration of the poor man's basic identity).

Yet, this defensive manoeuvre could not fully satisfy him. Shashanko remains pessimistic about the future. This pessimism might be related to another aspect of his personality: his holding the British as the ideal. Not only had his ambition always been to study in England, but also during the conversation he often referred to what was happening in England: how the position of Asians had changed with reference to their acceptability and affiliations, how they now participated in British politics. The colonial past probably still lingers within Shashanko's heart,[15] and he is vexed with the conundrum of Indian politics as it stands today. Indeed, he considers Christianity a realistic and relatively more acceptable religion than Islam. The discrepancy between the present state of England and his internalized ideal, and his constant unconscious comparison with this ideal, may be a secondary source of dissatisfaction.

Barun seemed a happier person. There is no apparent reason for him to be happier, as far as his financial, social or political situation is concerned. He is ostensibly not as well off as Shashanko. Nevertheless, Barun has a mission in life, and he seems alive with it. Notably, Barun was one of the few in my sample who did not start his narration with memories of his homeland and did not dwell on its past glory.

His narration was characterized by three main themes. Firstly was his emotionally charged and vivid description of the tortures inflicted on women. It is interesting that he spoke more of the torture of women than of men. This might have stemmed from my gender, assuming my greater sensitivity ('as a woman, you would feel ...'), or from his personal preoccupation.

Secondly was his fervent idealism that he declared had been with him from his very early days. He even suggested it was a tendency brought forward from a previous life. 'I think I was a bit unusual from the very beginning; maybe from my previous birth. I always had in my mind the words of Swami Vivekananda who instructed his followers to devote their life for the benefit of others.' Barun had been inspired by Subhas Chandra Bose and Vivekananda, as well as by Abraham Lincoln. I found this last influence interesting, as he admired the role of Lincoln in supporting the blacks, a minority community in America. How did he reconcile the idealization of a man supporting the minority community in America with his own anti-minority role in India, I wondered. Then it struck me that probably Barun had in his mind the minority community, not of India, but of Pakistan and now Bangladesh. Psychologically, he is still in the pre-migration phase of his life. One might say he has never come out of that time and place.

Thirdly was his dislike of Gandhi and impassioned admiration for Godse, Gandhi's assassin. This was, of course, closely bound to his ideal of Hinduism and his perception that Gandhi's efforts to reconcile the two communities were hypocritical and motivated by the selfish purpose of maintaining his image as 'Mahatma'. To Barun, Godse's act was one of meritorious sacrifice for the ultimate benefit of the country.

Barun has never stood for election. He is an activist in constant pursuit of information that reveals the negative qualities of the Muslim community. While he is unequivocal in his idea that the Muslims are the root of India's troubles, he still upholds the higher values of humanity. For a person in danger there is no religion, he said, and he acted on this, saving the lives of Muslims during riots. He still prays for the Muslim man who lent him a hand in need. Yet he has no confusion or guilt about his dislike of the community. He seems certain as to where they are acceptable and where not.

Both Barun and Shashanko discerned the enemy in the Muslims following the political canons of Hindutva. Nevertheless, their reasons were different. For Shashanko, the motivating force was apprehension, deprivation from a smooth and glorious life, confusion, desire for success, grievance against those responsible for his personal loss and resentment against those who usurped higher positions by exploiting their religion. Thus, his life-view grew out of personal rancour supported by narcissistic considerations.[16] His ideology was held within a relatively personal frame: his professional as well as political career. He was propelled by a fear of losing: losing control, position and property—a fear that grew out of his personal trauma of dislocation. Probably he was uncomfortable also with his own aggression towards the constructed others, hence the repetitive declaration that he did not hate Muslims.

Barun was committed and unequivocal in his aggression. He had always been straightforward, he claimed, even when threatened. 'Those who know me know that I cannot be moved by fear,' he declared. 'Write down all I say,' he insisted. His confidence probably came from multiple sources. One was his unfailing conviction that he was right; a moral strength. The second was his interpersonal network, the social contacts of various degrees of intimacy, which included both the communities. Indeed, he took pride in his thorough knowledge of Muslim culture and his ability to pass for a Muslim. There was a third source–an offshoot of these two–that contributed to set Barun apart from his fellow believers. Barun claims that his life has been steered by Vivekananda's philosophy that one should sacrifice oneself for the welfare of others. In trying to reconcile love for others with hatred for Muslims, Barun found a way to hate for an altruistic reason.

With this understanding, we can try to reconstruct the developmental dynamics of Barun's declared anti-Muslim and anti-secular stance. Young Barun witnessed violence and brutality at a very sensitive age. The episode of the truck full of dead bodies was a turning point. At that time, he was about fourteen and though already habituated through his social work to do 'troublesome jobs' like assisting in cremation and cleaning neighbourhoods, he was naïve about sexuality, particularly sexual violence.

Specifically, I think that this sensitive teenager's wrath was overdetermined. One source of anger was simply the humanitarian reaction at the sight of the perishing bodies. It was simple anger at those who had tortured and murdered innocent people of his religion. A second and more complex source of hate was, probably, directly related to his seeing the naked mutilated female corpse. Barun told me repeatedly that this scene did something to him. The intensity of his reaction was apparent from the youngster's sudden decision to document the event photographically. I consider this gesture of paramount psychological importance.

Let us visualize the situation of young Barun as an enthusiastic member of a team of social workers faced with a truck full of dead bodies. Here Barun was exposed to shocking sights: the most terrible being the naked mutilated body of a woman. This dead woman was probably Barun's first exposure to stark sexuality. And what an exposure it was! The body, that could have been a sight of beauty the subject of a teenager's fantasy, had been violated and rendered lifeless by others in an act of vengeance and cruelty.

What could be the impact of this scene on the teenage boy?[17] Sexuality and aggression are two aspects of personality that oppose each other in the conscious state, yet are often intertwined in one's unconscious. When a young child is exposed to a sexually violent scene, a number of strong emotions are likely to be generated in him that would, however, immediately be repressed. Based on the theoretical discourse,[18] I shall try to trace the tentative path of the emotions aroused by such an experience. The first overwhelming emotional reaction of any sexually mature person to the sudden sight of female nakedness would be sexual excitement. But such a sight, by itself, may be sufficiently disturbing for a naïve youngster.[19] In the case of violent sexuality, the excitement may immediately be replaced by twofold guilt: the natural guilt of a normal teenager at his surge of excitement on seeing an uncovered body;[20] and the guilt emerging out of the conflict between aggression and sexuality, from the realization that the source of excitement is unacceptable and unnatural: the perishing body, a mutilated corpse. The sexual sensation, if any, would immediately be severely condemned by the super-ego. Indeed, for a boy in his early adolescence the entire experience would be too pungent and likely to crush permanently aspects of his softer sentiments. It is likely to even result in a chaotic disarray of his sense of security and attachment as a covetable corollary to sexuality. The resultant upsurge of emotion, already unavailable to language, would be further complicated by the boy's probable identification with the aggressor; the unconscious sadomasochistic impulses lurking within are likely to be strongly stimulated by the view of the tortured body.[21] This in turn would receive further admonition from the super-ego. Under the circumstances, the boy would have a strong urge to undo his impulsive feelings. Memories of his emotional turmoil would be pushed into the unconscious, and whatever traces came up to the conscious level would immediately be repressed. At the same time, cautionary defensive measures would be taken by the boy's traumatized ego, one of which would be to generate extreme hate towards the original aggressor, because through hate the maximum distancing of the self from the aggressor would be possible.

One can never be sure if this is what happened to young Barun. There were two significant features in his presentation that might serve as non-verbal clues. One, was his insistence on my looking at him while placing his palms on his chest and around his stomach so that I could appreciate exactly where the body had been mutilated. Was this an indication of his re-enaction of the scene in his mind: an unconscious preoccupation with viewing it and thus coping with trauma through repetition? Two, was his focus on documentation. He told me a number of times that he was a recorder of events; he wanted to show me the documents so that I would know he was telling the truth. I wonder why he had this concern with keeping documents as proof? One hypothetical reason might be that the documents served to pacify his own super-ego that could be excessively punitive if his complex emotional history was laid bare. The photographs could serve to prove to himself that he was not guilty. There was a third feature as well. He mentioned more than once the vermillion in the woman's hair, signifying her married status as a Hindu woman. I am not in a position to relate it confidently to the Oedipal complex and the sadomasochistic desire originating therefrom. I have too little data about Barun's childhood at hand. Prima facie, however, the married status of the woman might have added to his discomfort.

In sum, it may be said that Barun, as witness to a scene of sexualized violence at a tender age of fourteen, had enough cause to suffer severe trauma and, hence, to face strong rejection from his own super-ego that did not accept his natural upsurge of libido mingled with aggression.[22] The guilt generated in turn could be cured by a secondary hate[23] using the mechanism of projection: in this case the conviction that the Muslim community is the epitome of cruelty. It may not be too illogical a conclusion that Barun's altruistic tendencies, present from his early days, took a different turn, chose a different object after this shocking event. The appeal of the stringent principles of active Hindutva for him probably lay in this need to handle such perturbing feelings. I am reminded here of René Spitz's notion of 'derailment of dialogue' in the context of traumatic moments in one's life. Spitz suggestsed that trauma with stimulus excess may result in internal chaos that is handled defensively with remembering parts of the trauma a bit too much, and acting against it at the same time.[24] Indeed, Barun did not have to move far from his habitual pattern of altruism and sacrifice. On the one hand, he retained his natural generosity and compassion for humankind, and on the other, he simply projected outward, the aggression and violence. He started counting the killings and sexual assaults perpetrated by Muslims that would serve the dual purpose of vicarious unconscious gratification and atonement, thus procuring the appreciation of the super-ego for being a meticulously moral and righteous person.

A *Note on My Own Confusion*

A special note about Barun at the end of all this. A friend of mine, who read this part of Barun's story, seriously doubted my proposition. He suggests that the entire chain of events might be concocted; the 'fantasy of a fundamentalist'. Being a politically involved person, this friend asserts that he knows people who have a tendency to describe sexually loaded imaginary stories of torture by the other community, as if they themselves have witnessed it. The narrative feat of Barun, my friend thinks, is partly politically motivated, and partly an imagination. I could not completely deny his perspective. Of course, when I listened to Barun, I did not feel the descriptions to be false, though at places, it may have been exaggerated and coloured. Yet, after this suggestion, I am uncertain, since in hindsight, I feel that there might have been some verbal and non-verbal features that could be interpreted as cues to his fantasy. I admit that my reaction to Barun's story could be erroneous. Yet, I decided not to change my position, since, even if Barun's story was partly false and fantasized, the comments I have made about his unconscious focus would continue to remain probable. Only its origin in reality would shift from the experience of sexualized violence to some other real component of his personal history, unknown to us. However, with the inadequate data at hand, I can end only with the question and not with the answer.

BALANCE IS MORE THAN MONEY DEEP: ACHINTYA AND TARAPADA

We have discussed a pair of respondents who had similar experiences and another pair whose political and ideological attitudes were similar; and have shown how they differed in their inner interpretations of religious discrimination and intention. For some respondents, however, religion was never a salient domain of life. Balance in such persons came from their natural sympathy for fellow human beings. Here we discuss two men who, though poles apart in the external aspects of their lives–financial, political or experiential–shared a common core, both of them having resolved the aggression generated in Partition with similar grace.

Achintya's Story

Achintya has probably had the most successful career among my respondents. Equipped with professional qualifications coupled with honesty and intelligence, he has held very high positions in the corporate sector in India and abroad. Even after retirement, he remained active and was associated with a number of social service organizations. When I contacted him , he invited me to his flat in an upper-class neighbourhood of south Kolkata.

I went to his place on the appointed morning. Achintya was a sturdy and pleasant looking man. He appeared confident and at ease. He was dressed informally and greeted me with a warm smile. He spoke deliberately and slowly; he had the air of a person of authority who was habituated to being obeyed. He enquired if I would like to ask him any questions. When I told him I wished to know about his life—before, around and after partition—he smiled and nodded, 'Ah, I understand. You would prefer me to guide you along my memories.'

Achintya's family lived in a village of Barishal. The majority of the village people were caste Hindus, but many Muslims also lived there. The family was educated and rich with plenty of land. People called them 'the educated babu family'.

Achintya's grandfather was a kaviraj, but he did not make a lot of money. His father was very enterprising. He was interested in land as property, and acquired plenty of it. They were not concerned about future livelihood, but wanted the children to become refined through study. Achintya's father died early, and the elder son who was fifteen years senior to Achintya became his guardian. This brother was an excellent student and an educationist.

> 'The times were quite different. We were not concerned about our future or career, as you have to be now. We had land and we thought that was sufficient. That would truly have sufficed if Partition had not taken place. But we knew we had to study, both for our own development as human beings, and as worthy descendants and keeper of the heritage of our family.'

Achintya spoke of the general political atmosphere of the period in the context of the freedom struggle, and famous leaders of the movement like Anupam Sen of Chandrahar village and Monoranjan Gupta of the *Jugantar* group. Achintya described how young children at that time were recruited by the leaders as messengers and spies. In the same context, he recalled other important persons in the locality, his school and friends. He also mentioned the condition of the Muslims. 'Most of the students were Hindu. The Muslims were rarely educated and were often extremely poor. They were employed as farmers by the rich Hindus, or as anglers, or boatmen. Many lived by cutting palm trees and selling molasses.'

Then Achintya recounted his own involvement in the freedom movement, and his adventurousness. In 1942, he had already become seriously involved in the secret activities of the freedom fighters. His father was aware of it and tacitly supported him. Achintya was arrested and released on bail, but was interned at home. Therefore, he could not sit for the Matriculation examination. At this time his father suddenly passed away. The Sub-Divisional Officer (SDO), who was his father's friend, arranged to shift Achintya to the precincts of a certain religious order, a closed resort where he was apparently free, but a constant watch could be kept on him. The SDO arranged matters so that he could sit for the examination, yet no law was violated.

Achintya spoke about his parents and family in general. 'My father was a supporter of education for all. He also used to support the freedom fighters. He secretly saved the lives of quite a few. He forbade us to tell Ma anything. "Women cannot keep secrets," he would say.' Theirs was a relatively liberal family, Achintya said. His mother and aunts too were literate. They used to read the *Ramayana*, and books like *Manasamangal* and anything else available for women. They were homemakers, concerned with the family, but used to help others in the village on various occasions. His mother was active and socially sensitive, though within limits. Being a natural extrovert, Achintya was only moderately close to his mother. 'I had relatively less interaction with Ma. She stayed at home and I remained outside. I remember she used to read the *Ramayana* continuously for one month.' In a different context, he spoke about his elder sister and about his brother and sister-in-law. He described the selflessness and saintly character of the latter couple and was very proud of them. He was quite emotional as he spoke about his family.

Achintya spoke about communal relations before and after the disruption. 'Father had helped a number of meritorious Muslim boys to continue their studies. Two of them graduated and became Presidents of the Union Board. They told my mother, "Don't worry, nothing will harm you while we are here." That is why we did not come to West Bengal immediately. Then one of these two men was murdered as he tried to save Hindu families. Twenty-one Hindus were killed in a single house and this noble man tried to intervene. The Muslim thugs killed him. After that, we were a bit afraid and started our attempts to shift our family here.'

Achintya pointed out that the rioters came as a rule from distant places. The local Muslims could not think of harming their neighbours, as relations with them were excellent. During the Durga Puja traditionally arranged in their house, the Navami festival was observed by the Muslims. They sang the 'zari songs' through the whole night and took food only at three in the morning. They did not take rice; they consumed lots of sweets, coconut, other fruits, and chira or pressed rice. They even took the *prasad*, the food offered to God during worship, and then distributed to the devotees, which usually Muslims would not accept.

Some practices of superstition and discrimination also prevailed. These were, Achintya mused, the odd and irrational elements of life. For example, Achintya's father used to travel overnight by boat. The boatmen were Muslim and they cooked for him. Yet, the same boatmen were not allowed inside the house. 'Actually, I think that financial status was more important. Most of the cases of violent interaction involved either financial strife or some personal issue like intercommunity romance,' observed Achintya.

He recalled an incident of prejudice. 'Discrimination had penetrated every stratum of social existence. Resistance is not that easy, but we tried to resist. A boy was sitting for *namaj* with his hands outstretched, and a Hindu boy put some dirt on them. We came and spanked the Hindu boy, but the Muslim boy came to us and said, "It's nothing, babu. Don't beat him like that. We poor fellows are accustomed to these. It is not that serious." Actually, you know, the poor of either community were not very belligerent, generally. The rich and the powerful designed the scheme.'

In 1946, Achintya's elder brother was teaching at a college. He had a close friend and colleague. Both of them were involved in various social activities. Achintya went to stay in the professors' hostel with his brother after the examinations. Then a problem cropped up. 'On the fourth day of my visit, the SDO, who was a family friend, came and said, "There is a case against you, flee for your life." Those were bad times; communal mistrust prevailed. It was a case of abduction of a Muslim girl. The fact was that this girl was originally Hindu, but forcibly taken away by a Muslim fellow who married her. Dada and his friend rescued her and kept her in the quarters of the professors' hostel. The Muslims had converted her, but that was not a point of concern for Dada. They were trying to rehabilitate the girl within her paternal family. However, the SDO insisted that we should leave the place right away, because communal sentiments had to be considered. Therefore, we left as we were, literally in one set of clothes. The SDO took the responsibility of informing our family.'

Achintya and his brother decided not to go back home immediately, but travel to Kolkata where they had relatives. They bought tickets for Sealdah. At the Darshana border, Achintya's brother suddenly changed his mind. He had a student residing nearby who had requested him a number of times to visit his place. They got off the train and went to this man's house. After they had rested, this student told them of his wish to establish a college there, if Achintya's brother would accept some responsible position there. His brother decided to stay on.

Achintya clearly adored this brother. 'My dada and I have been associated with a large number of organizations. Many of them are educational institutes. Not that Dada had much money. Shyamaprasad Mookerjee, who knew Dada, told him, "You are mad. How are you going to earn your own livelihood?" But Dada did what he thought right. He is a very well-known person in the neighbourhood.'

Achintya spoke of his further adventures. 'We had intended to return to Barishal after things cooled down a bit. Then I came to know that I had been charged under the Arms Act and could not go back immediately. Thereafter, the struggle began for me. Of course, after some time I surreptitiously went back. Just before Partition, when there was widespread confusion all around, I smuggled seven revolvers into Barishal and gave them to my family.' Achintya laughed as I expressed my surprise. 'Oh, yes, I was a bit daring. Used to do what you could call unscrupulous things. I had very good aim too. However, a few months later the police came to know and seized the revolvers.'

Soon, Achintya's family decided to migrate. They did so gradually, over almost five years. In the context, Achintya recalled how frightened the entire Hindu population had become. Many had their children wearing two dresses all the time, one on top of the other, lest they had to leave home at any moment. In response to my enquiry, Achintya spoke of the rioting and violence in Kolkata and described his involvement in it. In one incident he was wounded by a splinter in his leg and in need of immediate medical attention. No hospital would take him in, but a young nurse arranged for his admission to R.G. Kar hospital. She said he looked like her brother and in fact admitted him by falsely stating that he was her brother. 'Those days everybody could be every other person's brother or sister.' He suffered prolonged after-effects from the wound and was afraid he would lose his leg. He expressed gratitude towards the doctor who had taken special care of the youth and saved his leg.

After his release from hospital, he continued with his studies. He graduated, and with the intention of supporting his family, he also equipped himself professionally. In the meantime, he had joined the Student Congress. He was an executive member and was strongly committed. Here he mentioned some of his political contacts and spoke of the vow he had made to serve the country as long as he lived, which he had always kept.

Regarding his feelings about the Muslim community, he said, 'I had many Muslim friends and never had any ill feelings. Many were in the Student Congress ... Many still come to my house and stay with us ... . You see, the riot episode [referring to the event in which he was injured] was not because of hatred from any side. It was due to the violent atmosphere that prevailed at that time. The feuds were often just a response to attacks by hooligans but they took communal colour. You have to fight if you are attacked.'

At this point Achintya expressed a lament for the lost land.

He had a mental image of his homeland, he said, and would not tarnish it by seeing the Barishal of today. In fact, he had already refused one opportunity to visit his native land. Talking about this, Achintya became a bit pensive, but then recovered and came back to his narration.

He recalled how in 1971 they had sent relief to Bangladesh. They used to move secretly across the border. 'Never got over the habit of doing dangerous things,' Achintya remarked, laughing.

Achintya was very fond of his granddaughter. I asked him what his reaction would be if this granddaughter were to marry a Muslim. He paused for a while pondering the issue. 'I am not sure,' he said. 'They are different in certain ways. The culture is different. Of course I would not object if that were her choice ...' I sensed that the interview was over, and requested him to help me make contact with other possible interviewees. He immediately promised to talk to some prospective respondents he knew and let me know.

A few days later Achintya called to say he had made an appointment for me with a man in an organization he was associated with, and offered to take me there by car since he was going there too. On the way, he talked to me on various issues, distantly linked to Partition, the present political scenario, my work, and handed me an article on Partition, which he had photocopied for me from a journal. Then suddenly he told me, 'You know, I've been thinking about what you asked me the other day. I tried to visualize it. Then I found the true answer. No, I will not feel the least bit of resistance if the boy my granddaughter marries is humane, generous and flexible. But I will object if she marries a fundamentalist person, Hindu or Muslim, one with a narrow outlook.'

Tarapada's Story

Tarapada lives and works as a tailor in a suburb of Kolkata, in a small one-roomed hut with tiled roof. He works single-handed with only his wife helping him. He cannot afford to keep a helper.

I contacted him through one of the local residents who spoke highly of him as a 'good and honest man who tries to do well to others'. I went to his place on the stipulated date. The room was filled with pieces of cloth. Two sewing machines stood near the wall. This is his workshop as well as his bedroom. In a small extension on one side, his wife was preparing the midday meal. Tarapada is a short and slender person with high-powered spectacles and a broad smile. He lives with his wife and two children who are studying in local schools. Though poor, he has an appearance of dignity and confidence. He started talking as soon as I told him my purpose. 'I have not much to tell you, but since you ask me, I will tell you whatever I remember,' he said.

Tarapada is from Brahmanberhia. He had lost his father at an early age, and his widowed mother somehow managed to bring them up. Tarapada was the first son born after two sisters. He was studying in Kumilla town at the time of the Noakhali riots. His maternal uncle worked at the 'Collectory' there. Tarapada was about eight years old. He could remember the days following the rioting at Noakhali. 'I remember we used to pick flowers, a few of us boys used to get up by four in the morning and go to the station, which was about fifteen minutes' walk from our home. One such morning we saw refugees pouring in from Noakhali, they were fleeing from their villages, men, women, children and youngsters. The children had nothing on them; some of the women wore only petticoat and blouse, no sari; I remember it vividly. Many of them were soaking wet; they had stayed submerged in a pond for a long time and dared to come out only when the violence stopped. We ran back and contacted our local club–it was named The Bandhab Club–the volunteers were already at work. They put the refugees in the school building: hoards of men and women placed in small rooms. We assisted the volunteers in distributing relief. I remember a second lot of distressed people coming after some time.'

In 1947, Tarapada's family decided to migrate. His family did not face any direct assault from the Muslims. Their locality had a brahmin majority. Yet, everybody started migrating, and Tarapada's family followed suit because they usually did what the brahmins did. Also, the local influential Muslims advised them to leave. After a protracted journey with fellow villagers, they reached the border of West Bengal. Initially they had thought of staying with a relative. But the place was already overcrowded as other uncles and aunts had come over from East Bengal. Therefore, the children were placed at an orphanage at Banipur while Tarapada's mother stayed for a few days with her brother. In the meantime, refugee colonies were being established.

Tarapada had to struggle through life in West Bengal. His studies were interrupted. 'I had studied in school at Kumilla. But here in Banipur I could not manage. There were a number of big boys who bullied us. I tried to go to Raharha Ashram, where they educated children, but I could not get admission. I was never very good at studies. We did not have contacts. I understood that my studies had to be discontinued. So I thought of getting a job to help my mother. She was staying with a nephew at this colony in Belghoria. I joined them and started working. After all I was the son.'

Tarapada started working at a tea stall. He, and his younger brother who also took some menial job in Burrabazar, earned around seven rupees a month. They gave the entire amount to their mother who miraculously managed to 'feed the five mouths something' every day.

Despite poverty, Tarapada has maintained his self-respect. 'I could not prosper. But I never went for the relief or dole given by the government. Mother forbade us. She thought that it was equivalent to begging. I loved and admired her greatly. She was poor but had lofty ideas. In the meantime, I learnt work from a tailor. I also got a labourer's job at a Cotton Mill when I was sixteen. I worked as a tailor in my free time. The mill was shut down in 1980. From then, I have been jobless and have to live on my tailoring.'

Tarapada had many mouths to feed. He married late, because though his elder sisters were married, they were widowed soon after. At one time, he had 13 people depending on his meagre earnings. He got his brother married first and then he himself married. He has two sons and a daughter. The elder son is now

25, he is a driver. Tarapada refuses to take money from his son; he will need it for his future, he says. Tarapada mourns his brother's decision to live separately, but has accepted it.

Tarapada has nostalgic memories of the harmony and peace in his village. 'It was a remote village. We had very few facilities. Almost everybody of our caste was poor. We had some land that yielded crop that lasted for eight months. The rest we had to manage somehow. Nevertheless, there was a kind of closeness among all of us. We felt that any person from our village was like a blood relative. Here everything is different. Nobody cares for others.'

Tarapada has been in politics. He was a member of the undivided Communist Party of India and then of its Marxist faction. He was an active member of CITU, the Left trade union. He was involved in the workers' union in his factory, and tried to address the needs of his poor fellow labourers. He tried his best to organize livelihoods for as many workers as he could, and within his humble capacity extended help to those 'who were more wretched' than him. 'But I never took any advantage of being a party member', he said as I enquired after his present connection with local party leaders. 'My mother always taught me not to exploit any connection. At our Mill, there were more than 3,000 labourers. We all became jobless. I did not try to get anything for myself alone. Our demands were for all. We, the common workers, could see that the leadership was on the wrong path, but we could do nothing, nothing really.' Even today, he is committed to socialism.

I asked him what the impact of Partition had been on him. He initially said that at the time of Partition he had been so young that it was difficult to judge this. Then he said, 'I would have been no less poor had I stayed there. So I do not know if I lost anything. Maybe I would have studied, or maybe not [pause], but then Partition made me mature and forced me take the responsibility of my family during all our woes. I think that is a positive outcome.'

This unassuming man was surprised when I asked him about his attitude towards Muslims. 'Nothing special. What is there to think of? There are good and bad people in all communities. We had both Hindu and Muslims as our neighbours in Kumilla. Here also, we had both in our union. One should never be conservative. I have nothing special to say for or against them.' I asked him how he would feel if one of his children were to marry a Muslim. He smiled. 'I would tell them to be sure of the person–the girl or the boy, whoever. It is the person who is important, not the religion. After all I would feel worse if they married a narrow-minded Hindu.'

Then he paused for a while and volunteered that he had never believed in God and therefore the issue of religion was never important to him. I asked him if under dire circumstances he had not prayed to God. 'No,' he said. 'It was strange, I understand, but my mother always said that there is nothing higher than humanity. "Do something for fellow people if you can," she would say. I have never prayed to God, not in any distress. But I have tried to do whatever little I could for my fellow workers. Of course, that was not much.'

The Core Similarity

The dissimilarities between Achintya and Tarapada lay in their socio-economic placement: before and after partition. The single confirmed reality that followed Tarapada from the 1940s into the twenty-first century was his struggle for existence against the enemy called poverty. Achintya never tasted poverty, though he did witness it before and after Partition. He emerged from a politically aware, enlightened and affluent family, one of the landed, educated gentry of East Bengal, and became a highly successful professional.

Both Achintya and Tarapada had lost their fathers before migration. But Achintya received emotional and social shelter from others. In any case, he migrated at a more mature age and had his elder brother to guide and protect him. Though missing the smooth life of Barishal, Achintya was able to pursue a professional career and struggle his way to success. He was in financial trouble for a brief period after migration. Subsequently, by merit, honesty, determination and rationality, he stepped up steadily to very high position in the corporate sector. Tarapada was a mere boy when he had to migrate with his helpless mother and younger brother. He could not finish even his primary education and worked as an unskilled labourer. At certain points of his life, he had to eke out a living, particularly after losing his job along with thousands of other labourers in the late 1980s, when a number of cotton and jute mills on the two banks of the Ganga were closed. The closure of an industry is, to people like Tarapada, like the sky falling. It has direct implications for their daily ration of rice and dal. Achintya, on the contrary, belongs to the class that decides to close down the industry, even if with a genuine sigh, or at least accepts the closure as an inevitable sequel of industrial sickness understood in terms of numbers, pie-charts and diagrams.

Achintya has wide social and political connections owing to his family reputation, his profession, and his sincere humanitarian and rational approach that rarely fails to draw respect. Tarapada's world is confined to a narrow lane in an underdeveloped extension of Kolkata, and at best occasionally to the local party office where again he is not one of the frontline members. It is a small world with mundane problems. Achintya has a broad-spectrum personal history; Tarapada, in his own expression 'has virtually nothing to say'.

The exposure to the 'adventure' of the freedom movement and a rich family culture taught Achintya to thrive in the concept of patriotism. Therefore, he had his share in the glory of independent India. Tarapada was so busy feeding his family that he never enjoyed the security that could have been at least symbolically his through the independence of his country. Because of his earlier connection with nationalist leaders of importance, Achintya grew up in a constructive-nationalistic set-up. Therefore, apart from being politically involved, Achintya came to be socially active as well. He has been devoted to 'social work' related to poverty alleviation, education of the poor and the distressed, as well as providing vocational activities to women and disadvantaged children. Tarapada had no scope to 'donate' his money and service, nor could he call his battle against poverty 'social work'. It was simply 'work' that he had to do for himself and his family.

To explain why I have juxtaposed the lives of Achintya and Tarapada, apparently so far removed from each other, I would like to focus on the similarities in the feelings I had as I interviewed them. Both of them had a rational and brisk mode of talking, a no-nonsense kind of attitude coexisting with their politeness. In the case of Achintya, one might think that the confidence came from his merit and success. Contrarily, Tarapada was ostensibly intellectually less potent, living in a humble condition, jobless for the last two decades, 'uneducated' and surviving on the meagre earnings from his single-handed tailoring business. His flexibility was not an associate of success in life.

Probably, for both of them, the clarity in thought emanated from their self-esteem; from the sense of responsibility and the non-conflicting endorsement from their conscience for doing the right thing. In Achintya, the transparency was coupled with greater confidence; in Tarapada, with greater humility. Achintya has money and power; his nobility lies in bestowing it on those who do not have it. Tarapada has neither; his dignity lies in not accepting donations given for selfish reasons from those who have money and power.

A comparison of their opinions regarding Muslims deserves attention. Apparently, Tarapada was clearer in his thought than Achintya. In response to my question about the level of social and personal intimacy with the Muslims that would be acceptable to him, Achintya spontaneously expressed some hesitation about the cultural difference, and later, with rational judgement, modified his statement. Being a sincere man, he pondered over my question and tried to reach an integration of his sentiments and rationality. On the other hand, Tarapada was unambiguous. He knew that the struggle for his daily existence was not related in any way to his religion. Therefore, he simply felt that religion did not matter.

In fact, both of them considered religion irrelevant in judging the quality of a person. Both emphasized the humanitarian characteristics of the persons they knew. It was not only a matter of not believing in God; during my interviews I have seen how believers and non-believers alike fumbled over issues relating to superstition and prejudice. What rendered Achintya and Tarapada different from most of the lot was a broader vision beyond the tendency to perceive others in terms of stereotyped categories. To achieve this, they did not feel the need to submerge negative perceptions of individual Muslims, nor did they exaggerate the positive characteristics of one or the other religion. The simple and convincing statement of Tarapada that 'good and bad people exist in all communities' is not, psychologically, that simple.

Achintya and Tarapada had their own yardsticks for judging people. From my short acquaintance with them, I do not know if and where else in their lives they harbour prejudice and irrationality. On the issue of religion, however, both of them were relatively free from confusion. Negative interaction with some persons belonging to the Muslim community had not compelled them to define people in terms of their religious identity. There was an ideal for both of them to pursue. For Tarapada, it was the socialist ideal and serving the deprived. Indeed, Tarapada's own struggle for his daily bowl of rice revealed to him directly and poignantly the irrelevance of superficial characteristics like religious faith. For Achintya, this ideal was related to his involvement with the freedom movement: he was bound in service to the concept called the 'country'. Achintya reached the same conclusion as Tarapada through rationality and empathy. One might say that both of them tried to extend their selves beyond the trivialities of external appearances.

This pair is unique in one sense. In the case of the earlier pairs: Dipendu and Manish, Shashanko and Barun, the emphasis was on the individual's exposure and experiences as determining his interpretation of the event of Partition. The cases of Achintya and Tarapada seem to present evidence to the contrary: that openness, non-prejudicial attitude and flexibility are, at least in some cases, independent of the developmental and social context. How does a psychologist reconcile this contradiction? I submit that, however discrepant their apparent experiences may be, both these persons had a kind of self-respect and sense of responsibility that they had obtained through identification, Tarapada from his mother and Achintya, predominantly from his brother, but perhaps from other relatives too. The absence of grievance and blame, the rather placid and dispassionate way of accepting what life brought, coexisted with a distinctive ability to relate to people and to exude sufficient warmth. Probably these persons did not so ardently need to create an enemy; they had the inner calm and resources to neutralize the aggression in a balanced way within themselves.

Such rational thought and emotion are related to the development of a non-punitive super-ego. Healthy super-ego development requires a relatively smooth identification with the role model or the ego-ideal, which in turn needs to be rooted in reality.[25] The super-ego is usually strongly judgemental and generates guilt by pointing out that one has wronged in thought or action. The dictum of the super-ego is most frequently directed towards the libidinal and aggressive modes of thought, and perhaps the complex generated from aggressive thoughts is much more damaging than that by libidinal ones. To obtain a genuine balance in personality, one needs to have developed a basic sense of trust and security; the conviction that one is acceptable and lovable, despite transient aggressive encounters. This sense of security, originating in early infancy experiences, would give rise to an accepting and understanding inner guardian, the benevolent super-ego. This is the ultimate source of self-esteem that comes from proper appropriation of gratification and frustration. This may be considered the key element in management of aggression.[26]

Achintya and Tarapada evinced a relatively clear processing of aggression. Though directly involved in communal riots, Achintya could look upon communal hostility as a situational response devoid of undue rationalization or projection. Tarapada also witnessed the torture inflicted by Muslims on Hindus and had seen refugees pouring in from Noakhali. His own family had migrated owing to the worsening situation. Even so, he could look upon it with tolerance; as an event for which some persons of a particular community might be responsible, but by no means as a reason for rejection of the entire community. The ability to be free from stereotyping and to perceive the inter-communal conflict as a reaction to immediate events and not a characteristic of the generalized designated 'other' came probably from an internal harmony that gave Achintya and Tarapada balance and clarity of perception unmarred by either affluence or poverty. So, contradictory as the lives of these two persons were, their paths were not antagonistic.

As I discussed the characters included in this chapter with my friends and colleagues, different views and perceptions emerged. I acknowledge all of them as examples of various facets of truth and consider their validity at par with mine; I do not intend to claim that my perspective is nearer the *truth* than theirs. Some suggested that the pre- and post-partition social class of the respondents was largely responsible for their perceptions. Some wanted me to consider them in terms of their political ideology, since it is the value system that is the ultimate guide to human decision-making and behaviour. I, however, chose a relatively non-specific criterion to group the respondents, that is, their predisposing personality. To perform this grouping, I depended on the information that I was able to gather about their past, but also substantially on the non-verbal and verbal messages that I received with my heart, eyes and ears. The suggestions of my friends were internalized by me while listening and reconstructing and are reflected in my final interpretation. All along, I have remained aware that the 'truth' may be perceived in completely different ways as well.

May we, however, from the exposition of this particular angle of interpretation, at least tentatively conclude that the reported emotions and the distortion of the entire memory of Partition, personal or collective, is a kind of attempt to deal with the chaotic feelings, particularly those of aggression and love, generated by the inherent contradictions of the situation? As we study in depth some prototypes of individual reactions to Partition, we close in upon the various streams of thought cutting across the emotional history of the country as well. Hereupon two pertinent theoretical issues arise. One is the construction of the collective self, its communal, secular or independent nature, particularly in the light of the soft violence experienced by roughly one-half of the population of West Bengal in the early years after Independence. The second is the tracing of its impact on the socio-political atmosphere of the state. From a psychological perspective, this would entail a generalization from the individual to the culture, into which I shall venture in the next chapter.

Notes

1 Anna Freud strongly posited that everyone employs a characteristic repertoire of defence mechanisms, though in varying degree. She highlighted the fact that defences are erected not only against the upsurge of instinctual impulses, but also against the affects associated with it. A. Freud. 1937. *The ego and the mechanisms of defence* (London: Hogarth Press): 34. This defensive configuration creates a permanent mark in the individual's characteristic management of situations and results in the development of relatively permanent character traits. Reich calls it '*charakterpahzerung*: the armour-plating of character. See W. Reich. 1949. *Character analysis* (New York: Oregon Institute, 3rd ed.): 145.

2 I borrow this concept from the early theory of perception by Edward Bradford Titchener. He suggested that the perception of a physical stimulus depends on two sources of determinants: one is the core or the sensation of the basic stimulus; and the second is the context, the perspective residing within and outside the individual and provides the meaning to the stimulus. These terms have become obsolete with respect to the theme they were initially introduced; but they may be used to connote the significance of the perspective in case of social cognition. Translated to social perception, the event in its neutrality, if there can be any, is the core; and the context comes from the social-historical moment and from within the individual's personality. See E.B. Titchener. 1910/1928. *A textbook of psychology* (New York: Macmillan).

3 It is intresting to note that Manish actually said 'three nation-states'. When he was talking to me, it was of course, India, Bangladesh and

Pakistan. But during Partition, there were only two: India and Pakistan. But can it be so that he never thought of Pakistan and Bangladesh (East Pakistan) as one nation state? I wonder.

4 Cf. S. Freud. 1915-1916/1961. Introductory lectures on psychoanalysis. In J. Strachey, ed. and trans., *The standard edition of the complete psychological works of Sigmund Freud*, vol 15 (London: Hogarth Press). Freud compared the spontaneous memories of early childhood with the creation of personal myths in which historical facts are falsified according to one's wishes.

5 We may try to understand this selectivity during recollection by drawing upon Wilfred Bion. During the delineation of psychoanalytical epistemology Bion discussed Poincaré's notion of disparate facts being gathered together to form a generalized meaning of an event. While it seems to us that a cause might have been obtained, actually the memory itself is a tempotral phenomenon where past is recalled to fit the present. See for a critical discussion of Bion in this context, V.S. Mondrzak. 2007. Trauma, causality and time: Some reflections. *International Journal of Psychoanalysis* 40, 463-74.

6 All psychological theories agree that anxiety is a normal phenomenon with a signalling function. At the same time, excessive or over-generalized anxiety lies at the root of psychopathology. While psychoanalytically-oriented psychologists emphasize the anxiety generated from uncontrollable instinctual upsurge: cf. E. Jones. 1913. The psychology of morbid anxiety. *Papers on psychoanalysis* (New York: Wood & Co), the behavioural point of view also highlights the pervasive nature of anxiety developed from specific trauma through the process of generalization; J. Wolpe. 1958. *Psychotherapy by reciprocal inhibition* (New York: Stanford University Press). Reducing anxiety by binding it to specific situations and ideas or by exerting 'control' has been recognized as a preventive/curative measure, although disagreement may ensue regarding the recommended techniques.

7 From the psychoanalytical perspective, order as a personality trait has been associated with management of anxiety arising out of aggression. The personality characteristics of Dipendu and Manish evinced this organized orderliness. However, the paucity of data about their childhood prevents us from directly associating their traits of orderliness with their personality development.

[8] See E. Erikson. 1959. *Identity and the life cycle* (New York: Norton). In this book, Erikson relates the development of basic trust (or mistrust) to the quality of early mothering and ability of the child to regulate the mother's response. The sense of control on the availability of resources (milk or love) serves as the prime factor of trust development. The child who has been over-gratified, that is, provided without any active effort on its part may develop into a passive dependent individual. On the contrary, inadequate gratification of early oral need develops inability to put confidence in the world or in oneself.

[9] In some cases, when aggression cannot be expressed adequately, it may turn upon oneself, in a form of physical or psychological self-injury. In some, this has inhibitory effects on expression of achievement and talent as well. While narcissistic desire for self-expression and domination resides in the background, the apparent feature is of relative submission and non-achievement. Freud has explained the inhibition against achievement in 'those wrecked by success': S. Freud. 1916/1957. Some character types met with in psychoanalytic work. In Strachey, ed. and trans., *The standard edition of the complete psychological works of Sigmund Freud*, vol 14. See for further reference, C.O. Oberndorf. 1939. The feeling of stupidity. *International Journal of Psychoanalysis* 20. See also O. Fenichel. 1946. *The psychoanalytic theory of neurosis* (London: Routledge and Kegan Paul): 183.

[10] From a psychodynamic point of view, passive anger may be expressed as stubbornness, and also as moralistic manipulation. See Fenichel. 1946. *The psychoanalytic theory of neurosis* (London: Routledge and Kegan Paul): 279.

[11] See J.K. Swim and C. Stengor. 1998. *Prejudice: The target's perspective* (San Diego: Academic Press).

[12] Ganga Sagar Mela, an annual Hindu festival when thousands throng to a southern island of West Bengal to bathe in the sea on the last day of the month of Poush, mid-Dec to mid-Jan. Ganga Sagar Mela at the Winter Solstice, when pilgrims bathe in the sea.

[13] The concept of secondary elaboration comes from Freud's explanation of the dream phenomenon. It refers to the reported components of a dream, which were probably not present even in the manifest content of the actual dream, but unconsciously added to the recalled content to render the dream 'story' a psychological order and congruence. See S. Freud.

1900. The interpretation of dreams. In J. Strachey, ed. and trans., *The standard edition of the complete psychological works of Sigmund Freud*, vol 5. Here I have used the term in a similar connotation in the context of recall of childhood events.

14 I borrow this term from H. Rorschach. 1921. *Experiment in Rorschah.* Trans. as *Psychodiagnostiks* (Bern: Hans Huber Verlag, 1942). In the elucidation of actions associated with ambiguous stimuli, the respondent occasionally forces a meaning and organization that is unlikely and cannot be reconciled with the stimuli. This indicates an intolerance of ambiguity, a lack of ability to perceive details or an anxiety about assimilating uncertainty.

15 This refers to the idea that the political as well as the psychological space in so-called postcolonial countries contain the colonial hegemony within their essence, so that they become mimics of the first world. See A. Chaudhury, D. Das and A. Chakrabarti. 2000. *Margin of margin: Profile of an unrepentant postcolonial collaborator* (Kolkata: Anushtup).

16 One may, in this context, refer to the distinction between narcissistic and anaclitic object choice. While persons engaging in anaclitic object choices tend to pursue mother-figures or father-figures as their love objects in the hope these parent-substitutes will fulfil the needs of their ego-libido, people governed by the narcissistic object choice invest their libidinal energy in aspects of themselves. See S. Freud. 1914. On narcissism: an introduction. In J. Strachey, ed. and trans., *The standard edition of the complete psychological works of Sigmund Freud*, vol 14: 69-102. While both kinds of object choices may ultimately be conceived of as serving the purpose of the self, anaclitic object choice is characterized by a relatively greater identification with others and is therefore more expansive in nature.

17 A few studies have focused exclusively on the reactions of the witness to violence, particularly of the child witness. Among the few references most are concerned with family violence issues. See, e.g., M.S. Rosenberg. 1987. Children of battered women: The effects of witnessing violence on their social problem-solving abilities. *Behavior Therapist* 10, 85-89. There are however indications that witnessing violence on unknown others, particularly under organized political dominance as during war, may be as traumatic as being under fire or personally victimized.

18 See R.S. Pynoos and K. Nader. 1989. Children's memory and proximity to violence. *Journal of the American Academy of Child and Adolescent Psychiatry*

28, 236-241; C.R. Pfeffer. 1996. *Severe stress and mental disturbance in children* (Washington, D C.: American Psychiatric Press); A. Douglass and T.A. Vogler, eds. 2003. *Witness and memory: Discourse and trauma* (London: Routledge).

19 I refer to Freud's one significant tenet that we are afraid of our own uncontrolled emotions more than we are afraid of any external situation. See, e.g., S. Freud. 1926/1959. Inhibitions, symptoms and anxiety. In J. Strachey, ed. and trans., *The standard edition of the complete psychological works of Sigmund Freud*, vol 20: 77-175.

20 S. Freud. 1905/1953. Three essays on sexuality and other writings. In Strachey, ed. and trans. *The standard edition of the complete psychological works of Sigmund Freud,* vol: 125-243.; M. Klein. 1975. Love, guilt and reparation and other works. *The writings of Melanie Klein (1921-1945),* vol 1 (London: Hogarth Press): 344-70.

21 F. S. Friedenberg .1956. A contribution to the problem of sadomasochism. *Psychoanalytic Review* 43, 91-96; W. Arndt, J. Foehl and F. Good. 1985. Specific sexual fantasy themes: A multidimensional study. *Journal of Personality and Social Psychology* 48, 472-80.

22 Such upsurge can be called 'natural' as it receives a sort of endorsement from cultural practices and ideas. See for discussion on cultural meaning of sexualized violence, K. Lawrence. 1997. *After the lovedeath: Sexual violence and the making of culture* (University of California Press); D.M. Horvitz. 2000. *Literary trauma: Sadism, memory, and sexual violence in American women's fiction* (Albany: SUNY). Indeed, culture's attitude towards sexualized violence against women is ambivalent to say the least.

23 Jones commented that though it seems in most cases that guilt is primary and hate is its cover, in fact there is a deeper layer of hate beneath the façade of guilt as well. Jones further points out that the fact that guilt originates from hate and is relieved by hate is an example of the 'isopathic principle', which means cause cures the effect. See E. Jones. 1968. Papers on psychoanalysis (London, Ballière, Timball and Cox): 307.

24 The concept of 'derailment of dialogue' refers to the sudden break in a habituated pattern of attachment as a result of traumatic events, often a mixture of sexuality and aggression and stimulus overload. Since the derailment can result in complete disarray of both libidinal and aggressive drives, there may develop a frantic effort of perverse concerns, sometimes in the form of partial repetition of the trauma, while keeping at bay the

chaos that could have resulted from full appreciation of the traumatic moment. See R. A. Spitz. 1964. The derailment of dialogue stimulus overload, action cycles, and the completion gradient. *Journal of American Psychoanalytical Association* 12, 752-75. Spitz initially stated this concept in the context of infantile trauma. But later researchers have demonstrated that the dynamics is equally applicable for adolescents also. See L. J. Kaplan. 1995. Perversion and trauma: from paradoxical memory to narrative memory. *Canadian Journal of Psychoanalysis* 3, 177-198.

[25] The concept of super-ego and its complex role in the management of anxiety has been clarified in Freud's later writings, particularly in 1920/ 1955. *Beyond the pleasure principle*; 1923/1961. *Ego and the id*; and 1926/ 1959. *Inhibitions, symptoms and anxiety* in J. Srachey, ed. and trans., *The standard edition of the complete psychological works of Sigmund Freud.*

[26] The importance of this sense of security in tolerance of aggression has been underscored in the research of Ainsworth. She suggested that the behaviour of the secure child is reflected in its response to the mother on return from a brief absence, in its welcoming and willingness to cling after the supposed rejection. See M.D.S. Ainsworth ans B.A. Wittig. 1969. Attachment and exploratory behaviour of one year olds in a strange situation. In B.M. Foss, ed., *Determinants of infant behaviour*, vol. 4 (London: Methuen). More or less the same notion has been discussed in different language by Klein as 'introjection of the good object', by Erikson as 'basic trust' and by Yarrow as 'confidence in mother'. See M. Klein. 1923/1948. Infant analysis. In Klein, ed., *The writings of Melanie Klein, (1921-1945)*, vol. 1; E. Erikson. 1959. *Identity and the life cycle* (New York: Norton); L. J. Yarrow. 1967. The development of focussed relationships during infancy. In J. Hellmuth, ed., *Exceptional infant* (Seattle, WA: Special Child Publications).

5

The Self in Partition and Beyond

Keeping time, time, time,
In a sort of Runic rhyme,
To the throbbing of the bells—
Of the bells, bells, bells—
To the sobbing of the bells;
Keeping time, time, time,
As he knells, knells, knells,
In a happy Runic rhyme,
To the rolling of the bells—
Of the bells, bells, bells:
To the tolling of the bells—
Of the bells, bells, bells, bells,
Bells, bells, bells—
To the moaning and the groaning of the bells.

Edgar Allan Poe, 'The Bells'

I LISTENED INTENTLY to the tolling of the bells: the bells of golden memory, of happiness and pain. I moved back and forth between the past and the present with the people I interviewed. Now it is time I summarize my interpretations and bring the discussion to a close.

DATA AND INTERPRETATION

I am aware that the data I collected was inadequate for the depth of interpretation I would have liked to achieve. The inadequacy was threefold: in terms of the breadth of categories studied; the number of respondents; and the depth of data. In the first place, the present study is limited to a specific social layer. I have concentrated on the upper caste bhadralok Hindus, the respectable, mostly educated people, and have missed out the large section of landless labourers, belonging mostly to the Scheduled Castes. The entire scenario for the lower caste might have been framed in different terms and guided by different psychological principles. In particular, the meaning of violence would have differed for them. Their exclusion from my study is related partly to the methodology I adopted. Since I drew largely upon psychoanalytical premises, which in turn are dependent on communication, it was imperative that I should understand my interviewees' emotional language and vice versa. It was not really a matter of class or caste per se, but of culture and its linguistic products.

Secondly, to what extent am I justified in commenting upon the 'psychology of soft violence' on the basis of some two dozen interviews? Of course, the greater the exposure the greater is the reliability; but in qualitative research, the justification comes less from sheer number and more from the authenticity of understanding and treatment of the data.[1] As I used clinical methodology, I may have reason to be moderately satisfied with my results, as I felt I had achieved a kind of saturation in terms of the emerging relevant concepts. However, I have remained cautious about generalizing too broadly, except in those domains where almost all the respondents presented a similar face. The recounting of the pervasive fear, or the attachment to the homeland were some such near-universal examples.

I have particularly abstained from commenting seriously on the issue of gender difference, as identification of any characteristic experience of soft violence distinctive to women, so prominent in brutal violence in terms of rape and mutilation, has eluded me. The comparison of female and male perspectives would be a different work altogether with a different mindset. Another interesting aspect of the gendered perception of violence has been hinted upon by Nilanjana Chatterjee where she rightly points out that the picture of Muslims as violent always referred to the male Muslims, thus being essentially stereotypical.[2]

My third and main concern is about the depth of data, not only in terms of details of the events, but also the extent to which I could gather information on significant childhood experiences. (I use the phrase 'depth of data' in the same sense as psychoanalysis is termed 'depth psychology'). The careful reader will notice that though I have analysed defensive patterns as manifest in the reconstructions, I have less often touched upon their origin in developmental dynamics within the 'family drama', that is, on the specific psycho-sexual stages involved in the formation of the patterns. Whenever I have commented on these, it has been by way of post-hoc theoretical justification, and mostly presented in notes. The reason is obvious. I was hesitant to comment on the temporal genesis of the manifest patterns of defensive modes of these individuals when I did not have access to the detailed nuances of their growing years.

I am, therefore, aware that what I am trying to present here may constitute no more than a fiction whose task is to produce a whole collection of 'effects of the real'.[3] Nevertheless, I am not discouraged. Since none of our perceptions may be ascertained as really 'real', we can in fact, do little else. In addition, I rely on the assumption that this very 'misreading' of the past may have been the cornerstone of the refugee identity as well; that is, it is anchored in experience so far as the victims of Partition and other observers share the same misreading.

I need to report a second kind of difficulty as well. Within the purview of my emotional connection with the respondents, I faced a moral dilemma. Often during my interpretative work, I have paused to ponder whether I am doing something unethical. Javeed Alam criticizes any endeavour to persuade a respondent to recount a traumatic experience.[4] I believe, however, that most of my respondents welcomed the dialogue; they were happy to talk about the past and to be part of a research project. A more serious hesitation arose from the psychodynamic interpretation I made of their narratives, the way I re-presented their emotions and experiences. Every psychologist encounters this difficulty when reporting a living clinical case. While all of my respondents knew explicitly that their stories would be documented and may be interpreted, they were not aware of the theoretical stances that may be taken and the final content of interpretation. In this regard, I am aware that just changing the name and some other particulars may not protect against the individual getting hurt if the interpretations are distasteful to her or his sentiments and incongruent with her or his thought processes.

On the credit side, we have achieved two things. Firstly, we have an improvisation in the methodology for the study of traumatic memory, as far as it connects the collective and the personal developmental with regard to 'soft violence'. Secondly, we see glimpses of (or conjectures about?) the nature of the 'self' in Partition: the 'self' in its individual existence as well as in its collectivity. These two are inseparable, as the improvisations in methodology were offshoots of the way the respondents chose to reveal their selves to me.

NARRATIVES OF SOFT VIOLENCE

I feel the need to repeat here that the study of *soft violence* holds a *special* place in the *complete* understanding of *politically induced* trauma. It is not that pain and fear are understated in the related literature, but commentators have rarely highlighted the qualitative difference between the experience of soft violence and brutality. Rather, these two have been traditionally envisioned as differing only in intensity, soft violence being a milder form of hard-core violence. Even in narrations of violent trauma of the European Holocaust and other renderings of brutality, sufferers have only hinted at the distinct nature of the two kinds of pain.[5] My contention here is that we need to be sensitized towards the unique nature of soft violence and the methodology for its study. I intend to highlight a few characteristics of the narration of my respondents, in terms of style as well as content, and critically consider the approach for elicitation of such narrations.

Reactions to soft violence may be suppressed or distorted if there is explicit or implicit research emphasis on encounters with the horrific. Under extreme events of mass destruction and displacement, when dramatic stories of violence are spread by rumour and titillating gory details are dug up and splashed in the media, the sufferers of soft violence, already burdened under their indefinable fear and awkward guilt, are further cowed down. They hesitate to reach out to the outer world and to reveal their confused identities. It takes active support on the part of the researcher to prod them out of their apologetic stance. The term 'active support' in this context does not imply a greater degree of probing into emotions, but, contrarily, a non-directive mode of interview, with emphasis on free narration and reflective listening to encourage exploration of subdued sentiments. The researcher will be rewarded by a richness of psychological insights once the initial hesitation of the respondents is removed.

As a listener, I recognized certain patterns among the narratives, and I consider these the spontaneous organizing components of personal narration, at least under the stated conditions of soft violence. The interpretative endeavour of the researcher should follow the track suggested by such patterns. For each respondent there was a *discernible mould of presentation:* an arrangement of content that revealed the person's internal principles for the communication of self-related themes.

I found two basic styles in the sequencing of the events. For one group, the events were bound by chronology, that is, the entire presentation followed the temporal order of events. Paramesh, for example, started with the description of his home at Jessore. He narrated his family situation, his sufferings as a fatherless boy, the small enjoyments of village life, nature and social relationships, the fishing adventures and the games, and the humiliation of his mother owing to her dependence on her in-laws. He proceeded to tell me how he strove for academic success and took up a job in West Bengal. Then he described the worsening situation in East Bengal, how his family had to be brought over, his financial and other struggles, and how finally he got over the crisis. The narration followed the course of events in time. I would say the association followed the dictums of the rational self that held on to the linearity of temporal order: the antecedent-consequent version of causality. The word 'rational' here is not identical with 'anti-emotional'. It is not to say that Paramesh, for example, did not speak of emotionally significant accounts. Indeed his spontaneous exposition strongly affected me, as when he spoke of how his aunt had spitefully pushed his mother when she was carrying a pitcher full of water home from the pond, and the water fell on the ground. I could identify with the struggling boy who had to take up odd jobs and had various bad and good encounters with his temporary employers. However, the mind that peeped through all the joy, sadness and striving was a structured one, anchored in ordered time and place.

Additionally, the persons belonging to this group often attempted some kind of logical theorizing about the political and social events they had witnessed. They took recourse to rationalization in trying to organize the confusing circumstances and formulate an understanding of them, often in terms of causal relationships.[6] With them, I had the feeling of leafing through a book on history.

For a second group, the association of the elements was bound by reference to the emotional self, that is, by the affective salience of the event to oneself. The narratives in this group were characterized by an apparent mixing up of events; they in fact grouped together those episodes that had evoked similar emotions. When Pranab spoke of the deprivations he had suffered in life, he recalled the loss of land property owing to in-family litigation in the late 1930s followed by the loss of property in 1948 owing to Partition, and spoke immediately after of the financial deprivation he suffered in 1986 owing to delay in obtaining pension from the West Bengal state government. Rekha spoke about every event of her life in relation to her deceased husband, whom she had clearly worshipped. She remembered the respect they had enjoyed among both the communities and quoted her late husband when describing communal relations. This was followed by the recounting of her husband's attitude towards social issues, how he compared the two countries, and how she was happy with the decisions he took. For her, the personal self was a reflection of her late husband's self. I have noticed this kind of association by emotion somewhat more among women, though I am not in a position to comment confidently on gender difference in sequencing based on my small sample. Indeed, it is possible that the sequencing of organization varied with the educational status and exposure, since in general the women I interviewed had less formal education and less exposure to the world at large than the men.

The narrations also differed in their detailing of events with reference to external versus internal criteria. While a mixture of both was present in each case, for some, the task of narration was primarily to provide me with as much information as they could; for others, it was more to present their selves to me. Those belonging to the first category gave me facts about the geography and history of Bengal, the political issues that cropped up and led to Partition and its aftermath. Their own feelings, the joy, the pain and the fear, were relatively less discernible in their spontaneous narration. Interestingly, not all of them belonged to the earlier category that followed a chronological sequence of narration. Some organized their memories in terms of their emotions, but still provided elaborate factual details. An example was Ramananda. Like his father, he too is a lawyer. He started his narration with the conditions of the legal world under British rule and gave details of his father's efforts to assist the freedom fighters by providing them with legal advice. Then he talked about the gap in ethical-social judgements between the 1920s and the 1990s. Though he jumped over seventy years across the bridge of professional ethics, his narration was strangely devoid of emotion; it was crammed with legal instances and factual details.[7] In contrast, those of the second category spontaneously elaborated their own emotions and reactions to events before, during and after Partition. For this second group, the communication of their own happiness and pain was most important, occasionally at the cost of factual authenticity.

The tendency towards either facts or emotions is not necessarily rooted in personality disposition alone; I consider it the product of both disposition and habit. Indeed, some whose spontaneous narrations were anchored in facts turned out to be equally eloquent about their feelings after I enquired into more personal issues. It was, therefore, not necessarily a result of any inhibition on their part, but simply a style of self-presentation. I suppose, if a content analysis of words could be performed on the narratives, those of the first category would have been found to use more often the phrases 'I saw' and 'it happened', and the second category 'I felt' and 'I thought'. Such observation goads us towards considering the linguistic nature of the self. It is possible that the development of thought process and language from childhood as well as from later status and profession contributed to the specific mode of presentation.

The narratives further differed content-wise in their relative emphasis on the role of significant others, in terms of interpersonal bonds. In other words, the quality of the respondent's 'object relation' was reflected in the narrative. In psychodynamic terms, good object relation means a capability to form an adequately loving but not unrealistic representation of the 'other' in oneself. It further presupposes an ability to accept one's own and other's hostility; the acceptance of human limitations without succumbing to narcissistic inflation or its opposite, deflated self-image.[8] We have observed in earlier chapters how differences in individual object-relation patterns determine the perception of the 'enemy', related or unrelated to Partition and communal issues. Indeed, we can very well discern two categories of people: one sensitive to interpersonal stimulation and receptive to the warmth of human love, and the other whose psyche does not seem to be particularly populated by human faces. Despite a number of intra-psychic conflicts, Sudhanya possessed a powerful support against all stressors: his sensitivity towards the emotions of other people: 'I have always been oriented towards other people's sentiments. I thrive upon the love I have received from them.' In contrast, Ashok, a retired government officer, summarized his life-view in the following statement: 'I have been assigned some duties and I have completed them. I don't find much meaning in letting myself go and allowing others in. After all, man is alone. We never understand each other.' Again, while object relation served as a kind of defensive and protective function for some, it was relatively stable and conflict-free for others like Achintya, Madhabi and Tarapada. Thus, not only is the extent of object relation capacity relevant; its qualitative nature and situatedness within the entire personality configuration is also of importance.

From the scanty data I had, I could not say that the women I interviewed were more interpersonally sensitive and had better object-relation capacity. Though the women dwelt more on relationship issues and sentiments, much of these were self-related; their sensitivity to others was not more prominent. Just like the men, some women were more and some less 'other'-oriented.

I consider this diversity of narrative modes as a reflection of differences in cognitive style,[9] resulting from a complex interaction of dispositional and experiential factors. This style may not be too fixed, at least not for everyone. Yet, a search for this style is methodologically significant, because the exploration of such factors through an analysis of linguistic behaviour may provide clues to the curious diversity of the human mind. In my study, I considered all these points only post-hoc; but I can foresee a design of research whereby narrative style, language and content may be related to temperament and habit across the trajectory of development.

SCREEN MEMORIES

During the free narration, many respondents inserted one or another event, often out of context and in a casual tone. Sometimes this was some distant childhood happening, at other times an incident in adulthood. But it was always unexpected at the moment within the course of the narration and not connected to the preceding theme. I refer to Dipendu's Hoomwala, Manish's Uddhab-dada or Shashanko's Ramesh: trifling memories that provided cues to significant intra-psychic designs. Though apparently unrelated to the issue at hand, that is Partition, I do not consider them irrelevant at all. They are probably types of 'screen memory', that is, a consciously tolerable memory that unwittingly serves as a cover for another associated memory that would be emotionally painful if recalled.[10] Time and again, I suspected that these recollections, which sometimes seemed like mere gabble, bridged the individuals' unconscious affects and their rational presentation of content in response to my request.

Let me give here another example of such memory. Madhabi was describing how, post-Partition, she decided to contribute to the household income by knitting sweaters for army men and selling these through an organization. She got 50 paise per ball of wool used. She was quite emotional as she recollected the hardships she and her family underwent at that time. At this point, she spontaneously shifted to another story. I present it verbatim.

'At Khidirpur we used to stay in a rented house. We spent 22 years there. A ghost lived there as well,' she said all in the same breath. I could not resist an exclamation of surprise and her granddaughter sitting nearby became embarrassed. Madhabi, however, continued dispassionately without acknowledging anything unusual about it. 'Our home was beside a lotus pond. It was a two-storey building. Our bedroom was on the first floor. They said that the house had been built over a graveyard. We heard people walking on the roof, real sounds of boots. Sometimes it was the ringing of bells; I heard these especially when I studied late at night.' I enquired about her reaction to these supernatural happenings. She replied, 'If I became particularly afraid, I used to lie down and go to sleep. Gradually we accepted their presence. Otherwise, it was a nice house. One day my husband was coming up the stairs late at night. He bumped into somebody whom he could not see. The doorkeeper said he had seen batasa [a round-shaped sweet, like a wafer, made of sugar or molasses] falling from the roof—real batasa.'

Later on, Madhabi told me that she had always believed in God and led a religious life. She had faced many tragedies: the loss of her husband, son, son-in-law. Yet, she had found the strength to cope and accepted the undesired event with calm. I think, through the sudden insertion of the supernatural as she relived the unpleasant days of hardship, she was trying to assure herself (and me) of her major coping resource in life, her belief in a supernatural reality, that actually covered many painful losses.

One of the problems of screen memories is that these are handed over to the listener at the unconscious whim of the narrator. Could I have deduced more if I had goaded my respondents to a more elaborate discussion of such memories? I am not sure. Probably, verbal prodding with a rational stance would not, in most cases, have elicited anything of greater value. The unconscious does not respond to beckoning; it peeps through when it succumbs to its own pressure for discharge. As an interviewer, I could not drag it out; I could simply be alert enough to catch it when it spontaneously expressed itself.

The concept of 'screen memories' is essentially a psychoanalytical one; I have encountered little reference to it in any other approach to narration. The use of such out-of-context memories to understand the processing of painful incidents is, therefore, not a well-documented technique in trauma research. Either earlier researchers did not encounter such 'memories' or they found these irrelevant and omitted them from documentation. Of course, prolonged psychoanalysis of trauma victims has long been known to elicit screen memories. Sometimes, the memory of trauma itself serves as the screen.[11] The discussion of how such memories, however, may arise during a surface-level interview, and how they facilitate an understanding of the person, is largely missing from the literature. Since such memories appeared quite often in my interviews, I tend to pay them serious attention.

In the history of psychology, more than once, a development in one area from a particular perspective has been neglected by other 'schools', and its relevance understood and accepted only much later. This is particularly true when a cognitive psychological approach has been taken, for example, in the exploration of autobiographical memory. That the entire psychoanalytical narrative is a kind of autobiographical memory and its analysis, though framed in a different dialect and logistics, could be useful for the understanding of such memory is usually not acknowledged. Similarly, certain findings of the cognitive approach, for example, flash-bulb memory or the reminiscence bump, have been consistently neglected in psychoanalytical understanding. Such phenomena, when appearing in the course of analysis, may have been subjected to undue attention and over-interpretation, unnecessarily confounding the entire theorization. I suggest that, at least in the case of memory studies, the tenets of psychoanalysis need to be integrated carefully with the phenomenological and neurophysiological findings highlighted in the cognitive approach. This might bring about a much-needed breakthrough in understanding the function of memory.

PERCEPTION AND 'TRUTH'

In my perspective on studying Partition and soft violence, I intend to highlight a singular issue that renders the psychological viewpoint different from other approaches. I refer to an awareness of the lack of verifiability of the contents of narration: events or affects.[12] I have emphasized 'psychological truth' in lieu of the objective truth-value of recalled incidents and reactions, and suggested a kind of dissociation between two types of truths: external and internal. This is an opportune moment to clarify this distinction with an eye to the adopted methodology.

External truth with reference to the remembered past connotes a near-exact repetition of events as these happened and were recorded by a neutral observer. Any attempt to grasp this truth assumes two mechanisms: one, a recorder that retains the accurate image; and the other, a replicator that can reproduce the recorded item. The absurdity of such an assumption is obvious. There is no organismic information processor that is independent of the properties of the dynamic recording and reproducing system. There is no camera that does not take into account the angle at which it is set. All remembered incidents and feelings are functions of the recording and retrieving self. In the last resort, therefore, it is this 'self' that becomes of crucial importance. Thus, the very notion of externally verifiable truth reduces to absurdity; only internal truth, which again is ever-changing, persists.

The last statement requires elaboration. The self that records events is not a fixed instrument. It is not a static camera, but a moving one, a dynamic eye that tries to capture its target from different angles and, like a film director, edits it to suit one's taste. The volatile character of the self is again not under conscious control. While the self records the external world, it itself evolves under the experiences it goes through. As a result of this growing up process, its angles shift from a one time period to another; the events and feelings recorded at one phase of life acquire a different tinge when recovered at another phase. What was trauma at one juncture now becomes resource, what was courage and adventure appears to be imprudence and foolhardiness.

Therefore, the experiences and perceptions of a person at a certain point in life may be altered in the perception of the same person at the time of reporting, although the person is completely honest to himself or herself at both points; he or she is not deliberately falsifying facts. Consequently, a gap is created between the experiencing self and the declared self at a later randomly selected time. I find an echo of this confusing realization, of negation of times, in Borges' writings: 'that the present is indefinite, that the future has no reality other than as a present hope, that the past has no reality other than as a present memory'.[13]

THE SELF IN PARTITION

This understanding of our position launches us into our main discussion: the notion of the self in Partition. Before dealing directly with Partition, however, we need to examine the concept of 'self', such a confusing yet oft-used term in academic psychology. It has two connotations, depending upon the perspective from which it is viewed.[14] The first is rather easy to understand. Used in terms like self-concept, self-perception or self-esteem, it refers to the constellation of characteristics that one perceives in oneself and evaluates against idiosyncratic reference points. The second refers to what some psychologists call the 'actual self' to which the above self-perception refers: it is supposed to have a relatively independent existence. The former is cognitive in nature and may be considered as a theory about the object of observation called 'self'.[15] This object of observation, the 'actual self', is presumably the active agent that enjoys and suffers the flow of events over the entire course of life.

The distinction, however, poses a problem. When I am talking of the 'self of the partition victims', is it the self that suffered the event, is it the self that the narrators think they possess, or is it a third one that emerged gradually in the course of narration? It could be all three, or even more than three as each evolving self cuts across others to generate a plethora of patterns: each residing in a locus of moments. Each pattern of self-presentation corroborates certain characteristics and negates others, and with each alteration, suspends or warps the earlier 'self' in favour of a new one.

I submit that the configuration of the self of the partition victims, particularly those of soft violence, will be designed differently from the self of those with different experiences in life. Certain overarching emotions engulf the human mind under given circumstances and all of them contribute conjointly to the development of the self. At any given cross-section of time, the normal self from a distance appears apparently intact, smooth and well organized. Under scrutiny, however, it reveals a mosaic of discrete experiences that form a gestalt. Every single grain of the design contains a history of rupture, a violation.[16]

The civilized front presented by all of us hides a traumatic history of encounters with the 'other'. Every trauma leaves its unique fingerprint on the personality pattern. This is true for the partition experience as well, if we consider the historical event a significant assault on the self: an encounter that created an 'other' within. We may relate this to what Gyanendra Pandey wrote in the context of the Partition of India: 'The discourse of "civilization" may be described as a discourse—negatively—of violence. Violence is civilization's other.'[17]

When we focus on the nature of the self in Partition, it is as if we scrutinize one particular block of the entire design, one artificially isolated portion of the totality. In this process, we hope to trace the development of the self vis-à-vis its 'other'. This approach has its advantages and liabilities. Centring our attention on one arbitrarily defined aspect magnifies and clarifies its details; at the same time, it offers a clue to the mode of organization operating within the total personality. The risk is that the observer may overlook the entirety of the being and judge every reaction from her own locus of interest. Thus, when an inference about the totality called self is drawn based on such selective scrutiny, a false over-generalization may take place. Yet if one tries to avoid the generalization by limiting oneself to each specific situation, without moving to previous or succeeding events, or without making any theoretical projections, the effort becomes fragmented. Such an over-cautious study is not only constricted, but also misleading, as it contravenes the basic rule of human cognitive and affective development: that of the shaping, de-shaping and re-shaping of one's identity with experience.

Since the quality of my study depends upon the maturity of my compromise in this dilemma, I consider my decision with care. In outlining the self of the victims of soft violence during Partition, I abide by some basic principles. The first is being sensitive to individual differences. Indeed, in Chapter 4, my attempt was to drive home this very notion of individual differences in the processing of the partition experience among people with varied dispositions and destinies. Yet, one can always look for the commonalities as well. The message communicated to all the individuals through the shared experience is the binding source of these commonalities. I have already described how terror was the prime and singular message in the soft violence at the time of the Partition in Bengal. Accepting the risk of over-generalization, I have presumed that the unique characteristics of the self in Partition would be built upon this fear.

Another principle I follow in my endeavour is to define a collective self: one beyond individual variation and beyond additive conglomeration of the individual selves. Here we shift from ontology to epistemology. Let me start with the ontological characteristics first and then gradually proceed towards the collective self. The most pertinent discussion is R. D. Laing's description of ontological insecurity in response to any destabilizing experience. 'Fear' and 'lack of control' were the crux of my respondents' experiences of Partition and uprooting, and this was bound to generate a strong sense of insecurity in the developing psyche. This 'ontological insecurity' is in turn associated with a number of reactions. Depending on the developmental stage they were at the time of the experience, their reactions were expressed in various habitual and defensive modes. For some, this experience of lack of control imprinted a life-long sense of uncertainty on their psyche; for others, it was a step to maturity. Whatever the individual outcomes, the trauma of confusion and paralysing fear destabilized most of my respondents, at least temporarily. Laing has elaborated the symptoms following such experience of lack of 'realness, aliveness, autonomy and identity'.[18]

Laing observed that under ontological insecurity, with the incongruence between the expected and the real, the emergent feature is a sense of 'unrealness': a disbelief in what is happening. In spite of such denial, ultimately the reality shows through, and the individual attempts in 'contriving ways' to be and become real, to keep himself and others psychologically alive. In sum, he tries to prevent loss of the self. Laing further noted that it is not true that under duress one necessarily withdraws into oneself so that external realities cannot touch one. In fact, these touch one to a greater extent. However, in spite of the overflow of emotions, one is unable to share these with others. This concept is particularly relevant to our methodology, as it implies that the much-heralded 'withdrawal' as a reaction to trauma is not actual withdrawal of the psyche, but an abstention from reporting, which is congruent to the issue of 'silence' of partition victims that I shall shortly take up.

The reactions to ontological insecurity come in three stages: through three kinds of symptoms. One is 'engulfment'—where any deep interaction—interpersonal or intra-personal in nature, generates the fear of being overpowered, engulfed, devoured, destroyed. A second impact recognized by Laing is 'implosion'. Here the fearful avoidance of the reality is enhanced, as it is perceived as intrusive, breaking into pieces whatever identity one has built up. In this phase, one shuts oneself inside a self-created prison, so that the apprehended disaster does not come about. These two modes of reaction have been reported by my respondents in the description of the benumbment they experienced when scenes and news of violence unfolded before them. The 'pin-drop silence' of this period is not only an external silence; it is an inner silence as well. The third and final phase of Laing consists of 'petrification and depersonalization'. In discussing petrification, Laing refers to the motives of the perpetrator. Petrification is a 'magical act whereby one may attempt to turn someone else into stone ... and by extension where one negates the other person's autonomy, ignores his feelings, regards him as a thing, kills the life in him' (p. 46). Petrification makes the person a non-person; an object, possessing only physical life, without an identity. Laing observed that for his patients, petrification was followed by depersonalization, where one loses one's self: one's inner reality. Such depersonalization has been reported in a number of victims of genocidal schemes.[19] Our respondents, however, did not really reach this final phase of depersonalization and destruction of identity, although the assault left a mark, a fracture. This was probably because: *(a)* the phase of petrification was a short one; *(b)* once the victims migrated, the fear was substituted by a constructive struggle to accommodate to the new life; *(c)* they were young and had the strength to fight back and a future to look forward to; and *(d)* they had not directly suffered physical violence. But the trauma could not be integrated within the personality; it left a vulnerable point and hence was suppressed. I submit that mass displacement following petrifying fear generated a *culture of insecurity*. The characteristic features of this culture would presumably be similar to those of ontological insecurity, but would be expressed as the predominant characteristics of an entire generation, and transmitted to some extent to the next generation as well. The collective migrant self was built upon this culture of insecurity.

The consideration of the 'collective self' follows from here. The term 'self', though usually used in the sense of intra-individual properties, may be extended to define an intra-group identity as well.[20] This extended self presupposes two human tendencies: the search for 'social identity'[21] and 'self-categorization'.[22] The former refers to a human being's inherent social nature and the loss of identity when deprived of membership of the group. Self-categorization is an extension of the same tendency, where inclusion in a group necessitates exclusion from other groups. Thus the 'in-group–out-group' feeling is generated. This is the 'collective self', contained within the cultural milieu. If, until now, I was engaged in demonstrating how the individuals experienced and processed emotion, now I am in search of culture as well, or the emotional and social characteristics of the culture derived from the experiences of the migrants. The point is, am I in a position to trace the boundaries of such an overarching 'self', particularly considering the *idiographic* approach I have so long preferred?

I would say yes, with two qualifications. Firstly, this collective self will not actually apply to everybody at every moment; it is a self in process that we usually encounter. Secondly, the two aspects of the self—the self perceived by the observer and that conceptualized by oneself—may not be the same. Nobody knows which one is truer or closer to the 'actual self', if there is any. Thus, as I said in the Chapter 1, the entire effort is a 'reconstruction of reconstructions'.[23]

Among the defining characteristics of the migrant population is the intra-psychic fragmentation that occurred as a result of the petrifying experience and loss of identity.[24] When, in later life, rehabilitation was achieved more or less successfully, the trauma of this fragmentation was covered with various defensive modes, predominantly with partial repression, rationalization and isolation. Depending upon the intellect and early emotional exposure of the individual, these defences were used with maturity or unscrupulousness. What I found in my respondents' narrations were therefore not the direct experiences of fragmentation; these had been plastered over in the last sixty-odd years. But one could see the defences in operation, the patchwork and signs of hurried repair. A related feeling was that of marginalization as a member of the community. One major reaction to this marginalization and insecurity was a collective identification where the feelings of the individual were merged in the feelings of the mass. The transcendence from the individual to the collective self, the identification with 'we' probably assisted them in partially resolving the issue; they could, at least on the surface, anchor themselves to the collective identity. The memory of the desperate pushing for space on the steamer or the truck, the thronging crowd on the station platform, the wordless noise of thousands of people, all contribute to a feeling of a dumb identification with the swarm.

Western culture per se has been known to be more individualistic, emphasizing personal identity formation, while Eastern culture is more inclined towards a collective existence[25] and is more diffuse in nature. In India, the collective style of life was punctured to some extent by the colonial invasion, but most families, particularly in the villages, remained bound in an interpersonal cohesion: decisions were joint, individual development was within the framework of the family.[26] Therefore, under duress, the collective self may have emerged with relative ease. Persons who have a shared history may more readily be bound in a commonality than those with discrete existence or arbitrary bonding.[27]

In this feeling of being a part of the mass, one feels a part of history as well; one's individuality merges into the collective reality. This merging serves two psychological purposes. One is the silencing of personal pain, the anonymity of the crowd serving as a mask for oneself as well, and the other is the strength of identity one gets from confronting a hurdle together, particularly in the face of uncertainty about one's decision.

I have talked earlier about the silence within the narratives of partition memory. This was a typical kind of selective silence: throughout these sixty-odd years the victims of Partition have expressed their sentiments in discrete bursts of personal reaction to various events in life, and also sporadically in some literary and dramatic efforts. Rarely has anyone attempted to integrate these short-lived emotions into a consistent historical whole. Most writers on the Bengal Partition have noted this confusion in recorded history, oral or written, so far as the feelings of victims are concerned. The silence has been commented upon by Ashis Nandy,[28] who considers that the violence of Partition 'has never been a subject of any firm or intense scrutiny, either by journalists or by scholars. The violence associated with the birth of the two largest nation-states in South Asia remains till today, an invisible one. After a brief splash in the newspapers of the time, it quickly sunk into oblivion.'

Sandip Bandyopadhyaya comments on the under-emphasis on the trauma of Partition:[29]

> The tendency to forget or to overlook this unpleasant part of the history of Partition has led to the formation of a number of stereotypes, and provided a set of readymade categories to be used for understanding the catastrophic event that Partition was. The result is that while the total history of Partition remains unexplored, an alternative version has meanwhile evolved. And more significantly, this alternative discourse, both in oral and written forms, has at its centre a big question mark.

Debesh Ray confronts the question of absence of genuine feeling regarding partition issues in contemporary Bengali literature:

> 'Why then, are Bengali short stories and novels hushed on the issue of Partition and independence? Did writers consciously turn away from the great event that had displaced the history, the existence and the future of Bengal from its habitual axis? Was this owing to the intrinsic nature of writing developed over nearly a century, of

> expressing the inner versions of focal events? Or is this silence a *cultivated forgetfulness*?'[30]

The feelings, observers agree, did not die a natural death. They were buried alive through repression. And the repressed, as a rule, returns, perhaps in another garb, as seen in our narratives. Once out of the situation of terror, on this side of the border where the persecution of the faceless other is no more felt but where one confronts an equally unpalatable uncertainty about future livelihood, the anger is unleashed. They can now engage in the restoration of self-esteem constructively or destructively.[31] This is the time, I think, of actual transition from the individual to the collective self. This is what gives the refugees a determination to the extent of obstinacy, impulsiveness to the extent of headstrongness; this is what makes the migrant population sensitive, unreasonable and impetuous.[32]

This is usually the moment ripe for political activity. Individuals seeking refuge in collectivity are easily drawn towards the 'party', formal membership being a source of comfort in their background of uncertainty. In West Bengal, the neighbourhoods inhabited by the refugees have been known to be particularly 'politically aware'; could this term be another name for the collective attempt to regain lost identity?

With this assumption of political involvement as being partly an aspiration towards a stable identity and self-categorization,[33] I try to understand the socio-political scenario of West Bengal since Independence. Bengal in 1947 already boasted of being intellectually progressive and politically active; however, the vestiges of terrorism remained and provincial egotism was raising its head. It is in this backdrop that the refugee influx hit West Bengal, coming on top of two other recent events that caused turmoil: the political confusion following the 1942 Quit India movement, and the great famine. The vulnerable economy and low morale of West Bengal was shattered by the final blow of the refugee problem. The depressed, troubled and demoralized people of West Bengal were unable to sympathize genuinely with this new population and in fact considered them the ultimate troublemakers. They rejected these rootless people, yet at another level identified with them to some extent and introjected their anxiety: the refugees representing what might befall them as well if they did not hurry to protect whatever they had. This is probably the first occasion when one half of the Bengali self started hating its other half: the otherness took a concrete shape. Thus, the Bengali 'self' was partitioned. If Bengalis in general shared the pain of division, it was undoubtedly the refugees who bore the brunt of it. They were searching frantically for a foothold, a space that would provide them not only social but also psychological security.

This was the sentiment that the Congress leaders in West Bengal probably missed. And, this was the sentiment that the leaders of the Communist Party utilized to the fullest. Thus there was in the 1950s a mass identification with the leftist ideal—with or without comprehending its theoretical and practical implications. Following the second upsurge of migration after 1971, and the coercive measures of the Congress government at the Centre after the declaration of the Emergency, the Communists graduated from being a strong opposition to become the ruling party in West Bengal in 1977. I try to identify, though in a brief and incomplete way, some of the psychological determinants of political developments in the then West Bengal.

Among my respondents, I find that political affiliations were determined by three factors. One was age. Many of those who were late adolescents or early adults at the time of migration had already formed political views, often linked to those of the various factions of freedom fighters. A good number of them were moved by the combination of spirituality and pragmatism in the doctrines of Gandhi and therefore supported the Congress; they persisted in the same belief in later life, ignoring the gulf between the later activities of the Congress and the ideals heralded by the Gandhi they adored. Some of them changed positions in West Bengal and inclined towards Marxism. Indeed, many political prisoners changed from being terrorists or Gandhians and became Marxist in jail in the 1940s. Others who belonged to the Forward Bloc or Anushilan Samity in East Bengal also remained actively or morally aligned with leftist politics later in their lives.[34]

A second influence was the political atmosphere of the localities or colonies the refugees settled in. Here often the leftist leaders were prominently available to help them: sharing their joys and woes, their struggle for survival. The moral fibre of the Communist Party, its linkage with the soil, its humane face, was probably most palpable in these leaders. A large number of families became their followers as personal love turned into impersonal ideal.

A third influence was related to the second one, but operated on a wider scale: the refugee rehabilitation issue. It was the leftists who led the movement against the Congress government in West Bengal in favour of the demands of the refugees.[35] The history of the United Central Refugee Council (UCRC) (including establishment of squatters' colonies)[36] is closely intertwined with the history of the Communist Party. From 1959, the UCRC was dominated by leftist leaders. Involvement with this movement gave the refugees not only a source of identity, but also a chance to unleash their suppressed aggression and a specific target to blame instead of the previous nameless faceless enemy. This provided a source of relief; a psychological breathing space after the numbing fear.[37]

Another appeal of the Communist agenda may have lain in the 'image' or 'stereotype' of socialism. When an individual embraces a theoretical stance as one's own, it is rarely a result of thorough critical analysis of all of its tenets, but owing to an immediate relevance of some of its components to the personal life—an internalization of certain aspects of its made-easy 'slogans'. The socialist approach, viewed from a perspective of popular understanding, emphasizes scientific judgement and rationality as the desired approach to the world.[38] Under the prevailing uncertainties of communal disharmony, rationalization was, we have seen, a major mode of defence.

We have observed earlier how in certain individuals personal irrationality and impulsive emotionality belied the rational stance adopted publicly. This, as I have already asserted, is not to say that the person in question was dishonest; indeed it is an excellent example of the internal split between the individual and the collective self,[39] whereby the person is 'true' to both of his selves that contradict each other.

The active, structured and well-defined socialist doctrine, presented to the migrants as devoid of conflict and confusion and carrying the assurance of a humanitarian goal was exactly what they needed to regain a sense of security. If they had suffered the trauma of forced weaning from the motherland, the socialism of the day was like a nourishing foster mother, providing the comfort and love they craved. It is no wonder that the migrants would be attracted to this doctrine.

Let me qualify this. The leftist politics was anti-establishment and oppositional by nature. Indeed, some authors point out that quite soon UCRC started to talk not only of refugee welfare, but also forwarded anti-imperialist commentary about world affairs, thus projecting both a global revolutionary and progressive face.[40] This revolutionary image probably served a psychologically pertinent purpose: it provided scope for the silenced aggression to express itself, through identification with the rebel. Social psychologists have observed that group identification is best retained when the sentiment of anger and injustice is the binding force.[41] Commitment increases when people conglomerate as a result of negative aspersions being made against them; negative identities are stronger than positive ones. Thus, the stigma of being 'Bangal', 'refugee' and 'Communist' helped to develop a strong bond of group identity[42] that remains intact at least in some persons even today. I have mentioned that socialism was like a nourishing mother, but was it a 'good enough' mother? Could it recover the 'true self' of the Bengali community, the confidence in a stable existence? Or was it a temporary balm, yet another illusion that might break into pieces under scrutiny? I have yet to resolve this question.

A second question stares me in the face. If the Bengali soul had been fragmented, if one part of it, as I have claimed, had started to hate its 'other', why did West Bengal never become a strongly communal state? Why, in spite of the fact that Bengalis are proud of Shyama Prasad Mookerjee, did the Hindutva concept not win strong ground here? Why did the refugees not give vent to their anti-Muslim feelings more strongly after coming to West Bengal, although many of them did harbour such negative feelings? I can only offer a shaky psychological hypothesis in addition to the numerous political ones. I anchor this paradox to a couple of issues. The first is, once again, the very impact of soft violence, that is, the confusion about who the real enemy is. Since most of the migrant Hindus were never sure if the Muslims were truly their personal enemies, the anger against the community could not nurture itself into violence with its sap drawn from personal vengeance. There is, however another probable reason. This refers to the stereotype of the nature of the Bengali community as labile: also designated as 'effeminate' by some authors. I shall try to explain my point below.

The culture of Bengal has always been seen to be deeply philosophical as well as emotional: soft and melting with the Baul, Agamani and Bhatiali songs, the image of the mother pervading. The Bengali language is deemed soft and musical to the ear. Bengali images of gods and goddesses are derivatives of north Indian ones with a rounding of the face and limbs. Even when worshipping Kali, her maternal image is highlighted, although she might be a mother who is moody, *pagli*, and occasionally destructive. Perhaps the Bengali culture saw itself as a more feminized one,[43] not a warrior's culture at heart, attempting to neutralize the sharp edges, yet trying to compensate for the softness with an aggressive intellectuality. I presume that this stereotype, serving as a frame of reference for Bengali culture, exerted its self-fulfilling effect[44] and influenced the political scenario of Bengal.

When we talk about the 'effeminate Bengali', the tone is usually derisive. But isn't it an out-of-date patriarchal imperative that men must be manly? A number of observers of Indian culture in general have tried to relate the personality of Indian people, particularly men, to the psychosexual development patterns of traditional Indian society. Indian men, it has been said, on the one hand were attached too closely to the mother, at least physically. Particularly during infancy and early childhood, the identification with the father is rendered almost impossible owing to the distinction between *andarmahal* (the inner quarters which was the women's world) and *barmahal* (the outside world, where men prevailed). On the other hand, the psycho-social structure of society forces a separation between the mother and the son when he reaches late childhood and adolescence, thus disrupting the bond.[45] Usually, the negative impacts of such identification, for example, undue narcissistic concern, unaccepted yet unavoidable feminine identification and development of a binary mother image as either a powerful goddess or a shrunken degraded woman have been stressed in earlier writings. I subscribed to this concept earlier, considering the Bengali psyche a simple specific case of the greater Indian selfhood.[46] However, while reconciling such concepts with my present findings, I want to hint at a different possibility.

Most of the above characteristics have been observed on the basis of north Indian samples where political and geographical conditions caused a greater degree of dissociation between the feminine and the masculine and between the inside and outside. Although Bengali culture shares some of these elements with other parts of India, its differences must be taken into account. Owing perhaps to the sultry weather, the geographical characteristics and the social structure of pre-colonial agrarian Bengal, the compartmentalization of inside and outside was never as watertight as in certain other parts of India.[47] The direct influence of Muslim purdah was also less stable and pervasive. In this sense, perhaps the eastern and southern states are more comparable. The relatively greater intermixing of the two sexes in Bengal resulted in an acceptance of femininity and submission in men in a relatively positive light. Valour as expressed through assaultiveness and honour killing was never the cardinal trait of Bengalis. They identified more with accommodation and adjustment, sometimes cleverly and sometimes not, allowing things to run their own course, submitting occasionally out of lethargy, and at other times thanks to an intrinsic sense of balance and flexibility. I submit that the concept of radical Hindutva might be too dis-cordant to the Bengali ear. The majority of Bengalis would not respond spontaneously to the strong binary distinction between the good and the bad divisions of the self; the 'split' would be incomplete. If the Bengali stereotype is one of non-aggression and tolerance, an inevitable corollary is avoidance of extreme measures, particularly physical assault. This has probably served to prevent major violence. The accommodative and non-aggressive traits of Bengalis—the silent grit that helps survival—are sometimes reflected in the form of humour, an integral part of Bengali literature, drama and movies, and sometimes in the form of romantic dreams, stepping out of reality in order to adapt to reality.

I know I am treading on shifting sands in positing the above; yet I intend to pursue and explore it further, as it is related to a crucial problem of India today. I refer to the increasing communal animosity and violence that has been sweeping the face of the country in the last two decades. How much risk does Bengal hold? In the face of the new communal crisis in the country, Bengal cannot deny its past and has to operate upon the experience it has gained from Partition. Total communal integration, where all memories would be obliterated, is not only utopian; it is also undesirable as it entails denial of experienced pain. Bengal today has two options. It can choose to follow the course of retaliation and counter-retaliation; and opt for a binary social existence. The other option is to accept a mode of inter-communal living in which there would be no simplified answers, no fixed structure, but a continuing quest for a true self born out of, yet extending beyond, suffering and falsehood. The pain of fragmentation, now a matter of the past, has to be recovered from memory, reconstructed time and again to serve as a caution against the destructive impulse, and utilized to develop a restorative orientation towards a new kind of orchestrated community: towards a coexistence of opposites to create a multilayered synchrony. Perfect harmony and stability may never be reached, but the efforts themselves would live on. The process of search itself would be the product of search: an action that would keep humanity alive. As I look back upon the psychological history of Partition, I can see that such feats have already been performed at the individual level. Small personal victories have already been won, victories not over the constructed or even the concocted 'other', but over one's own aggressive and destructive tendencies. Is it only wishful thinking that Bengal would use its so-called 'submissive' persona not to tolerate injustice, but to create a new mode of living?

GOING BEYOND

Time has passed. The refugee Bengalis were gradually incorporated within the mainstream, the rigid division between the Bangal and Ghoti melted with time. Socialism changed its face. The politics of West Bengal has seen 'Paribartan' change. The Hindutva concept is yet to take root in the soil of Bengal. America is being mimicked in nightclubs, in the 'booze' culture, in the music the present generation listens to, in the ideals they set. The globalized, technologized Bengali psyche will soon lose its direct touch with the partition experience. We shall see only the work of memory on subsequent generations: the introjected old in interaction with the new. As the good and bad effects dissolve in the course of years, as social customs redefine themselves, as old political doctrines are served in new bottles, it is this memory alone that will bind the past generations with the future, till Partition becomes a myth: a legend. Perhaps the true meaning of the partition experience will be unfolded only when it becomes a legend because it is in the process of mythification that the time-tested essence of any experience is consolidated.

> 'I am old and infirm,' said Beena. 'You have come to meet me today, maybe I will die tomorrow. I do not know what use you may have for this old woman's gibbering, but remember one thing. I have given you my memory of pain. If I die tomorrow you must remember that a

part of me has remained with you, inside you, all who have outlived me in this country.'

Beena died a week after. I have a part of her in me. We all do.

Notes

1 H. F. Wolcott. 1990. On seeking and rejecting validity in qualitative research. In E.W. Eisner and A. Peshkin, eds, *Qualitative inquiry in education: The continuing debate* (New York: Teachers College Press): 121-52; see also N. K. Denzin and Y.S. Lincoln, eds. 1994. *Handbook of qualitative research* (Thousand Oaks, CA: Sage); J. Morse. 1994. *Critical issues in qualitative research methods* (Thousand Oaks, CA: Sage).

2 Nilanjana Chatterjee. 2012. *Interrogating victimhood: East Bengali refugees narratives of communal violence*, http://www.pstc.brown.edu/chatterjee.PDF, accessed on 12 Oct.

3 Gayatri Chakravarti Spivak. 1999. *A critique of postcolonial reason: Towards a history of the vanishing present* (Kolkata: Seagull): 203.

4 'Remembering partition', a dialogue between Javeed Alam and Suresh Sharma. 1998. *Seminar* 461.

5 See D. Laub. 1992. An event without a witness: Truth, testimony and survival. In S. Felman and D. Laub, eds., *Testimony: Crises of witnessing in literature, psychoanalysis and history* (New York: Routledge); see also T. Todorov. 1996. *Facing the extreme: Moral life in concentration camps*, trans A. Denner and A. Pollak (New York: Holt).

6 Rationality has multiple meanings, and its use in different contexts may cause confusion. Amartya Sen sees it as a tendency to subject one's choices, actions, objectives, values and priorities to 'reasoned scrutiny'; see A. Sen. 2002. *Rationality and freedom* (Delhi: Oxford University Press). For my participants, however, this scrutiny often came post-hoc; that is, as a justification, sometimes impulsive and unreasonable after the events have taken place. Under such conditions, it is no longer rationality, but rationalization.

7 The tendency to talk about factual or descriptive details only may be compared to the responses one gets in certain clinical cases, when the

respondents are asked to construct a story with Thematic Apperception Test cards. Instead of imagining a story and focusing on the feelings of the people in the cards, they tend to describe what they are seeing. Such response styles are supposedly related to the defences of repression and isolation.

8 'Object relation' implies the capacity to form and maintain friendly and loving relationship with others with a minimum of inappropriate hostility. This function of the ego has been elaborated by a number of psychoanalysts. Some essential references are: K. Abraham. 1924/1953. *Selected papers on psychoanalysis* (New York: Basic Books); E. Kris. 1951. The development of ego psychology. *Samiksa* 5; M. Klein. 1955. *New directions in psychoanalysis* (London: Tavistock); D.W. Fairbairn. 1966. *Psychoanalytic studies of the personality* (London: Tavistock).

9 'Cognitive style' refers to the characteristic style or manner in which an individual manages one's cognitive tasks. Some usual dimensions of cognitive style are levelling *vs.* sharpening; field dependence *vs.* independence; reflective *vs.* impulsive. In the perspective of narration of life-history, it seems that additional dimensions like 'systematic *vs.* random' and 'self-anchored *vs.* other-anchored' could be hypothesized.

10 S. Freud. 1899/1962. Screen memories. In J. Strachey, ed. and trans., *The standard edition of the complete psychological works of Sigmund Freud* (London: Hogarth Press), vol 3: 301-22. Screen memory in context of traumatic experience and their recuperative role has been discussed by N. C. Marucco. 2007. Between memory and destiny: Repetition 1. *International Journal of Psychoanalysis* 88, 309-28.

11 E. Glover. 1929. The 'screening' function of traumatic memories. *International Journal of Psychoanalysis* 10, 90-93.

12 See D. Spence. 1982. *Narrative truth and historical truth: Meaning and interpretation in psychoanalysis* (New York: Norton).

13 Jorge Luis Borges. 1983. *Labyrinth* (New York: Modern Library).

14 For a review of the psychological theories of self, see E. R. Hilgard. 1949. Human motives and the concept of the self. *American Psychologist* 4, 374-82; and M. B. Smith. 1978. Perspectives on selfhood. *American Psychologist* 33, 1053-63. For a discussion on the nature of the two perspectives of self, see A. Aron and E. N. Aron. 1986. *Love and the expansion of self: Understanding attraction and satisfaction* (Washington, DC: Hemisphere. For psychoanalytical perspective on self, see H. Kohut. 1985. *Self-psychology*

and the humanities (New York: Norton).

15 S. Epstein. 1973. The self-concept revisited or a theory of a theory. *American Psychologist* 28, 404-416.

16 Ego development necessitates frustration and violation of infantile desires. It is through the ability to withstand series of small and big assaults and to accommodate non-fulfilment of wishes, that one learns 'delay of gratification': a sign of maturity. See S. Freud. 1923/1961. The Ego and the id. In Strachey, ed. and trans., *The standard edition of the complete psychological works of Sigmund Freud*, vol 19 London: Hogath Press. 3-63.

17 G. Pandey. 1999. *Memory, history and the question of violence: Reflections on the reconstruction of partition* (Kolkata: Centre for Studies in Social Sciences): 9.

18 R. D. Laing. 1959. *The divided self* (Harmondsworth: Penguin).

19 See D. L. Niewyk, ed. 1998. *Fresh wounds: Early narratives of holocaust survival* (Chapel Hill, NC: University of North Carolina Press); R. J. Lifton and E. Markusen. 1988. *The genocidal mentality: Nazi holocaust and nuclear threat* (New York: Basic Books).

20 For a thorough discussion of research on the 'self' in collectivity, see R.F. Baumeister. 1998. The self. In D. T. Gilbert, S. R. Fiske and G. Lindzey, eds. *The handbook of social psychology* (New York: McGraw-Hill): 680-740. See also for a discussion on the self in individual and social context, M.R. Banaji and D. A. Prentice. 1994. The self in social contexts. *Annual Review of Psychology* 45, 297-332.

21 For a discussion on the social identity theory, see H. Tajfel. 1978. *Differentiation between social groups: Studies in the social psychology of intergroup relations* (New York: Academic). See also H. Tajfel and J. C. Turner. 1979. An integrative theory of intergroup conflict. In W.G. Austin and S. Worchel, eds, *The social psychology of intergroup relations* (Monterey, CA: Brooks-Cole): 33-48.

22 For a detailed discussion of the self-categorization theory, see J. C. Turner (1987). A self-categorization theory. In J. C. Turner et al. 1987. *Rediscovering the social group: A self-categorization theory* (Oxford: Blackwell): 42-67; see also J. C. Turner. 1999. Some current issues in research on social identity and self-categorization theories. In N. Ellemer, R. Spears and B. Doosje, eds, *Social identity: Context, commitment, content* (Oxford: Blackwell): 6-34.

23 This attempt to reconstruct is the strength and weakness of all

interpretative endeavour. Krishna Sobti speaks about the distortion of memory in the context of Partition , and its use in history, in an interview with Alok Bhalla: 'I think that when a historian decides to take sides, he can justify anything. Memories of those times can always be justified. In the histories of the Partition, "culture" is one word that has been abused constantly and mercilessly.' See Krishna Sobti. 1997. *Memory and history* (Delhi: Orient Longman): 66. Although aware of the danger, I have decided to take sides.

24 See G. Kudaisya. 1998. Divided landscapes, fragmented identities: East Bengal refugees and their rehabilitation in India, 1947-79. In D. A. Low and H. Brasted, eds., *Freedom, trauma, continuities: Northern India and independence* (Delhi: Sage): 73-90.

25 The stress on individuality in Western culture has been discussed by a number of psychologists. See, e.g., G. Hofstede. 1980. *Culture's consequences: International differences in work-related values* (Thousand Oaks, CA: Sage).

26 See D. Sinha. 1988. Family scenario in a developing country and its implication for mental health: The case of India. In P. R. Dasen, J. W. Berry and N. Sartorius, eds, *Health and cross-cultural psychology. Towards applications* (Newbury Park. CA: Sage). For a discussion of Indian family dynamics from a psychoanalytical perspective, see A. Roland. 1988. *In search of self in India and Japan: Towards a cross-cultural psychology* (Princeton: Princeton University Press).

27 See B. Simon. 1997. Self and group in modern society: Ten theses on the individual self and the collective self. In R. Spears et al., eds, *Introduction: the social psychology of stereotyping and group life* (Oxford: Blackwell): 318-35; L. Gaertner, C. Sedikides and K. Graetz. 1999. In search of self-definition: motivational primacy of the collective self, or contextual primacy? *J of Personality and Social Psychology* 76, 5-18.

28 A. Nandy. 1997. The invisible holocaust. *The Hindu*, 24 August.

29 Sandip Bandyopadhyaya. 1996. The riddle of partition: Memories of the Bengali Hindus. In R. Samaddar, ed., *Reflections of the partition in the East* (Delhi: Vikas), 59-60.

30 D. Ray ed. 1999. *Raktamanir haare*. A collection of Bengali short stories on partition and independence (Delhi: Sahitya Academy), 25. My translation, italics added.

31 A large number of studies and memoirs on life of the refugees and their

subsequent trauma and struggle for survival, including negative experiences from humiliation to rape and murder have been illustrated in many works. Since the post-Partition context was not the focus, I have omitted many references here. Some significant studies are, however, Manas Ray. 2000. Growing up refugee: Memory and locality. In Pradip Kumar Bose, ed., *Refugees in West Bengal* (Calcutta Research Group): 163-9: Nilanjana Chatterjee. 1992. *Midnight's unwanted children: East Bengali refugees and the politics of rehabilitation.* Unpublished Ph.D. dissertation, Brown University; Arun Deb. 2000. The UCRC: Its role in establishing the rights of refugee squatters in Calcutta. In Pradip Kumar Bose ed., *Refugees in West Bengal.* (Calcutta Research Group): 65-79. Kamla Patel. 2006. *Torn from the roots: A partition memoir*, Uma Randeria trans. (New Delhi: Women Unlimited). Uditi Sen has discussed different images of refugee women in Calcutta: 2011.Spinster, prostitute or pioneer? Images of refugee women in post-partition Calcutta. EUI working paper MWP 2011/34 (Italy: European University Institute) Retrieved from *cadmus.eui.eu/bitstream/handle/1814/.../MWP_Sen_2011_34.pdf?.* M. M. Rahman and W. Van Schendel. 2003. I am not a refugee-rethinking partition migration, *Modern Asian Studies* 37; Tathagata Roy. 2001. *My people, uprooted: a saga of the Hindus of eastern Bengal* (Calcutta: Ratna Prakashan).

32 D. Chakrabarty. 1999. Nation and imagination: The training of the eye on Bengali modernity. *Studies in History* 15: 177-207. Chakrabarty has designated such characteristics as the 'refugee syndrome'.

33 I am indebted to the writings of Vamik Volkan for my thoughts on the psychology of political involvement. See V. D. Volkan. 1988. *The need to have enemies and allies: From clinical practice to international relationship* (Northvale, NJ: Jason Aronson); V. D. Volkan. 1997. *Bloodlines: From ethnic pride to ethnic terrorism* (New York: Farrar, Straus and Giroux).

34 Of course many were already attracted towards the new world view of Marxism. An account of the personal memory of pre-Partition Bengal and development of affiliation to Communism may be obtained in the Bengali memoir of Jayantanuj Bandyopadhyay. 2005. *Oparer chelebela. 1931-1947* (Kolkata: Subarnarekha).

35 S. Z. Donald. 1969. The social bases of Indian Communism. In R. Lowenthal, ed. *Issues in the future of Asia: Communist and noncommunist alternative* (New York: Praeger): 97-124.

[36] The UCRC was formed on 4 June 1950 in response to the Eviction of Persons in Unauthorised Occupation Land Bill that was to become the Act XVI of 1951. Its root may be traced back to the All Bengal Refugee Council for Action formed in 1948.

[37] Apart from the detailed outlining of leftist influence over refugees by Prafulla Chakrabarty in his *Marginal men*, a host of other writings have traced the development of left politics in the early stages through the refugee rehabilitation issue. See P. Chakrabarti.1999. *The marginal men: The refugees and the left political syndrome in West Bengal* (Kolkata: Naya Udyog). Also see, Abhijit Dasgupta. The politics of agitation and confession: Displaced Bengalis in West Bengal. In Sanjay K. Ray, ed, *Refugees and human rights: Social and political dynamics of refugee problem in eastern and northeastern India* (Jaipur: Rawat): 98-100: Nilanjana Chatterjee, Interrogating victimhood: East Bengali refugees' narratives of communal violence, web article, retrieved from http://www.pstc.brown.edu/chatterjee. pdf; Anasuya Basu Ray Chaudhury, Life after partition: A study on the reconstruction of lives in West Bengal, web article, retrieved from http://www.sasnet.lu.se/EASASpapers/33Anasua Basuray.pdf. The leftist influence among the refugees became prominent after 1958, when apart from CPI, the Proja Socialist Party and the Revolutionary Communsit Party of India also participated in organizing the refugees.

[38] I must hurry to emphasize that this statement is an oversimplification of the rich Marxist literature and theoretical contribution to the understanding of society. However, most people, when they declare themselves supporters of a particular doctrine, emphasize a chosen few oversimplified ideas, and hardly bother with the detailed ideology embedded in any comprehensive theoretical system. Most of my comments concern this popular understanding of the doctrine, as it exists among the thousands of supporters of the erstwhile ruling political party in West Bengal. This perception is far removed from that someone who has delved deeper into the concepts.

[39] In some cases the individual and the collective self within the same person compete for prominence, and often the person carries the split for life. See R. Spears. 2001. The interaction between the individual and the collective self: Self-categorization in context. In C. Sedikides and M. B. Brewer, eds, 2006. *Individual self, relational self, and collective self: Partners,*

opponents or strangers? (Philadelphia: Psychology Press): 171-98.

40 See Prafulla Chakrabarty. 1999. The *marginal men (Kolkata: Naya Udyog)*; also see Mohit Ray. 2009. Illegal migration and undeclared refugees - Idea of West Bengal at stake, Presented at National Seminar on 'Migration and Its Impact on Indian State and Democracy'–13 March 2009, Dept of Politics & Public Administration –University of Pune, downloaded on 12 Oct 2012 from http://www.bengalgenocide.comPaper_Bengal%20infiltration.pdf.

41 See for reference A. J. M. Dijker. 1987. Emotional reactions to ethnic minorities. *European Journal of Social Psychology* 17, 305-25; see also D. M. Mackie, T. Devos and E. R. Smith. 2000. Intergroup emotions: explaining offensive action tendencies in an intergroup context. *Journal of Personality and Social Psychology* 79, 602-16.

42 I remember in this context *Arjun*, a Bengali novella by Sunil Gangopadhyaya, where a young refugee who tried to be different from his fellow migrants by aspiring for higher education and cultural refinement was persecuted by members of the colony where he lived.

43 Mrinalini Sinha. 1995. *Colonial masculinity: The 'manly Englishman' and the 'effeminate Bengali' in the late nineteenth century* (Manchester: Manchester University Press), discusses how the concept of masculinity or absence of it played a major role in defining the Bengali self-image; see also Saraladebi Chaudhurani. 2011. *The scattered leaves of my life: An Indian nationalist remembers*, trans. and edited by Sikata Banerjee (Delhi: Women Unlimited; Kolkata: Stree). The original Bengali book was *Jiboner Jharapata* (1914); Saraladebi organized clubs where men wrestled and worked with clubs to develop muscles and become less effeminate and thus good material for nationalism.

44 I want to emphasize that although some sociological and psychological observations have supported the 'soft and submissive' Bengali culture, it remains an issue of contention whether such core characteristics are really present in the members of a given province or state. On the other hand, undoubtedly such stereotypes exist for every cultural group. Individual Bengalis may or may not reflect the features of the stereotype, but such beliefs have the capacity to influence behaviour as underlying cognitive givens and may be self-confirming. See for Theoretical understanding of such influence, G. Allport. 1958. *The nature of prejudice* (New York: Anchor Books).

[45] See S. K. Mitra. 1985. Indian personality: A perspective. *Samiksa* 37, 31-55; and A. Roland. 1978. Psychoanalytic perspective on personality development in India. *Samiksa* 32, 48-68. See also, S. Kakar. 1978. *The inner world: A psychoanalytic study of childhood and society in India* (Delhi: Oxford University Press); S. Kakar. 1997. The maternal feminine in Indian psychoanalysis. In S. Kakar, ed., *Culture and psyche: Selected essays* (Delhi: Oxford University Press): 60-73.

[46] J. Basu. 1990. An analysis of some stories of *Thakurmar Jhuli*—a Bengali fairy tale collection. *Samiksa* 44, 87-108.

[47] D. Chakrabarty, 1999. Nation and Imagination. *Studies in History*, 15, 177-207.

GLOSSARY

altruism A defence mechanism where service to others in a constructive way leads to one's own satisfaction.

autobiographical memory A memory system that contains recollections of episodes, events and knowledge from a person's own life.

cathexis In psychoanalytical parlance, the investment of libidinal energy in an object, person or situation.

client-centred therapy A type of therapy developed by Carl Rogers in 1940s and 1950s, emphasizing therapist-client connection and congruence, empathy, non-judgemental acceptance of the client by the therapist and unconditional positive regard as major agents of therapeutic change.

cognitive approach in psychology An approach where the emphasis is on understanding how information from the environment is processed by the individual; focus includes attention, perception, memory, thinking, decision making.

content analysis A method of textual analysis where the content of specified communication are analysed.

counter-transference In psychoanalysis, defined as the therapist's emotional responses to the client; it may be irrational and generated from the therapist's own complex. There are debates as to whether it is a hindrance to therapy.

defence mechanism In psychoanalytical parlance, the various techniques of the ego employed to resolve the conflicts between contradictory id impulses and between the id impulse and the super-ego.

depth psychology An alternate name for psychoanalytical psychology, coined by Eugen Bleuler, where the concept of the unconscious is addressed.

emic and *etic* Two modes of cultural account of human behaviour: *emic* means data viewed from within the culture to be studied; *etic* implies data viewed from an outsider's perspective. These two terms are common in cultural anthropology, but are used in other social sciences as well.

fixation A defence mechanism where the individual is fixated to an earlier phase of psychological development.

flash bulb memory Vivid, detailed and specific recollection from one's personal life of an event or situation that was of high emotional value.

free association A technique used in psychoanalysis and psychodynamic therapy where the client is asked to speak out whatever comes to her/his mind without judging its truth, rationality or moral aspects. This is expected to facilitate the change process in therapy by making unconscious material more available and by reducing resistance.

free floating anxiety A state of anxiety without any specific focus or triggering event; often seen in connection to generalized anxiety disorder.

Gestalt This German word means form or shape; in English it also connotes 'wholeness'. In psychology, Gestalt theory emphasizes the holistic and organized nature of perception and learning.

idiographic versus *nomothetic* These are two approaches to knowledge. *Idiographic* emphasizes the unique and the subjective, and hence more appropriate for the humanities; *nomothetic* emphasizes generalization and therefore is more commonly used in the natural sciences.

introjection A defence mechanism where the thoughts and feeling originating outside oneself are incorporated or felt as one's own.

libido As a psychoanalytical term, the force of the occurrences in the domain of sexual excitation; conceptualized as variable and quantifiable. Freud further qualifies the term 'sexual' to refer to all instincts associated with the notion of 'love' or attachment.

narcissistic and *anaclitic love* Freud considers two kinds of object choice: in *anaclitic* mode the individual chooses to love persons similar to her/his early love objects, often after the mother or the father. In narcissistic mode the individual seeks one's own ego in the love object and hence tries to find self in chosen objects.

object relation The phenomenon of being related and attached to other persons; in psychoanalytical parlance, it often refers to the infant's primary ability to connect with its mother, who is usually the first 'object'.

over-determination An effect (attitude, emotion or perception) being determined by multiple aetiological factors reinforcing and interacting with each other; also used to imply multiple levels of underlying facets or meanings of a phenomenon.

pathogenecity The ability of a pathogenic or causative factor to generate pathology/disease.

phenomenology In philosophy, the study of structure of experience or consciousness. It also refers to a movement in the history of philosophy based on the works of Edmund Husserl.

projection A defence mechanism where the thoughts and feelings originating in oneself are thought as being located in the outer environment.

psychoeconomics The psychoeconomic model of the mind assumes that there is a finite amount of energy available for mental works: if too much energy is invested in one, there may be lack in another; also the probability of a specific response depends on the amount of energy invested. Freud described this energy in terms of libido.

reflective listening A strategy of listening often used for client-centred counselling. It entails listening empathetically to the speaker and then reflecting it back to the speaker to ensure proper understanding.

regression A defence mechanism where the individual goes back to an earlier phase of psychological development and demonstrates behaviour of that phase.

reminiscence bump The tendency of older persons to remember events occurring around adolescence.

saturation (in sampling) In qualitative research work, e.g., non-probabilistic, the sample size is often not pre-determined and new participants may be incorporated till no new theme or concept appears in analysis. The point of no further new concept is known as saturation.

schema In cognitive psychology, an inner representation or mental framework for organizing information.

script A concept often used in transactional analysis, referring to the life plan we cherish and follow, often without our conscious knowledge.

snowball technique A non-probability sampling technique where the present participants refer their acquaintances as possible future participants of the study; thus the size of the sample rolls like a snowball and grows in size.

sublimation A kind of defence mechanism where unacceptable impulses and ideas are transformed into socially acceptable or even appreciated activities.

INDEX

aggression, 92 n18, 179-82, 197-98. *See also* anger; hate

anger, 92 n18. *See also* aggression; hate; refugee.
  and guilt, 56-57
  nature of, 42, 92 n19
  and Partition, xix, 20, 51, 53, 62, 75, 77

anxiety, 20, 92 n18, 112, 114. *See also* fear

Bandyopadhyaya, Sandip, 80, 99, 100, 107, 224

caste, xxix, xxxviii n21, 3, 167, 183, 206

Chakrabarty, Dipesh, xxv n14, 31, 121

closure, xxiv, xxvi, 116
  and Holocaust, 110-11. *See also* Holocaust
  lack of, 111-12, 123, 125
  and myth formation, 122

cognitive psychology, 6, 8, 24 n13, 215-16. *See also* memory; psychoanalysis

defences, xxviii, 16-17, 18, 20. *See also* silence
  and emotions, 42-44, 76-77, 149-51, 199 n1
  as mature, 65
  and memory, 53-56, 57-58, 101-03, 173-74
  super-ego, 25 n21, 75

desire
  and frustration, 41
  for homeland, 30, 31, 65-66, 67, 100-02, 120
  nature of, 40, 41-42, 90-91 n13

developmental approach, 14, 21

emotion, 30, 41, 43-44, 66, 116; *See also* anger; desire; fear; guilt; Partition

enemy. *See also* memory; Muslims, attitude to
  as faceless, 110, 113-16
  as the other, 10, 72-89, 153, 154, 212

Erikson, Erik, 15-16, 28,

fear , xxxi, 21, 92 n18

atmosphere of, 103-06, 114-16, 123-24
Ernest Jones, 42-44
nature of, 42-43, 113. *See also* uncertainty
during Partition, xix, 20, 21, 44-45, 73, 132 n37
Freud, Sigmund, 16, 69, 92 n21, 110.*See also* psychoanalysis

Gender, 213. *See also* women's accounts
of interviewer, 2, 5
masculinity, 206-207
in Partition, xvii, xxvi, n20, 206, 213 *See also* Partition
guilt, 94 n32. *See also* hate
for aggression, 54, 55-56, 181
and confession, 84-85
as coping, 85, 97 n44
and fear, 43. *See also* fear
for not suffering, 18, 71-72, 145
during Partition, xix, 145
reduction of, 95-96 n37
types of, 82-84

hate, 42, 73-74, 75, 76-77, 92 n21, 181. *See also* anger; defence. hate
history, xxiv
critique of, xxiii-xxv n9
as memory, xxvi-xxvii
oral, xxvii n13
of Partition, xii, xiii, xxviii, n25
and psychology, xii – xiii, xxiv
as subjective, xx, xxv

Holocaust, ix, xiii, 99, 111, 116, 121, 129 n23, 208. *See also* Partition
homeland, 98, 101-02, 106-09, 136. *See also* desire

identity, xx, 2, 63, 88-89, 124-26. *See also* self
interviewees. *See* narrative; respondents; women's accounts

Lacan, Jacques, 41, 43, 90 n13, 91-92,n17, 131 n27. *See also* desire
Laing, R. D., 45, 220
listening, x-xi, 9-13, 27 n18. *See also* methodology; psychoanalysis

memory, xxvi, xxxv n 8, 1, 109-10. *See also* defences; Partition
with age, xi, xvii
autobiographical nature of, 6-9, 128-29 n16, 215
in childhood and adolescence, xvi, 7
of the family, 34, 39, 157, 185
declarative, 6
distortion of, xvi, xxv, n14, 7, 8-9, 198
of emotion, 7, 29, n37, 98. *See also* fear; anger; guilt
flash bulb, 216
of food, 34, 63, 91,n14, 143
of freedom movement, 39, 184

memory (*cont.*)
  of friends, 35, 38, 136, 146
  Jorge Borges on, 217
  nature of, 31-35, 146
  and the other community, 35, 44-58, 61-62, 65, 143-44, 157-59, 170-71, 185-86. *See also* Muslims, attitudes to
  postmemory, xxxiii
  recall, 8, 19, 24 n11, 120
  recollection, xv
  reminiscence bump, 7, 216
  screen memory, 213-15
  retention, xiv-xv
methodology, xxxviii, 3, 208
  comparison with clinical technique, 17-18, 19-20, 206
  data, 206-07. *See also* narrative; cognitive psychology
  depth of, 205-06
  ethics of, 87, 207-08. *See also* narrative
  interview, xvi, 1-2, 3, 9-10, 19, 209
  interviewer's subjectivity, 2, 4-5, 11, 135,
  limitations of, xxi, 42, 134, 136, 182, 206-208,
  of listening, 209. *See also* listening
  nomothetic *vs* idiographic, 13-14, 222
  psychoanalytical, 6, 8, 14, 17, 18, 19, 102, 207
  qualitative, xiv, 23-24, n9, 206
  as reconstruction, 2-3, 17-18, 19
  respondents, 3, 7, 16, 206. *See also* respondents
  of self, 219-20
  of specific behaviour, 87
  of whole person, xiv, 13-14, 15, 101, 133-35
migration, 3, 4, 34, 37, 39,118, 123. *See also* memory
  cf weaning, 65-66
  decision of, 60-62, 103-06, 107-08
  lack of feeling during, 59, 60-62, 107
  memory of, 58, 60-62
  three stages, 108-09
Muslims, attitude to, 13, 21, 99, 72-89, 195-96. *See also* fear; hate; guilt; memory
  conflict-free, 88, 192
  contradiction in, 72-87, 114-16, 147, 173-74, 189
  friendships, 35, 113, 137, 139, 144, 188
  life-experiences and, 142-154, 166, 174-82
  as negative, 153-54, 178, 181;
  as the other, 41, 76,-77
  as positive, 88-89,139, 147, 158, 169, 171, 185-86, 193, 195-98

Nandy, Ashis, xvii, xxi, xxviii, 224
narrative, xxvii, 2, 7, 20-21
  confusion on Partition, 224
  difference, styles of, 65, 66-72, 100-02, 120, 139,142,

145-46, 157,160-61, 173-74, 209-13
effect of age, 39, 125
homeland, 102, 103
interpretation of, 5-9, 13-17, 208-16. *See also* methodology
life stories, xxx-xxxi, 5, 135-36, 145-46, 153-54, 161, 173, 177
nature, 1-2, 5, 13-14, 121-22
opening theme, 102
personality and , xx, 134-35, 142, 147, 149, 182, 183, 212
reception of, 9-13
reconstruction of, 17-22,148
and regression, 91 n16, 100
Roland Barthes, 5
as root metaphor, 14
and silence, 123, 223

Pandey, Gyanendra, 98, 128 n15, 218
Partition, vii, viii, ix, xxvii, xxxi, xxxii. *See also* memory
and denial, 107, 110, 206, 208, 216, 218. *See also* narrative; self
emotions. *See* fear; anger; guilt
gain from, 19
history of, xvii-xviii
cf with Holocaust, vii, ix, xiii-xiv
literature on, 31
memory of, xiv, 1, 30-42, 45-51
next generation, xxxiii
pathographizing, 18, 20,
Positive Illusion Strategy, 153
cf with Punjab, xii, xxiii, xxix, 4, 98-99, 103, 109
psychology of, xvi-xvii, xxvi n19
pain of, 98-99
positive effect on women, 70-71
as 'soft'. *See* soft violence
as surprising, xii, 117-19;
violence, xxiii, xxviii, 45, 51-52. *See also* violence
women, violence against, viii-ix
Zero Miss Strategy, 153
Pavlov, Ivan Petrovich, xi
post-migration. *See* refugee
psychoanalysis. *See also* cognitive psychology; defences; methodology
communication, 206
fear, hate, guilt, 43
as mode of discourse, xx, 17-18, 19
and interpretation, 6, 8-9, 16, 102, 110, 215
and object relation, 41, 65-66, 69-70, 212-13
Partition, xxxi n32
and phenomenology, 25-26 n22
psychoeconomics, 16
psychohistory, xvi, vviv, xxv, n17, xxxviii, 15, 16, 23 n9, 28

reality, xxvii, 21, 31, 35, 40, 59, 150. *See also* truth
refugee, xxxii, 207. *See also* identity; respondents
anger of, 16, 63, 65
experience of, 62-66

refugee *(cont.)*
fear, 99. *See also* fear
frustration, 66-67, 69-70, 108-09, 124-25
humiliation, 63-64
positive impact, 68-69, 108-09
rehabilitation, 63-65, 223, 225, 229
resilience, 67-68, 88, 125-26
respondents, xv, xvii, xix-xx, xxix, xxi, 1-5, 9, 32, 99. *See also* narrative
age of, xv, 7, 16
as aggressors, 54-57
and blame, 110, 114, 147
fear, 44. *See also* fear
vs Ghotis, 63
Henry Murray, 15
migration impact, 66-70
movement in time, 15
and nostalgia, 30-31, 100, 119-21
number of, 206
and politics of, 226-28
reactions of, 3, 183-89, 190-95. *See also* narrative
reasons for departure, 103, 104, 111
saturation in sampling, 206
trauma. *See* trauma
Roland, Alan, xxi

self, 33, 198, 217. *See also* Laing, R.D.
Bengali culture, 229-32
collective, xx, 208, 222
dynamic, 21
multiplicity of, 80
narcissistic, 212
and ontological insecurity, 220-22
in pre-and post-Partition, 20, 208, 217-19
postmodern, 21-22
western *vs* Indian, 223
silence, xii. *See also* narrative
as defence, 116-19, 123
and pain, 154
selective, 123, 223-25
about violence, 58
soft violence, xxiii, xxxi, 4, 21, 103, 123, 198. *See also* Partition; violence
difference from brutal, xix, 21, 71, 99-100, 103, 109-10, 125, 208
experience of, xi-xii, xxi, xix, 99, 145, 206, 208-16
nature of, xi
in politically induced trauma, 208
and self, 218-22
as slow process, 119.
super-ego, 18, 45, 54, 70, 76, 79, 94 n 32, 102, 180, 181, 197, 204 n25. *See also* defences

terror
engulfment reaction, 45
experience of, 105-06, 108-09
process of, 46-51, 123-24; *See also* fear
trauma, xiv,-xv, xxi, xxv, xxvi, 21, 110-112, 144, 149, 181-84,

198, 203 n24, 215, 218. *See also* silence; violence
truth, 9, 14, 23 n4, 14, 216-17. *See also* reality

uncertainty, 21, 109-16

violence. See also Partition; soft violence
  and defences, xiii, 55-58, 103. *See also* defences
  Gyanendra Pandey, 218-19
  during Partition, xviii, 51-57, 78-80, 99, 155-56,162-71
  news of, 45
  in Punjab and Bengal, xi, xvii, xxix, 4, 23, n5, 98-99, 144
  stories of, xviii-xix, xxx, n28
  threat of, 45-54, 104-05

West Bengal, xi, 85, 154, 157, 159-60,172, 176-79, 211, 226-32
women's accounts, 33-34, 37-38, 44-45, 62, 70-71, 80-83, 115, 117, 210-15